Lille

CITY GUIDE

Edition 3

Laurence Phillips

1.00

Bradt

www.bradtguides.com
Bradt Travel Guides Ltd, UK
The Globe Pequot Press Inc, USA

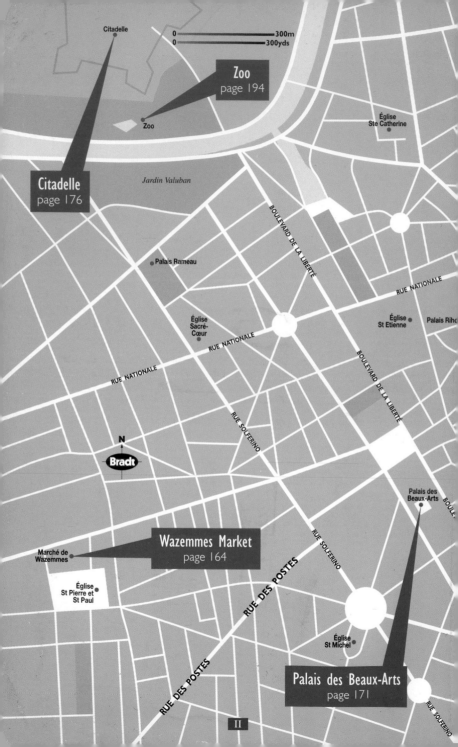

(MD)

▲ *The belfries of the north: civic buildings trump churches and cathedrals with their imposing towers, such as Lille's town hall (p.178).*

(P/Tips)

▲ Porte de Paris, a healthier name for what was once known as 'Sick Man's Gate' (p.182); (right) better late than never: the 19th-century cathedral of Notre Dame de la Treille, finally completed with a Millennium façade for the 21st century (p.187).

(DT)

(MD)

▲ The regal entrance to the Sun King's favourite garrison, La Citadelle, once home to Dartagnan himself (p.176).

(D/A/SP)

▲ (Above) Grand' Place hosts the annual Braderie - the ultimate flea market (p.12); (below left) fine cheeses in the old town.

(LF)
(MD)

(MD)

▲ (Middle right and bottom) Wazemmes market has stalls indoors and outside for foodie foraging (p.164).

▲ Surrender to your appetites: (top) follow the signs for cafés, crêperies and brasseries; (middle) indulge in home-brewed ale at Les Trois Brasseurs or home-made pâtisseries at Paul; or (bottom) stop for lunch at a pavement terrasse on Grand' Place.

(LP)

(LP)

(MD)

▲ Bienvenue a Lille: (top left) Artist Yayoi Kusama's gloriously camp Tulips of Shangri-La are the flamboyant welcome to Lille Europe Station; (top right) the Credit Lyonnais tower, dubbed the 'ski boot', stamps its authority on the city; (bottom) the real welcome is from the people - ever ready with an excuse for a party, such as this evening for Lille 3000 on Grand' Place.

Author

Laurence Phillips (🖱 www.laurencephillips.com) has been escaping to France since boyhood and has written many and varied guides to the country, most recently a companion to Robert Louis Stevenson's classic *Travels With a Donkey in the Cevennes*. He has been described by the French press as a charming *bon vivant* and by British critics as a witty and entertaining enthusiast. His passion for all things French has fuelled countless BBC radio broadcasts, including Radio 4's *Allez Lille*, and his is a familiar voice on travel and arts programmes. His 2009 collection of short stories *Garson Lazarre's Paris Confidential* is a satirical appraisal of the capital's expat celebrity circuit. In France, he has been honoured as a Commander of the Order of St Nectaire cheese and a Squire of the Confrérie des Sacres de la Champagne (although for the latter citation he was inscribed as Madame Laurence Phillips, which possibly makes him a Dame). Twice winner of the prestigious Guide Book of the Year award from the British Guild of Travel Writers, for this book and the *Bradt Guide to Eurostar Cities*, he combines wanderlust with a love for theatre and work as a critic, playwright and songwriter, and has written for the Royal Shakespeare Company. His stage work has clocked up more travel miles than the author, being performed on four continents, from the West End to the South Pacific.

Third edition November 2009
First published 2004

Bradt Travel Guides Ltd, 23 High Street, Chalfont St Peter, Bucks SL9 9QE, England;
www.bradtguides.com
Published in the USA by The Globe Pequot Press Inc, 246 Goose Lane, PO Box 480,
Guilford, Connecticut 06437-0480

British Library Cataloguing in Publication Data
A catalogue record for this book is available from the British Library

ISBN-13: 978 1 84162 296 5

Photographs
James Cridland/Flickr (JC/F), Dhote/Andia/Still Pictures (D/A/SP), directphoto.bz/Alamy
(d/A), Maxime Dufour Photographies (MD), Langrand/Andia.fr/Still Pictures (L/A/SP),
David Noble/Pictures Colour Library (DN/PCL), PeerPoint/Alamy (PP/A), Laurence
Phillips (LP), Photononstop/Tips Images (P/Tips), Tom/Andia.fr/Still Pictures (T/A/SP),
Derek Trillo (DT), A Vossberg/VISUM/Still Pictures (AV/V/SP), Yann Guichaoua/Pictures
Colour Library (YG/PCL), Zylberyng/Adnia.fr/Still Pictures (Z/A/SP)
Front cover Palais des Beaux Arts stairwell (d/A), Café display at Wazemmes Sunday market
(PP/A)
In-text photos Laurence Phillips; Daniël Leppens/Dreamstime; Davidmartyn/Dreamstime;
Thomas Nilsson, Sweden (photo: page 80); Flickr: a.goffard, apple94, amsfrank, austinevan,
Be Pak, DaffyDuke, Damien Roué, genevieveromier, jf1234, kikozbi1, ljcybergal, Sarah &
Iain, Stefan, SwedishCarina, tea bow, Thomas Claveirole, Tijani59, tofos59, vacation 2,
Wolfiewolf

Maps Steve Munns & Dave Priestley
Typeset from the author's disc by Artinfusion
Printed and bound in India by Nutech Print Services

AUTHOR'S STORY

Nobody was more surprised than I when Bradt decided to back my project to write a guidebook to Lille. On reflection, it made a certain sense. Bradt has a global reputation for revealing the charms of places often overlooked, and when first I began broadcasting and writing about Lille, even the French raised an eyebrow or two. On the original publication, as part of a guide to all the Eurostar cities, Bradt determined not to launch the title in Paris, London or even Brussels, but in Lille's Palais Rihour, imperial seat of the city's heyday well before its rediscovery as Europe's cultural capital.

To the outside world, the outside France even, Lille was a slagheap, a monochrome reminder of a failed industrial past. Echoes of Emile Zola's *Germinal* and simple metropolitan snobbery regarding northerners helped perpetuate the prejudices. I'd personally broken through the barrier when hitchhiking from the ferry-ports in the rain – I found myself in a contemporary Brigadoon, where bright lights and pulsating partying punctuated the midnight hour and positively punctured the propaganda. People were vivacious, generous and fun. Next morning, in the dazzling sunlight of day, the glowing beauty of gabled cobbled Flanders lay before me, a true European jewel in a contemporary cosmopolitan pleasure-ground.

Since opening and sharing my no-longer-secret address book, each new edition, each reprint, has chronicled the blossoming of a metropolis coming of age at the heart of Europe. No more need to explain. This once unmentionable city has become a point of reference for the rest of the Continent, with style magazines and travel gurus ever hailing the next discovery destination as 'the New Lille'.

FEEDBACK REQUEST

It has been, as ever, exhaustive, fulfilling and feel-fulling fun compiling and researching this guide. However, a restaurant is only as good as its last clean plate, and a hotel, shop or even museum may best be judged by the quality of its welcome. So I would appreciate any comments on your own experiences in Lille. Feel free to drop me a line at lolly@laurencephillips.com or write to me c/o Bradt Travel Guides, 23 High Street, Chalfont St Peter, Bucks SL9 9QE.

Contents

Lille Contents

ACKNOWLEDGEMENTS

Special thanks to my dining partners in Lille for letting me reveal their secret tourist-free tables; to those generous readers who emailed me with their own stories of this special city; to Vera Dupuis, her heirs and successors (especially Bruno Cappelle), for their unstinting support; to the editorial team at Bradt for reining in my ramblings, airbrushing my grammar and granting me the illusion of fluency; to my family and friends for bearing with me as I disappeared on yet another culinary and cultural expedition; and of course to my parents, Di and Ronald Phillips, for getting out the car and ferrying me from table to table, and wallowing in cholesterol when, as usual, the clock and the calendar said we'd never finish the infinite mealtime of summer.

DEDICATION

To Stéphane Fichet
who has had to endure my lyrical appreciation of so many fine meals, without the joy of actually passing a fork from plate to palate!

LIST OF MAPS

Preface

How can you fail to fall in love with a city that erects a statue to a lullaby? Although the *Internationale* was composed in Lille, the song the townsfolk took to their hearts was *Le P'tit Quinquin*, a sentimental patois melodrama of a poor lacemaker and her weeping baby. The statue, ravaged by a million scrambled cuddles and kisses, is a working-class *Madonna and Child* to melt the hardest of hearts. The town clocks still chime the tune each day at noon.

For years, Lille was France's best-kept secret. Despite charming cobbled streets, broad Flemish squares and the richest art gallery outside Paris, Lille was tucked away in a coal-mining region, scorned by Parisians and ignored by tourists. Then came Channel Tunnel trains linking Europe's key capitals, and the city was reborn. Lille may have a population of barely 220,000, but with literally millions of people now living within an hour of the city, it is an unofficial capital in its own right, deservedly chosen as the European Capital of Culture for 2004.

Lille 2004 was just the excuse Lille needed to kick-start another renaissance: a dozen brand-new and wonderfully inventive arts centres set up in remarkable buildings in towns around the city itself; the reopening of one of France's most beautiful opera houses; and a calendar packed with reasons to dine and dance until dawn, and a programme of performance, from Shakespeare to tango, to rival any capital city in the world.

Proof came with the very first street party. We all wore white as exotic images were projected on to the milling throng. Organisers had expected around 200,000 people to take to the streets and were quite frankly astounded when the best part of a million good-natured revellers managed to squeeze into central Lille. I tried to surf the human tide to see a thousand musicians perform the opening concert (Berlioz's *Chant des Chemins de Fer*, composed for the arrival of the first Paris-Lille train in 1846), but was swept away towards the main squares where artificial snow accompanied partygoers en route to the magnificent firework display by the Esplanade. Les showgirls and boys of the lamented Folies de Paris performed in the Chamber of Commerce, and the rest of us danced 'til dawn around the flames of square Foch, in the pink light of the Gare Lille Flandres and to the sound of *chansons* at the Hôtel de Ville.

The year was punctuated with many such explosions of high-octane bonhomie and the theme-party tradition is now confirmed as an essential

XV

part of city life in the 21st century. Like the Maisons Folies, the new Tripostale centre, the now reinvented Saint Sauveur goodsyard, beautifully restored churches, and the promise of more new urban parks, weekends of merrymaking are the long-term legacy of an unforgettable year. Eight million party animals can't be wrong! 2004 certainly pulled in the punters to the last, with a respectable 300,000 filling the squares and beyond for November's final knees-up.

Then came the decision – the party was not over. Cue Lille 3000, a biennial mini-me to the original festival. From an opening season in 2007 that brought India to Flanders, with the rue Faidherbe most memorably lined with elephants, through 2009's Europe XXL celebrating the 'new' countries and cultures of eastern Europe, the city is even now looking at the guest list for 2011.

A glance at the free listings magazine *Sortir* promises 100 events any Saturday night, from the national theatres and concert halls to smoky dives, film festivals and rock happenings. As for art, Lille can barely contain its national and international treasures: the city's cultural map embraces towns for miles around. For years Picassos and Braques have packed out the Musée d'Art Moderne at the Villeneuve d'Ascq campus; Roubaix's Piscine is home to a truly eclectic and thrilling art collection, worth a day or two of anyone's life; and Matisse's private pictures are an essential drive away at Le Cateau-Cambrésis. In the city itself, museums include the Palais des Beaux Arts, France's second collection after the Louvre, with its wickedly wonderful Goyas and splendid Renaissance treats, its deep-red walls and high ceilings being the perfect backdrop to a veritable banquet of masterpieces from the 17th century to the Impressionists. The Capital of Culture drew 387,000 art lovers to a prestigious Rubens exhibition, yet visitors at any time may see the artist's majestic *Descent from the Cross* in the Palais, or while away a weekend hour in a natural history museum so quaintly dated with suspended skeletons and tableaux of taxidermy as to provide other-worldly diversions from the vibrant good-time city.

Elsewhere this might be the stuff of stuffiness, but in such a youthful and exuberant university town there is always a definite buzz in the air, the vitality of youth amidst improbably quaint 17th- and 18th-century elegance.

Whether you are in Lille to meet up with friends, or just to celebrate your own special weekend; whether you are lifting a *bière blanche* in an *estaminet* or raising your fork in a Michelin-starred restaurant; whether you are admiring Old Masters in a museum or breaking bread with a young artist in his studio; whether you are among the crowds packing

Grand' Place on a midsummer night's free rock concert or listening to a chamber recital in a baroque salon: wander, wonder and wallow in a corner of the world that has always been a capital city of culture. Let music follow your footsteps into history, let your tastebuds tempt you from your chosen path. Let lunch segue into dinner, art deco streets lead you to the talents of tomorrow and the sounds of a lone midnight saxophone from an open window in the lamplight blend into a bedtime serenade in a city that, more than any other, knows the value of a great lullaby.

Laurence Phillips
lolly@laurencephillips.com

HOW TO USE THIS BOOK

Symbols

Symbols indicate the location of venues/sites/sights listed in the book (see pages 9–15 for more information):

VL   Vieux Lille

GP   Grand' Place to République

MK   Markets

S   Stations/Hôtel de Ville

🚊   Closest métro or tram stop.

e*   This symbol suggests the most direct route from the Eurostar terminus, using métro, tram and bus services.

Map references

These are listed in square brackets as part of the contact information for each site (eg: [2 G1]), and relate to the colour maps on pages 234–6 at the end of the guide. Map grid references for listings in the *Eating & drinking* chapter also contain their key number in brackets after the grid number (eg: [236 A3 (36)]). The key for all restaurants, bars and cafes on the overview and city centre maps can be found on the inside back cover.

Email & websites

Email or web addresses are published wherever possible. Where an establishment has a reliable website, we list the URL in order that readers may view photographs, current prices, menus and last-minute information before mailing.

Prices

Restaurant prices include all taxes and service charges. It is customary to leave a small tip (usually loose change) to reward good service. The price range indicates options ranging from a basic set menu to indulgence à la carte. In France all restaurants are obliged to display their prices outside the front door, and most will offer a set-price meal deal. Very expensive restaurants usually have a far cheaper *prix-fixe* menu at lunchtimes. All menu prices were verified within a few months of each other, so use them as a comparative guide.

Hotel room rates apply for single or double occupancy.

Prices quoted in the text were correct at the time of going to press.

Opening hours

Most restaurants open for dinner from around 19.30 to 23.30, and lunch from 12.30 to 14.00. City-centre bars usually stay open until after midnight, generally closing between 01.00 and 02.00. Where establishments open or close later than usual, it is mentioned in the text. With the exception of late-night brasseries, it is advisable to telephone in advance to make a reservation for dinner after 22.00 or for late lunches. Gastronomic restaurants tend to close for two to four weeks in summer.

In France, national museums close on Tuesdays, and city museums on Mondays, so do read the opening hours given in this guide carefully. Since no hours are set in stone, before setting out on a dedicated mission to any one specific museum or restaurant, phone ahead just to be sure.

Credit cards

Unless otherwise stated, most establishments accept payment by MasterCard or Visa. American Express and Diners may also be used at many hotels, restaurants and shops. Smaller museums and bars may refuse credit cards. Carte Bleu is a domestic alternative to Visa.

▼ *The Vieille Bourse – jewel box between the squares.*

LILLE AT A GLANCE

Location Northwest France, 45 minutes' drive from the Channel coast. By rail it is 35 minutes from Brussels, 1 hour from Paris and 1 hour 40 minutes from London.

Population 170,000 in the city; 1,125,500 in the greater metropolitan area

Language Predominantly French; also some Flemish. A composite patois Ch'ti may also be heard (see page 215).

Religion Principally Roman Catholic; also Protestant, Muslim and Jewish (see page 44)

Time GMT/BST +1 hour

International telephone code +33

Public holidays 1 January, 1 May, 8 May, Pentecost Monday, 14 July (national day), 15 August, 1 November, 11 November, 25 December

School holidays One week at the end of October, two weeks at Christmas, two weeks in February, two in spring, the whole of July and August

Climate Average temperatures: winter 6°C; spring and autumn 14°C; summer 23°C. For weather forecasts, check on-line weather services or dial 08 92 68 02 59.

Contexts

INTRODUCTION TO THE CITY

When French mayors go to French Mayor School, they all learn several key buzzwords. By far the most popular is the phrase '*Carrefour de l'Europe*' ('The Crossroads of Europe'). The crossroads of the silk route, the wine route, the tin route, even, I presume, the beetroot route. Almost every town in the country claims to have been, at some stage in its history, at the crossroads of Europe. A well-known resort on the Atlantic coast once seized the honour in a triumph of civic pride over orienteering. With so many mayors declaring crossroad status, the historic map of the Continent must have resembled a particularly virulent tartan.

Pierre Mauroy, unique amongst his mayoral colleagues, claimed the rank as a goal rather than mere heritage. Lille's mayor for 29 years, until handing his flaming torch in 2001 to Martine Aubry, Mauroy was most famously President Mitterand's first prime minister. Like Mitterand, Thatcher and Reagan, his was an iron will, and so, when the Channel Tunnel rail link was agreed, Pierre Mauroy persuaded the world that the shortest distance between two points was a right angle. Thus the Eurostar route was swung in an arc to create a new European hub. With a flourish of the presidential and prime-ministerial pens, Lille was transformed, Cinderella-like, from depressed centre of a mining district with 40% unemployment to France's third most powerful financial, commercial and industrial centre.

Mauroy's successor is equally worthy of the mantle that she inherited. Aubry's socialist credentials are unquestionable: the blood of Jacques Delors courses through her veins; she was the firebrand who seared the cause of women's rights on the national consciousness; and she is still cheered to the gables during gay pride parties and cultural events alike. But this corner of France, birthplace of the legendary Charles de Gaulle, has a tradition of social-reforming politicians. Jean Lebas, whose name graces the principal street of nearby Roubaix, was a much-loved mayor of that town, whose valour in two world wars is still spoken of with reverence, as is his institution of paid holidays for factory workers, introduced when he served as minister of works in the pioneering government of Léon Blum. Lebas died a hero, deported by the Nazis.

Politically, Lille may be French, but it was most famously the old capital of Flanders. Perhaps the town's heritage, being variously and successively Flemish, Burgundian, Spanish, Dutch, French, German, French, German and French again might have inspired Mayor Mauroy's ambitious vision to create the future of Europe in a town that had long been dismissed as a broken yesterday, arguing that in an era of Eurostar, Thalys and TGV, geography should no longer be determined by distance but by time. These days, Paris, Brussels, Amsterdam and even London might be legitimately classed as the suburbs.

Lille discovered the secret of eternal youth. Every year brings a new influx of first-time residents, youngsters from all over France, and from Europe and beyond.

And so Lille, the best-kept secret in the world, with a population of 170,000, became one of the great capital cities of Europe. She may not be the capital of any nation state, but a morning, weekend or lifetime in her company proves without doubt that Lille is the capital city of life. With its high-flying business community and university campus, Lille is where Europe comes to party. A former director of the Opéra de Lille told me how he would nip between Germany and Britain to arrange meetings with soloists and musicians during the working day, and how he mixed and matched choruses, soloists and orchestras from around Europe. After all, he argued, the audiences pop over from Cologne, Brittany and Kent; why not the performers? His successor doubtless agreed, and the first opera to be staged after the house's renovation was a co-production with the Théâtre de la Monnaie, Brussels's famous opera house.

The opera is not the only lure in town. With the legendary Goyas, Impressionists and Dutch masters at the Palais des Beaux Arts, a national theatre, ballet company and orchestra, not to mention scores of smaller theatres and music venues, Lille can offer the Saturday night sensation seeker as much as any town ten times the size. Serious shopping, from Hermès and Chanel to the fleamarkets, pulls in bargain hunters and the money-no-object fraternity alike. Good food, great beers, cider and locally distilled *genièvre* are the recipe for a legendary good-natured northern welcome. The introduction of city-centre stewards (recognise them by their colourful sweaters, jackets and caps), whose sole function is to offer help and advice to visitors, is merely the official recognition of a long-time trait. I was not the first stranger to find myself lost in the old town, ask for advice in a bar and be personally escorted by the locals to my destination, with handshakes and good wishes all round.

Perhaps this attitude is born of Lille having discovered the secret of eternal youth. With 150,000 students living in both the town and the dormitory suburbs of the campus of Villeneuve d'Ascq, 42% of the local population is younger than 25. Every year brings a new influx of first-time residents to be wowed by the city, youngsters from all over France, and from Europe and beyond studying at the business, arts, journalism and engineering faculties. Lille hands over to these same *arrivistes* the responsibility of producing the annual *Ch'ti* guide. The *Ch'ti* (named for the local *patois*) is produced by the business school and is the most comprehensive local directory you will ever find anywhere. Each year a fresh editorial team spends 12 months visiting every establishment in town. With honest, often witty reviews of every shop, photocopy bureau, bar, club and restaurant in Lille and the metropolitan area, the *Ch'ti* is a veritable bible. Until political correctness set in during the mid-1990s, the guide even rated local red-light streets with details of nearest cash and condom dispensers. Check out the number of 'C' symbols on the stickers in each restaurant window for an indication of the *Ch'ti* rating (C–CCCCC).

As such an international melting pot, it is sometimes easy to forget that Lille is also a real modern-day capital city. It is capital of a metropolitan area that embraces the former manufacturing towns of Roubaix and Tourcoing and urban areas straddling the Belgian border. It is also capital of the Nord-Pas de Calais region, with Vimy Ridge, Montreuil, the floating market gardens of St-Omer, the Channel ports and the tunnel only an hour's drive away.

Although the heritage of the region is generously displayed on the tables of Lille, this is also a country of tomorrows, with wonderfully ambitious projects breathing new life into the old mining district. Perhaps no more so than in Lille, where the uncompromisingly modern Euralille stands comfortably next to the Flemish squares and art deco shopping streets. In other cities the grafting of a new high-tech glass-and-chrome futurescape on to a historical landscape would jar like UPVC doubleglazing on a thatched cottage or ill-fitting dentures in a favourite smile. Lille's newest quarter, from the old railway station to the *périphérique* ring road, settles easily by its classical neighbour. Architect Rem Koolhaas was given free rein over the transformation of 173 acres of city-centre wasteland

▲ *The old town clustered around the new cathedral.*

reclaimed from the army. His brief: to create a city of the 21st century to greet the high-speed trains.

This new Lille Europe quarter is just one of the many welcomes that Lille showers on its visitors. If the Grand' Place is forever on the verge of a party, Vieux Lille is a portal to times past, the Citadelle and Bois de Boulogne are a living legacy of the Sun King, and the marketplaces of Wazemmes and Solférino are the pulse of modern life.

Walk back towards your hotel in the late evening, tripping down the *pavé* of the old town towards the magnificent belfry, passing the illuminated ornate scrollwork and carvings over the shopfronts. Look around you at the crystal lights reflecting a hundred diners, families, friends and lovers. Then surrender to temptation and head to the brasserie tables or jazz cellars to steal another hour or two of the perfect weekend.

Lille, capital of the past and beacon of the future, has found her time. As any self-respecting mayor would say, 'Welcome to the crossroads of Europe.'

HISTORY

Lille is a European capital of culture. In its time it has also been capital of Flanders, belonged to the Austrians, Spanish and Dutch, been governed by the royal families of Portugal and Constantinople, and served as the ducal seat of Burgundy, 500km due south. As this guide went to press, it was French.

Nestling in a loop of the River Deûle and its canals, and cornered by Belgium, Lille, in the administrative department of Nord, is capital of the Nord-Pas de Calais region. The region takes in the Côte d'Opale sweep of the Channel coast from the Belgian border, via the ports of Dunkerque, Calais and Boulogne, past the resort of Le Touquet down to the mouth of the Somme, and includes the ancient areas of Artois, Hainault and French Flanders. Always at the front row of history, this is home to Henry V's Agincourt, Henry VIII's Field of the Cloth of Gold and, more recently, those Flanders fields of World War I. Vimy Ridge lies beside the town of Arras and Hitler's V2 rocket bunker, now a museum of war and space, outside St-Omer. Napoleon stood on the cliffs and planned an invasion of Britain (which never happened) and Louis Blériot looked across the same expanse of sea and planned his historic flight across the Channel.

Lille has mattered since at least 1066, when l'Isle (The Island) was mentioned in a charter listing a charitable donation by Baudoin V, Count of Flanders, who owned a fortified stronghold on the site of the present Notre Dame de la Treille. At this time, Grand' Place was already a forum. In 1205, at the time of the Crusades, Count Baudoin IX was crowned king of Constantinople, and his daughters were raised under the protection of the French king, Philippe Auguste. The eldest, Jeanne, married Ferrand of Portugal. As the English and the Holy Roman Empire united with Flanders against France, the French captured Lille after the Battle of Bouvines, in 1214, and the city was given to Jeanne.

Throughout this time Lille had been earning its living through trade. The upper and lower Deûle rivers did not meet, so merchants from Bruges and Ghent, en route to major fairs in Champagne and beyond, were obliged to unload their barges and push carts through the town centre in order to continue their journeys. This staging post evolved into a market town, and textiles and fabrics changed hands, the city even giving its name to some products: Lisle socks – ever wondered where that name came from?

In 1369, Marguerite of Flanders married the Burgundian duke Philippe le Temoine. His ducal successor Philippe le Bon moved the Burgundy court to Lille in 1453 with the construction of the Palais Rihour. Less than a quarter of a century later, in 1477, Lille was handed over to the Hapsburgs when Marie de Bourgogne married Maximilien of Austria. Since the Hapsburgs were as pan-European as you can get, the Spanish King Charles V took on the mantle of emperor and therefore Lille and the Low Countries were considered part of Spain.

Of course, it wasn't too long before France came back into the picture – a couple of centuries after the Hapsburgs first got their hands on the city. In 1663 Maria-Theresa of Spain married Louis XIV, France's Sun King, who, claiming his wife's possessions in northern Europe, set about protecting the dowry, with the great architect Vauban building the fortifications that we know today. The famous five-pointed star-shaped Citadelle and the residential Quartier Royal that dominate Vieux Lille were created during the golden era of construction that began in 1667. During its seasons of favour as a Royal Town, the garrison was governed by both Vauban himself and another swashbuckling hero, D'Artagnan.

In the Bar La Liberté, he sang for the very first time the socialist anthem L'Internationale, a song that in the coming century would change the world forever.

This was not the end of the shuttlecock identity saga. From 1708 to 1713, Lille was occupied by the Dutch in a war over the Spanish succession and, in 1792, 35,000 Austrian troops laid siege to the town. However, Lille remained in French hands, and took its rightful place in the agriculture and education revolutions of the mid-19th century, with the completion of the main railway line to Paris in 1846 and Louis Pasteur becoming first dean of the Faculty of Science in 1854.

In July 1888, a local woodturner, Pierre Degeyter, embodied Lille's spirit of social reform and revolution when, in the long-demolished Bar La Liberté, he sang for the very first time the music that he had composed for Eugène Pottier's socialist anthem *L'Internationale*, a song that in the coming century would change the world forever.

In the two world wars Lille held out against the invading German armies for three days, both in 1914 and in 1940. Nine hundred houses were destroyed during World War I. During the Nazi occupation, the city's most famous son, Charles de Gaulle, famously led Free France from London. In 1966 the Communauté Urbaine made Lille the capital of a cluster of towns in the wider region, and in 1981 Mayor Pierre Mauroy became prime minister, laying the seeds of a public transport renaissance. The world's first driverless, fully automated public transport system, the VAL métro, was inaugurated in 1983; ten years later the TGV brought Paris within an hour of the city. In 1994, the Channel Tunnel Eurostar service enabled the new Europe quarter to become a continental hub. The 20th century ended with the reopening of the Palais des Beaux Arts, France's second national gallery, and the completion (a century behind schedule) of the cathedral.

The 21st century began with Mauroy handing over the city to Martine Aubry and Lille becoming European Capital of Culture in 2004. With characteristic forward planning and boundless optimism, the decision was made to continue the celebrations long past the date that Lille relinquished the European title. Lille 3000, a programme of biennial culture festivals, hit the ground running. The party is over, so long live the party.

Modern Lille

France's fourth largest city and third financial centre, river port, medical research centre and industrial zone is an unlikely success story. The area was crippled by unemployment when traditional mining and manufacturing industries declined, yet revived its fortunes in the age of the TGV. The capital of the vast Nord-Pas de Calais region, Lille is at the heart of a vast metropolitan area of 118 communes crossing national borders into Belgium.

A legacy of centuries of textile manufacturing is the city's current status as the centre of Europe's mail-order industry. Lille is also the principal textile-trading area in France. There are more law companies based here than anywhere else outside Paris, and it is the second city for insurance companies.

By contrast, the city's huge transient student population, coupled with the region's socialist heritage, means that, unusually in a city with such a large business community, left-wing causes are very much to the fore. Regular good-natured marches and rallies criss-cross the city, from Hôtel de Ville to Grand' Place and the stations, with a carnival air about them.

The Future

A new green park for the centre of Lille itself and the reinvention of an abandoned railway yard brings a breath of fresh air to a former city car park, and the Maisons Folies (see pages 189–92) rejuvenate towns across the region. Soon the slagheaps of the old mining communities could evoke echoes of Paris's famous glass pyramid as the nearby town of Lens, currently only really known for its *Sang et Or* football team, has been plucked from obscurity to open France's second Louvre. This satellite of the world's most famous museum will eventually house up to 700 of the nation's greatest art treasures in a new complex to be built at the former Théodore Barrois pithead: the northern talent for reinvention continues apace. A brand new casino is opening and *Gault Millau* gastro guides predict the next generation of great chefs will emerge from the cobbles of Vieux Lille.

▼ *Christmas comes once a year, but the big wheel on Grand' Place keeps the festivities turning until the end of January.*

Planning

THE CITY:
A PRACTICAL OVERVIEW

Lille has grown somewhat since its early years when it was clustered around the site of today's Notre Dame de la Treille. First, Louis XIV built his fortress on a virtual island in the River Deûle and commissioned a residential quarter next to the old trading district. As it sprawled in all directions, the city swallowed up neighbouring districts – those quarters that still bear the names associated with their own histories. On maps you will see **Lille Centre** around the main squares, with the university-lined boulevards known as **Vauban Esquermes** stretching westwards; to the south are **Wazemmes**, **Moulins** and **Lille Sud**; eastwards is the **Fives** district; and to the north are **Vieux Lille** and **St-Maurice Pellevoisin**. The neighbouring communes of **Lomme**, **Lambersart**, **La Madeleine** and **Hellemmes** are now very much part of Lille itself.

Lille is surprisingly compact and very easy to explore on foot – that is, if you are wearing your sturdiest walking shoes rather than the stylish footwear sold in a dozen exclusive emporia in the hilly and cobbled old town. Even without using the excellent public transport system, you can cross from one side of the central area to another in 15 minutes. To make life even easier for readers, we have divided the centre of Lille into four easily distinguished zones:

Vieux Lille **VL**

Vieux Lille is a very special place. Looming gables, cobbled streets, intoxicatingly wonderful street names promising golden lions, hunchbacked cats or freshly minted coins at every turn. Since the principal roads were laid out in sweeping arcs to protect the long-forgotten castle on the site of the old castrum fortified camp and many other streets were reclaimed from canals, no map will ever satisfactorily convey the geography of the place.

The first-, second- or fifth-time visitor should be prepared to surrender to fate and banish any dreams of short cuts. Getting lost is among the greatest pleasures that Lille has to offer its visitors, with so many entrancing little shops selling antiques, fragrant soaps and sumptuous linens that every journey brings its own diversions.

From central Lille it seems that all roads lead to the old quarter. The Parc Matisse may be the short cut from the station, and the Alcide archway on Grand' Place might seem an obvious entrance. However, the most comfortable introduction is from the rue de la Bourse by the distinctive belfry on place du Théâtre. A few paces lead to rue de la Grande Chaussée; an iron arm above the corner shop will point you in the right direction. Charles, Comte d'Artagnan, lived at numbers 20 and 26; you can see the old walls from La Botte Chantilly, the shoe shop on the ground floor. Turn right along rue des Chats Bossus and admire the fabulous Breton art-deco mosaic frontage of l'Huitrière restaurant. Continue across the place du Lion d'Or to the 17th-century rue de la Monnaie. Named after the royal mint, this is the oldest street and has many of the original traders' emblems above the regimented shopfronts. Like the rues Royale and Basse, it wraps around the cathedral, following the line of the moat. Houses of red Armentières brick and white Lezennes stone have doorways adorned with cherubs, cornucopia and wheatsheaves, all painstakingly restored in the 1960s.

Rue de la Monnaie links the market square of place du Concert with the main hub of the old town, place du Lion d'Or and the adjacent place Louise de Bettignies. The latter was named for a local heroine, a spy who died at the hands of the Germans in 1915. Number 29 is the Demeure Gilles de la Boë, a handsome baroque house dating from 1636 that once overlooked the inland port. Lille's name derives from its original position as an island between the upper and lower Deûle rivers, and the wealth of Vieux Lille comes from the thriving trade between merchants plying the two routes between Paris and the Low Countries.

Furthest from the town centre is the Quartier Royal, an elegant residential district commissioned by King Louis XIV, who fell in love with the town when the Citadelle was built. These roads were built to link the marketplaces of the centre with the fortress in the woods of the Bois de Boulogne.

The quaint narrow streets of Vieux Lille today feel wonderfully safe, with cheery groups of students in animated discussion, well-dressed couples window shopping arm-in-arm on the narrow pavements, and traffic insinuating turns at a snail's pace, ensuring that the quarter's refined charm never slips into stuffiness. Mind you, the indiscreet working girls by the old Porte de Gand are a reminder that any town with a military presence can never become too prissy! Three decades ago, the kerbside trade was the only truly thriving *métier* of the old town, but as Lille reclaimed its streets, art dealers and restaurateurs moved into the renovated buildings to create the enchanting realm of refinement that we know today.

Carnality on the plate and in the boudoir are not the only tastes catered for in this other world of 17th- and 18th-century houses and shops. No one should miss the pretty pleasures of saying 'I wish' to the latest fashions chez Michel Ruc on the rue des Chats Bossus, and 'I will', 'I do', 'I can't help myself' to the unrivalled confections of the Pâtisserie Meert on rue Esquermoise, just a whim and drop of the willpower away from the Grand' Place.

Grand' Place to République **GP**

Absolutely everything that matters in Lille begins on Grand' Place, from sunrise over the Vieille Bourse's morning market selling cut flowers and uncut antiquarian books, to shirtsleeved lunchtimes on the terrace of the Coq Hardi. You will not find the name Grand' Place on any map nor street sign – the square is now officially called the Place Générale de Gaulle, but the locals still refer to the place by its old, familiar name. The central column is a virtual sundial of life in the city. Carrier bags from FNAC and the Furet du Nord rest on tables during the 'any time, coffee time' of a contented shopper. Afternoon rendezvous by the fountains flow into evenings at the Théâtre du Nord, its posters proudly proclaiming Stuart Seide's latest season of Shakespeare, Pinter and Molière. Bars, beers and *bonhomie* beckon from all directions, but the goddess standing on the central column draws everyone back for a dawn onion-soup breakfast at a late-night restaurant.

The square is bounded by the performing arts, with the theatre dominating the south side and, to the east, the picture-book opera house on the place du Théâtre; westwards, the circular Nouveau Siècle building is home to the Orchestre Nationale. Many weekends see displays or entertainment on the Grand' Place itself. Perhaps a bandstand will have been erected for a concert, or a marquee set up to house an exhibition sponsored by the local paper, *La Voix du Nord*, whose elegant building dominates the square.

The main commercial districts of Lille fan out from the Grand' Place, a giant compass where all roads lead to shopping: chain stores, multiplex cinemas and boutiques line the rues de Béthune and Neuve. Since traffic was barred from these streets in 1973, visitors have been able to admire the art deco architecture above the shopfronts in the pedestrianised triangle between the stations, place République and the city squares. Along the rue Faidherbe are inexpensive shoe and clothes shops, including the wonderful Tati (see page 152); the wide rue Nationale has Printemps (see page 165) and the glitzier Parisian stores; and northwards, beyond the once-upon-a-time perpendicular-style belfry of the Chambre de Commerce, are hidden the picture-perfect boutiques and galleries of Vieux Lille.

But walk along the wide, traffic-free shopping streets south of the square to reach the Palais des Beaux Arts – the very magnet that pulls the world to the place République, providing an abundance of inspiration and fulfilment. How many visitors realise that the museum is but a gateway to the one-time Latin Quarter of Lille, a 19th-century haven of culture and learning? The boulevard de la Liberté was laid out when the original city walls came tumbling down in the mid-19th century. Originally named for the Empress Eugénie, this was the essential address for well-to-do families enriched by the industrial revolution. Textile barons and their ilk competed to build grander and grander mansions with grand staircases for grand gestures and grander entertaining, many with their own private theatres for after-dinner opera at home.

The place République itself is poised between the museum and the equally grand Préfecture, which was based on the design of the Paris Louvre. Notice the emblems on each wing: an eagle for the Second Empire, the letter N for Napoleon III. At the centre of the gardens is a stepped arena, providing a stage for musicians and a well of natural light for the métro station.

Markets: Gambetta to Solférino **MK**

Lille is a market town, never more so than during the Braderie of the first weekend in September. For 48 hours non-stop, the entire city sets out its stalls on doorsteps, pavements, trestles and pitches. Recycle your children's clothes for a few pence, rediscover stolen goods from that break-in in May and swap deco uplighters for 1960s lava-lamps in a tradition that dates back to the city fathers granting servants the right to earn money by selling their master's cast-off clothing once a year. A hundred kilometres of stalls appear every year, the métro runs all night long, and every hotel room for miles around is booked months in advance. The Braderie never sleeps and brasseries compete to sell the most *moules* and create the highest pile of shells on the pavement outside the front door.

A special map-guide is published for the Braderie and may be picked up at the tourist office.

Since the event is held only once a year, a happy alternative takes place every week in the Wazemmes quarter, 15 minutes' walk or two métro stops from the town centre. This is the market of markets and a Sunday morning institution (see page 164). A smaller market is held each Wednesday and Saturday at place Sébastopol. The Théâtre Sébastopol dominates the square. An entertaining explosion of architectural styles – Renaissance, Moorish, classical and sheer pantomime – this people's playhouse provides popular boulevard entertainment. From populist playtime one can turn to intellectual reflection, as roads south lead to the former Faculté des Lettres, once a centre of study, reflection and tolerance. The Protestant temple and the synagogue may be seen on rue Angellier. Whilst the secular university is now based outside the town centre to the north, boulevard Vauban is home to the Catholic university campus.

Between the two city-centre seats of learning, rue Solférino, the centre of Lille's student nightlife, is the starting point for any serious partying (see pages 124–5).

▼ *Braderie season, when every inch of pavement is the trading floor.*

Stations/Hôtel de Ville S

Not one station but two. The new Europe station welcomes the TGV and Eurostar and looks like the airports of tomorrow. Dominated by the boot-shaped Crédit Lyonnais building, this is the heartland of the new international business community. Constructed on land hived off by the military, there are hints of early fortifications scattered in the emerging Parc Matisse. The vast paved square of the place Mitterand is gradually being claimed by a generation of skateboarders, micro-scooter aces and mountainbikers.

Across the square is the Euralille shopping centre, an indoor alternative to the rest of the city. A few yards along avenue le Corbusier is the public transport hive: underground are two métro stations, and the tramway to Roubaix and Tourcoing; while at street level one finds the bus station, taxi ranks and the original 19th-century station serving all points local and beyond, and all speeds under *trèsgrands*.

The older Gare Lille Flandres was Paris's original Gare du Nord, moved brick by brick and stone by stone for the railway line's royal opening. The town elders, not wishing to appear satisfied with secondhand goods, insisted on building an extra storey onto the station façade to create an even more imposing frontage. The first train to arrive at the station was greeted by the Bishop of Douai, who blessed the locomotive, and by Hector Berlioz conducting the town band in a specially composed concerto, an event nearly recreated on the launch night of the Capital of Culture celebrations (sheer crowd numbers led to it being abandoned). Today, the place seems less grand, just the typical terminus hive of bars, cafés and eateries clustered around the fountains at the front of the station. Weekends see soldiers from the Citadelle flirting with students from the universities. After a while, the incongruous sight of a young lad with a sub-machine-gun at his belt, composing text messages on his mobile phone, seems perfectly normal. At the side of the station, on rue de Tournai, eating is cheap with *frites* stands and burgers. Seamier services are available behind the line of brasseries facing the station, with flesh offered shrink-wrapped in cellophane in shops and in lycra on the pavements around the rues de Roubaix and Ponts de Comines (see page 141).

Close to the motorway intersections of the ring road, Lille Grand Palais is a huge exhibition arena. The Zenith auditorium hosts major rock concerts and lavish musicals, and is the place to see international superstars such as David Bowie or Elton John.

Below the stations is the successor to the long-demolished St-Sauveur district, home to the 20th-century Hôtel de Ville. Further out to the east and across the railway lines is the district of Lille-Fives, which grew up as a town in its own right. Fives has its own brass bands, festivals and customs, including a wine harvest festival every autumn, when the little local vineyards produce *vin de Fives*.

Cutting a swathe from the Gares to the République is the only slightly seedy rue Molinel, the broad street a boulevard wide in its aspiration, an un-grand ribbon of otherness and improbable neighbours: catholic schools rubbing shoulders with kebaberies; travel agencies selling weeks in north Africa alongside artistic florists selling minature topiary in galvanised pots opposite nail bars and religious bookshops; the long-forgotten *schmutter* trade recalled by long-closed textile traders and thriving bespoke tailors and wedding couturiers. The fluctuating fortunes of the Molinel are told by the boarded-up and thwarted Monoprix supermarket at the station end of the road, and the new generation Tanneurs shopping mall where rue de Paris bisects the main road and the pedestrianised quarter spills down to the border. This is also where a modern reinterpretation of the Monoprix lives anew.

The other walk, along the avenue Le Corbusier from Lille Europe past the old station, then along the rue Faidherbe to the Grand' Place and the old town, is a gentle turning back of the clock as the architecture rewinds through 21st, 20th and 19th centuries to the 18th and 17th; 400 years of optimism, confidence and faith in the future, respecting the past.

WHEN TO VISIT

Lille 2004 was merely a shop window for a city with a talent for late-night partying. Some themed weekends inaugurated for the festivities have become regular events, and each year sees a string of *incontournables* the unmissable happenings that are the perfect excuse for a trip to Lille.

January
The big wheel turns on Grand' Place
Lille Film Festival
January sales (until mid-February)

February
Tourissima – the huge holiday exhibition at Grand Palais

March

Craft fair at Villeneuve d'Ascq

April

Robert Casadesus International Piano Festival
Paris–Roubaix cycle race
Lille Short Film Festival
Fortified towns open day at the Citadelle and other walled towns of the region (fourth weekend)

May

La Louche d'Or – soup festival in Wazemmes
The *Montgolfiades* – hot-air balloon meeting
Wazemmes International Accordion Festival

June

Fêtes de Lille – the town's giant mascots parade through the streets
Gay Pride Weekend – with free concerts
Fête de la Musique
Festival of Excellence – the market sells regional produce, from beers, ciders and floral-scented lemonades to farmhouse cheeses and delicious sweets
Independent Cinema Festival

July

Bastille Day (14 July) – much partying in the streets as summer holidays officially begin with fireworks and dancing for the French national day
Summer sales

September

The Braderie (see page 12) is Europe's biggest market (first weekend)
Lille Half Marathon
National Heritage Day – private buildings open their doors to visitors (third weekend)

October

The great circus festival with troupes and performers from all over the world

November

Tourcoing Jazz Festival
Mozart Festival (November–April)

December

St Nicholas's Day (6 December) – with parades and entertainment to launch the Christmas season
Christmas market in place Rihour and the big wheel on the Grand' Place
Roubaix's Braderie d'Art
New Year's Eve fireworks and partying on the Grand' Place

SUGGESTED ITINERARIES

If you are staying one day

- Walk through Vieux Lille

- Have a coffee or meal on the main squares

- Treat yourself to an excellent lunch

- Spend at least an hour at the Palais des Beaux Arts

- Stroll round the Vieille Bourse

- Go shopping: the old town for something special; the streets around Grand' Place or Euralille for more practical purchases

- Taste a selection of freshly brewed beers at Les Trois Brasseurs before catching the train home

If you are staying two days

- Vieux Lille – and the Musée de l'Hospice Comtesse

- The Palais des Beaux Arts

- Browse the bookstalls at the Vieille Bourse

- Wander through the magnificent churches

- Start your evening on Grand' Place and enjoy a performance at the opera, theatre or jazz club before hitting the late-night bars

- Have at least one bistro or brasserie meal with a local beer, and indulge yourself with a gastronomic treat at one of the gourmet restaurants

- Start the second day with breakfast at Paul or a walk in the Bois de Boulogne
- Shop for bargains: midweek at Roubaix bargain outlets; Sunday morning at Wazemmes market
- Explore the wider district for half a day: take the tram to Roubaix and La Piscine, or perhaps the modern art collection at Villeneuve d'Ascq
- Visit the smaller museums or catch an event or exhibition at one of the Maisons Folies

If you are staying three days or more

Do all of the above, but give yourself a full day away from central Lille to discover the attractions of the Métropole. Perhaps you might hire a car to visit Le Cateau-Cambrésis to see Matisse's own art collection. If your French is up to it, do take yourself to the theatre or a cabaret show.

TOURIST INFORMATION

Before leaving home, contact Maison de la France, the French national tourist office in your own country. Email via contact form on the website. All local online sites may be accessed via ⌂ www.franceguide.com.

TOUR OPERATORS

Check with Maison de la France in your own country for a full list of tour operators offering inclusive packages to Lille. Visit ⌂ www.franceguide.com and click on your country of residence. Alternatively you may contact the local office directly.

UK & Ireland

Maison de la France Lincoln House, 300 High Holborn, London WC1V 7JH ☎ 09068 244 123 (premium rate) ✉ info.uk@franceguide.com ⌂ www.franceguide.com ⊙ Mon–Fri 10.00–16.00 🚇 *Holborn*. An excellent one-stop shop for buying guidebooks, booking tickets for events & picking up the free *Traveller in France* reference guides, as well as plenty of advice.

The Association of British Tour Operators to France

⌂ www.holidayfrance.org.uk. Includes scores of companies offering holidays, travel & short breaks in Lille.

Major companies selling packages to Lille include:

Cresta ☎ 0870 161 0920 ⤴ www.crestaholidays.co.uk

Eurostar ☎ 0870 167 6767 ⤴ www.eurostar.co.uk

Leisure Direction ☎ 0870 442 8943 ⤴ www.leisuredirection.co.uk

USA

Maison de la France *New York* 825 3rd Av, 29th floor (entrance on 50th St), New York, NY 10022 ☎ 514 288 1904
e info.us@franceguide.com ⤴ www.franceguide.com; *Los Angeles* 9454 Wilshire Bld, Suite 210, 90212 Beverly Hills, CA ☎ 310 271 6665; *Chicago* Consulate General of France, 205 N Michigan Av, Suite 3770, 60601 Chicago, Illinois ☎ 312 327 0290

Canada

Maison de la France 1981 Av McGill, College Suite 490, H3A 2WP, Montreal ☎ (514) 288 2026 e canada@franceguide.com
⤴ www.franceguide.com

Australia & New Zealand

Maison de la France Level 13, 25 Bligh St, 2000 NSW, Sydney, Australia ☎ + 61 (0)2 9231 5244 e info.au@franceguide.com
⤴ www.franceguide.com

RED TAPE

European Union (EU) nationals need carry only a valid identity card or passport. For nationals of non-EU countries, passports are required. Nationals of some countries require visas. Check with the local embassy or consulate when planning your trip (taking into account the time it may take for visas to be issued).

For customs advice in France telephone ☎ 01 53 24 68 24 and in the UK ☎ 0845 010 9000. Within the EU there is officially no limitation for purchases destined for personal consumption by EU citizens, although there are recommended limits for cigarettes (800) and alcohol (90 litres of wine and 10 litres of spirits). Travellers from countries outside the EU must take heed of duty-free regulations and make a customs declaration and pay duty on items with a value of over €220. However, they may also claim approximately 15% tax discount on their purchases (see page 40).

Narcotics, some pornographic material, illegal drugs, weapons, live plants and ivory may not be carried across borders.

If you lose your passport, contact your consulate immediately. Most of these are to be found in Paris, although the UK and Canada have consular officials based in Lille (see page 38). Replacement passports may be reissued in France. However, if you are travelling within the EU (even if you are not an EU national) you may, under certain circumstances, be allowed to travel without your passport, subject to the discretion of the airline or carrier and immigration authorities, should you have acceptable alternative photo-identification.

TIME

From the end of March through to the end of October, Continental European time changes from GMT+1 to GMT+2.

GETTING THERE & AWAY

By train

Eurostar, from the UK, is a fabulous way to travel to Lille: 80 minutes from London St Pancras International, 70 minutes from the new station at Ebbsfleet and an hour from Ashford International. Each 400m-long Eurostar train can carry up to 560 standard-class and 206 first-class passengers from London to the heart of Lille in 18 air-conditioned carriages. Two train managers and teams of uniformed stewards look after passengers, welcoming arrivals and reminding would-be smokers that the entire train is ciggie-free. Two bar-buffet carriages, modelled on TGV bars, have space to stand and chat over a drink. Baby-changing rooms are at each end of the train, and there are toilets in all carriages. Pricier seats are spaced three abreast, one single, one pair; in standard class, two pairs. Groups of four passengers should request seats around a table. The more expensive compartments have several business-seating configurations, including a semi-private area for four or six passengers at the end of each carriage. Be warned, not all second-class tickets sold as 'window' seats are actually next to a window: around four places in each carriage are in fact against a solid wall. Regular passengers with a good book may not mind, but first-timers and anyone who thrills to a view will be disappointed, so do insist when booking that your window seat actually has a window, if only for the thrill of arriving back at the new London terminus.

Flexible fares are available in all carriages, but non-transferable tickets offer sensational value, with return tickets often costing less than single

ST PANCRAS

Returning to St Pancras is always an occasion. As the train pulls out of the tunnel that sweeps under the Thames and the city itself, the view across the regeneration lands of the Kings Cross goods yards is a feast of promise. Note the Grand Union Canal with its basin at the new Kings Place concert venue, the protected wildlife reserve at Canley Street, the British Library compound and the barcoded skyline of London, from the old Post Office Tower to the new Gherkin of the City and the plinthed pyramids of Docklands. Reigning supreme, are the gothic spires of St Pancras itself. Glide through the new glass box of the station's extension to the splendid archway of the original Barlow Shed, the ironwork now picked out in a British sky blue, the magnificent span perched on the warm red brick and white stone walls. For some passengers, the centrepiece is the lumbering statue of snogging giants looming over the platforms in chunky impersonation of a cinematic farewell. For me, the station clock itself is the more potent symbol of the timeless thrill of arrival and departure, of the tender kiss of parting and the balmy embrace of return.

fares. Self-print ticket option for online bookings. Leisure Select and Business Premier passengers enjoy more spacious accommodation and a three- or four-course meal served at their seat. According to the hour, a welcome glass of champagne may be offered, and a choice of wines served with the meal. The quality of onboard food is pretty good – an improvement on previous years. Vegetarian and other dietary requests should be made at least 48 hours in advance. For an inexpensive upgrade from standard class, consider travelling with a tour operator (see page 18), since deals usually include hotel accommodation. You may also upgrade in one direction or find day-trip and weekend promotional rates. One favourite deal has been the Saturday £42 Nightclubbing ticket offering evening outbound travel and returning first thing in the morning – a huge hit with party people or opera lovers who may leave London on any train after 16.00 on Saturday, arrive in time for a fortifying meal before dancing until dawn, sleeping through the return trip on the 08.36 from Lille and dozing in their own homes by the time their friends and families awake to the Sunday morning call of church and garden centre. Another new bargain is the £35 lead-in one-way fare.

A makeover, courtesy of France's pet designer Philippe Starck, restyled the carriages before the move from Waterloo to St Pancras. Train crews were also kitted out with a dress-down look that somewhat mutes the original glamour that marked out Eurostar as special. The onboard staff remain as professional, helpful and charming as ever.

From the regions, Ebbsfleet Station is easiest to reach by car (off junction two of the M25 near Bluewater shopping centre) and has a car park like a medium-sized continent. Ashford station, the original Eurostar base in Kent, has inexplicably been downgraded to a mere one Lille train per day. Through-rail tickets from 68 key UK cities, including Birmingham, Cambridge, Leeds and Manchester, are now available, changing at St Pancras. TGV, Thalys and Eurostar services from Paris, Brussels, Amsterdam, Cologne and other key European cities arrive at Lille Europe station, with some additional Paris services arriving at nearby Lille Flandres. SNCF, the French rail company, has online booking facilities (⏶ www.sncf.com). Within France, click the link for *prems* deals – discount advance-purchase tickets you can print from your own PC. UK-based travellers should go to ⏶ www.tgv.co.uk for similar discount fares within France. On any non-Eurostar service, remember to validate your ticket in the red or yellow machines at the entrance to the platforms. Rail Europe's UK and US offices sell all tickets, and Interail, Eurail and EuroDomino offer passes for unlimited rail travel across Europe. French trains have dedicated compartments banning mobile phones.

Onboard meals

Leisure Select and business passengers enjoy a full meal served at their seat, and in standard class the buffet bar offers a range of hot and cold snacks. An alternative to the trek to the buffet compartment for those encumbered with luggage, small children or delicious lethargy is an onboard picnic. St Pancras boasts a fresh food market as well as two Marks & Spencer food stores, offering a range of salads, snacks, sandwiches and sushi. A tip: when the branch opposite the Eurostar check-in is busy, nip along to the larger M&S store (next to Boots the Chemist) at The Circle by the domestic section of the station. A smaller selection of snacks is available from Boots the Chemist. For a similar treat on the return journey, Lille's Carrefour hypermarket (see page 165) is located just across the parvis François Mitterand from the station. As well as the obvious pâtés, cheeses, breads and sandwiches, this store has platters of prepared crudités and dips as a healthy option – at the back of the food hall, by the fresh veg. Do make sure that food complies with international regulations. During the UK foot and mouth outbreak, meat products were banned.

Cash & carry

St Pancras International sites most of its facilities before Eurostar check-in, so left luggage and bureaux de change should be checked out in the main station, where a bigger range of shops includes Foyles and Hamleys. Europe's longest champagne bar, more than a dozen restaurants (see pages 24–5) and pub grub are also 'landside'.

Eurostar's terminal is housed in the exquisitely reconceived undercroft of the splendid Victorian Gothic station. The restoration work is simply stunning, especially to we former 'locals' who recall this area as the province of taxi repair shops and earthy greasy spoon caffs. The departure lounge area has its café and restaurant-bar. There is free Wi-Fi available and a bank of workstations in the lounge. Some fun interactive screens on coffee tables and in brick alcoves on the walls allow exploration of Britain's national art treasures. There is also a mail box at the information desk for posting those last minute letters, cards and bills. An impressive selection of international newspapers is available at the WH Smith bookshop and newsagency. You may also print up a copy of any of scores of other daily newspapers from around the world.

Holders of the Eurostar frequent traveller card have an excellent private lounge with complimentary refreshments, bar, newspapers and mobile phone chargers, as well as Wi-Fi access.

Passport control, customs & security

Eurostar terminals run passenger security screening similar to that found at airports. The original plans for onboard passport inspections have been overtaken by more traditional checks by the appropriate authorities at arrivals as well as departures. Check-in is 30 minutes before departure (10 minutes for Eurostar Carte Blanche holders), subject to changing security regulations. Standard class ticket holders should allow half an hour, or even longer during peak travel periods. Two cases and one extra piece of hand luggage are allowed per person. Knives and other restricted items have to be registered before travel. So do allow extra time to check in.

Tickets

Tickets may be purchased directly from Eurostar, as well as at Rail Europe's counters and call centres. Rail Europe also offers internal European tickets for Thalys, TGV and regional trains. Many UK travel agents offer Eurostar tickets, although at the time of writing, Thomas Cook, publishers of the *European Rail Timetable*, no longer sell continental train tickets.

DINING AT ST PANCRAS

The new St Pancras International is a true destination station in its own right. It lives up to its dramatic architecture and, appropriately for the UK's premier link to mainland Europe, this is a continental-style *Grande Gare*. Just as Paris's Gare de Lyon has its celebrated *belle époque* Train Bleu restaurant, so St Pancras has two flagship dining places – the St Pancras Grand brasserie and the already legendary Champagne Bar. The latter encompasses around 100 yards of fizz, with a breathtaking selection of champagnes, from a glass of De Nauroy brut for £7.50 to a Dom Pérignon White Gold 1995 at £6,500 a jeroboam. For the quality of some of the wines the prices are certainly not excessive, and of course the setting, along a stretch of platform, is impressive. The spectacular railway-cathedral architecture soaring above the Barlow Shed, restored in all its 19th century glory, is a perfect place to toast a journey and turn travel into an occasion. An all-day menu features the obvious indulgent accompaniments to bubbly …

Here, even if you have not opted for an onboard upgrade, you may start your trip to Lille with flair: whether the full English afternoon tea of sandwiches, scones, cake and nice pot of Darjeeling with a glass of Pomery rosé for around £20, or starting the day with a smoked salmon, scrambled egg and champagne breakfast for £17.50 per person. Should you really want to greet the dawn in style, splash out on scrambled eggs, black truffle and chives on toasted sourdough, tea

Eurostar *UK* Travel Centre, St Pancras International, Pancras Rd, London NW1 ☉ 09.00–19.00 🚇 *Kings Cross St Pancras* ☏ call centre 08705 186186 (☉ Mon–Fri 08.00–21.00, Sat 08.00–20.00, Sun & UK bank holidays 09.00–17.00; a £5 booking fee applies to all phone bookings) ⌂ www.eurostar.co.uk; *France* ☏ 08 36 35 35 39

Rail Europe 1 Regent St, London SW1 ☉ Mon–Fri 10.00–18.00, Sat 10.00–17.00 🚇 *Piccadilly Circus* ☏ call centre 0844 848 4070 (☉ Mon–Fri 08.00–20.00, Sat 09.00–17.00, Sun (Jun–Aug) 10.00–16.00)

or coffee, freshly squeezed juice and a half-bottle of Krug Grand Cuvée at £97.50 for two.

Whilst the Champagne Bar has its all-day menu, the St Pancras Grand is the choice for hearty appetites, with full menus starting under £20. Kedgeree has always been my breakfast weakness, but all foodie vices are catered for. Romantics might opt for the Aphrodisiac menu with the requisite oysters, chocolate and bubbly at £45 (although the proffered parsnips would never be my choice of asparagus substitute!). Sunday options range from brunch to jazz in the evenings.

For a flavour of the quarter itself, rather than the anticipation of travel (remember, St Pancras has always been the blurred boundary of Kings Cross and Bloomsbury), the original station pub from the terminus's humbler days still has a local feel. Now known as the Betjeman Arms (after the poet, Sir John, who long campaigned for the station's preservation), this pub, serving traditional British grub, hosts Monday quiz nights, Tuesday sing-along sessions around the piano, offers pie and mash on a Wednesday and has live music on Friday evenings. Outside the pub, Martin Jennings's statue of Sir John is for me far more evocative of the spirit of the place than the Brobdingnagian lovers along the way.

Elsewhere on the station, you can find branches of Carluccio's Italian restaurant under the famous statue of the lovers kissing; Yo Sushi, Japanese conveyor belt eaterie in The Circle shopping area; and two branches of coffee shops familiar from the streets of Lille: Le Pain Quotidien (by Eurostar Arrivals) and Paul (opposite the sushi bar).

At least a dozen other cafés and food outlets, including The Fine Burger Company, Peyton and Byrne British patisserie and most of the main international chains can be found on the station.

The Champagne Bar and St Pancras Grand may be found on the upper concourse (✆ 020 7870 9900 🖰 www.searcys.co.uk/stpancrasgrand; *Champagne Bar* ◷ 07.00–23.00; *St Pancras Grand* ◷ 11.00–23.00).

🖰 www.raileurope.co.uk; *USA* ✆ 1 877 456 RAIL (09.00–21.00 EST)
🖰 www.raileurope.com; *Canada* ✆ 1 800 361 RAIL (09.00–21.00 EST)
🖰 www.raileurope.com

St Pancras Station 🖰 www.stpancras.com

Rail information
SNCF ✆ 08 36 35 35 35 (from France) 🖰 www.sncf.com
In all other countries contact Rail Europe (see above).

By car

From the UK you have to cross the Channel or the North Sea, either by boat or through the Channel Tunnel. Most ferries ply the busy route from Dover to Calais, with journey times averaging 90 minutes; the tunnel claims a 35-minute crossing on the same route. However, you must also allow for check-in times, queuing and visits to the terminal buildings. Slower overnight services operate from Hull.

Best value is often to be found with package deals from tour operators, but an excellent place to shop for bargain cross-Channel fares is ⏚ www.aferry.to.

Cross-Channel operators

Eurotunnel ☏ 0870 535 3535 (UK); 08 10 63 03 04 (France)
⏚ www.eurotunnel.com. Eurotunnel operates the Channel Tunnel service for motorists. At the terminal near Folkestone, motorists are directed to drive aboard the special trains that carry cars through the tunnel. It is easy & by far the most efficient route, since you need not even leave your vehicle. Of course, the ferries offer a wider range of entertainment, with restaurants, bars & children's play areas, but the advantage of the tunnel is in the saving of time & effort. Free Wi-Fi in the terminal & lounges.

LD Lines ☏ 0844 576 8836 (UK); 0825 304 304 (France)
⏚ www.ldlines.co.uk. Newest arrival on the short crossing, LD took over the Dover-Boulogne service from the much-missed Speed Ferries in early 2009.

Norfolkline ☏ 0870 870 1020 (UK); 03 28 28 95 50 (France)
⏚ www.norfolkline.com. Has up to 10 crossings a day between Dover & Dunkerque, with a journey time of around 2 hours. Also runs 3 ferries per week from Rosyth near Edinburgh to Zeebrugge, an hour from Lille. Ferries arrive on the continent late morning after an afternoon departure from Scotland.

P&O ☏ 08716 645 645 (UK); 0825 120 156 (France)
⏚ www.poferries.com. Operate the biggest fleet crossing on the Dover–Calais route with the largest ships. A round-the-clock service means that passengers can turn up at the port & drive straight aboard. Also run a service from Hull to Zeebrugge, leaving the UK at 19.00 each evening & arriving at the Belgian port, just 53km from Lille, at 08.30.

SeaFrance ☎ 0871 423 7119 (UK); 08 25 04 40 45 (France)
🏠 www.seafrance.com. The French-owned & managed Dover–Calais ferry is proud of its 'Continental flavour'.

After the crossing

From Boulogne, Calais or Dunkerque take the A16 then A25 motorway (signposted for Lille). From Zeebrugge take the N31 (via Bruges), which leads to the A17 motorway, and then the A14 (which becomes the A22 as it crosses the French border). Remember that Belgian motorway signs may list Lille by its Flemish name, Rijsel. At Marcq-en-Baroeul, leave the motorway and follow the N356 into Lille.

By air

Lille Lesquin Airport, for domestic and continental European flights, is 8km from the town centre (see page 47). However, visitors from UK regions and beyond Europe may fly direct to Paris's Roissy-Charles de Gaulle Airport and take the 51-minute TGV train to Lille from the station at the Air France terminal. Air France (🏠 www.airfrance.com) sell through-tickets to Lille. Alternatively, flights to Brussels airport, across the border, connect with a rail link to Lille in under 40 minutes. Ryanair fly in from across Europe.

▼ *Arriving in style at Lille Europe.*

HEALTH

No inoculations are required to visit France. Citizens of EU countries should carry an EHIC (European Health Insurance) card, available from post offices. This enables the traveller to claim reimbursement of medical and pharmaceutical expenses in the event of illness or accident. Nationals of other countries should arrange necessary private insurance cover before travelling. Insurance is recommended for all travellers to cover additional costs such as repatriation or extra nursing care.

See also *Useful numbers* (page 44) for emergencies.

Travel clinics & health information

A full list of current travel clinic websites worldwide is available on ⌘ www.istm.org/. For other journey preparation information, consult ⌘ www.nathnac.org/ds/map_world.aspx. Information about various medications may be found on ⌘ www.netdoctor.co.uk/travel.

Pharmacies

Pharmacies are easily identified by the green-cross sign and are open during usual shopping hours. Out of hours, condoms may be purchased from supermarkets and vending machines. Details of out-of-hours opening are posted in pharmacy windows, and may be obtained from the police.

WHAT TO TAKE

Apart from Marmite (and you'll probably find that in the *cuisines du monde* aisle at the supermarket), there is virtually nothing essential that you could wish to take that cannot be found in Lille. Perhaps the only exception is plug adaptors. Electricity in France is 220 volts; appliances use two-pin plugs. Adaptors are freely available from airport and station shops before you travel.

MONEY & BUDGETING

Currency

The euro constantly plays dynamic games of cat and mouse with Sterling and the US dollar. The single European currency, the euro, is divided into 100 cents (often referred to locally by the old French term 'centimes'). Notes are valued at €5, 10, 20, 50, 100, 200 and 500. In practice many shops may refuse to change the three largest denominations (and, considering that they are worth upwards of around a hundred dollars or £70 each, it would be foolish to carry them with you). Change higher-value notes at banks or supermarkets. Coins are worth 1, 2, 5, 10, 20 and 50 cents. A good way to get rid of too much heavy loose change is to use self-service stamp-printing machines in post offices. All notes bear uniform designs featuring architectural images, but coins carry national emblems (monarchs' heads for Spain and Belgium, the Irish harp, sundry symbols of the French Republic, Leonardo da Vinci's works for Italy). No matter what the motif, all coins, like the notes, may be used anywhere in the euro zone.

Budgeting

As befits a student city with exclusive shops, Lille may be savoured by all budgets. But how much money should you expect to spend?

Rock bottom

If you really want to keep your hand from straying into your pocket you can manage on as little as €35 per day – by staying at the youth hostel, eating one inexpensive set meal at a modest bar or restaurant and making your own breakfast. Bread costs around 65c a loaf; cheese, pâté, water and beer are very cheap at markets and supermarkets. Don't use public transport – sit outside and enjoy people-watching on the squares and visit those sites that do not charge for admission.

Modest

Neither hardships nor extravagances at under €60 a day. Using two-for-one hotel promotions, a simple hotel room could cost you as little as €20 per person per night. Allow yourself €30 for meals, including a delicious set menu at lunchtime (when restaurants are cheapest), a *flammekeuche* or *moules-frites* evening meal and a couple of beers or coffees around town. You'll have change for sightseeing and public transport.

Fun

A daily allowance of €100 gives you a better hotel room, and budgets for a delicious lunch and a good brasserie or bistro dinner, drinks at cafés and bars around town and a good deal of sightseeing and travel.

Indulgent

Spend €150 each day, and enjoy a good three-star hotel room, a gastronomic set menu, a hearty lunch, a good day's sightseeing and an evening out.

Extravagant

From €300 upwards you'll be able to afford a luxury hotel room, an à la carte meal at a Michelin-starred restaurant twice a day and as much shopping as the chauffeur can carry!

Of course, these prices do not include shopping for clothes, jewellery etc. But I have been as thrilled by an unexpected find at Wazemmes market as others have been at Bulgari and Cartier!

▼ *Gare Lille Flandres – one up on Paris.*

GARE DE LILLE FLANDRES

Lille for visitors with limited mobility

Philanthropic may well have been the adjective that has linked the centuries of Lille but, despite a grand tradition of hospices for the poor and needy, jumble sales for servants and retirement homes for Renaissance hookers, you can't get over the sheer ubiquity of the cobbles. Just as the *pavés du nord* play havoc with the bruised bottoms of thousands of cyclists each season, so those stones and steps that line the old quarter provide a challenge for wheelchairs, walking frames and sticks. No wonder one mercifully short-lived trend in 2008 was for an oxygen bar where flavoured air was served to guests through masks.

Having myself walked the streets of the past with the zimmer frames, rollators, sturdy crutches and canes of the present, I can testify to the awkwardness of the city centre. But the city is not entirely off-limits to disabled guests. The central pedestrianised area is easily user-friendly, parks are well laid out, there is flat access to cinemas and most restaurants around the squares and back streets have heated outdoor terraces. The shopping malls are well-equipped, so a restaurant table near those or the department stores provides a practical alternative to the toilet problem.

PLANNING A TRIP

The national tourist office website has the usual info: ♿ www.franceguide.com then follow the links: Practical Information > During Your Stay > France for Disabled People. Contact the departmental tourist office (see page 38) and ask for the *Handi-Tourisme* brochure or listings.

GETTING THERE

By rail

Of course (as very few major organisations understand), there are many and varied limits and levels of mobility. Transport authorities often like to

▲ *Refreshing the parts even the mètro cannot reach, the bus network runs through the old town and out as far as Belgium.*

lump all differently-abled travellers as 'wheelchair users'. Whilst it is easy to book a train or plane for a full-time wheelchair user, a person of restricted mobility who may perhaps be able to walk a few yards on the flat with a frame or stick, but cannot climb the steep step into a railway carriage without a ramp, nor board a plane without level access, could face long interrogation and explanations as some booking clerks do not have a pre-ordained key-stroke on their reservation software that recognises any disability which does not involve a conventional wheelchair.

Eurostar

St Pancras Station is well equipped to support disabled passengers, with lifts to all levels, and a gentle sloping travelator to platforms for those with powerful brakes! Eurostar has a special fare for wheelchair users, and a companion if required, with a designated space in each of the two central carriages. Ramps can be arranged for boarding these two carriages only, as when the platforms and trains were being designed for the move to St Pancras, no allowance was made for the width of second class doors in relation to the company's pre-ordered ramps. Eurostar is, albeit gradually, getting there, but some front-of-house staff at St Pancras are in need of some modern awareness training in dealing with differently-able punters. Onboard train and platform staff, however, seem uniformly lovely, kind, helpful and not at all patronising. Contact Eurostar directly for information (see page 24).

Those extra customer service lessons for those behind desks may be learnt from their counterparts at Lille Europe station, for travellers travelling from Lille to the UK or within France.

Service Accès Plus

This excellent semi-privatised service (☎ 0890 640 650 (then press 1) from France only ✉ accesplus@sncf.fr 🖥 www.accesplus.sncf.com 🕐 07.00–10.00) is extraordinarily efficient. Cheery and intelligent young staff offer the friendliest of welcomes. Find the reception desk at Lille Europe station, next to the ticket office. Contact Accès Plus an hour before travelling to arrange assistance. Advisors can also help plan your journey in advance and suggest alternative routes and facilities. A mini-boutique in the Lille office offers everything from plasters to notebooks and condoms – how refreshing for disabled guests to be regarded as human! Arrive at the lounge and reception area 30 minutes before departure to be accompanied all the way to reserved seats on the train. The train manager will be informed as to your needs, and a team member will be waiting for you at your destination if you have booked onward travel in France. When travelling by TGV make sure that you choose a duplex train if possible and ask to be put in a carriage with an elevated floor. This mini-lift system makes for dignified and comfortable boarding in a wheelchair. If your train is delayed or journey disrupted, call the helpline from your mobile phone on ☎ 0890 640 650 (then press 2). Passengers with hearing disabilities can text on ☎ 06 10 64 06 50.

Lille Europe station

Lille Europe station has a good system of lifts – although be aware of two alternative exits from the station. Should the lift down to the parvis Mitterand and Euralille be out of order, take another lift up to viaduct level and walk back down the av Le Corbusier.

By Car

Ferry and Channel Tunnel operators are very helpful. Explain your requirements when booking (see page 26) and arrangements may be made for your car to be parked onboard near a lift or flat, with wheelchair access to the passenger lounge. Just check in an hour before your crossing. Eurotunnel is the easiest option of all since you do not need to leave the car during the 35-minute crossing. Onboard the train the WC is not wheelchair accessible, so use facilities at the terminal before departure.

By air

Let airlines know special requirements at the time of booking. Lille airport is equipped with lifts and ramps for access to aircraft, has adapted toilets and telephone kiosks and supplies wheelchairs. There are ten designated parking spaces near the terminal.

GETTING AROUND

Métro & trams

The métro system is excellent, with level platforms and lifts from street to booking hall to platform level at every station. Brilliant. When a lift is to be taken out of order, for maintenance or other reasons, this will usually be announced on the ⌂ www.transpole.fr website. Click on '*se deplacer*' then '*reseau accessible*'.

Buses

Whilst most French buses are traditional touring coaches with several steep steps and not adapted to the needs of disabled passengers, Lille's Transpole network has done sterling work in opening up the network to all users. 90% of city buses are fitted with platforms that can be lowered for easier boarding. The following routes are fully accessible: 1, 6, 9, 12, 13, 14, 17, 31, 40, 41, 42, 43, 44, 50, 51, 54, 55, 73 and the two Citadine services. Lines 3, 4 and 20 are partially accessible.

Driving & parking

Blue badges issued in any EU country may be used in France. You still have to pay, though.

Overground rail

Accès Plus (see page 33) may also be able to assist with train journeys across the region. As well as both Lille Europe and Lille Flandres, the service is also available at Arras, Boulogne Ville, Calais Frethun, Calais Ville, Douai, Dunkerque, Lens, St Omer, Tourcoing and Valenciennes. Ask about accessibility at rural stations before travelling.

ACCOMMODATION

In France, the definition of accessible hotel rooms can be flexible. I know of one hotel, some 500km south of Lille, which boasts a fully adapted room with handrails in the en suite and all facilities up to international standard. The problem is that it is on the first floor and there is no lift. No independent hotels or B&Bs in central Lille are listed in the 2009 *Handi-Tourisme* guide (see page 31), but there are several *gîtes* and *chambre d'hôtes* suggested for the outlying metropolitan area. However, even if they have not been granted the official label, large chain hotels all have reasonably accessible rooms and most can provide properly adapted accommodation. Remember to specify your precise requirements when booking. Many apartment and suite options have wet-room bathing options with no step to the shower. Do check for recent changes, as most hotels in the city are undergoing a rolling programme of improvements. Be warned that some older, taller hotels may have a lift, but it may not reach the ground floor. Extra questions to ask when booking: does the lift run from street level to the room with no steps? Can it take a wheelchair? Is there flat access to the breakfast room?

EATING

The annoying truth is that most seriously *gastronomique* addresses come complete with doorstep. But, if a helping hand with one step or two can be arranged, nothing is impossible. Whilst only Au Bout des Doigts (see page 111) in the centre of town gets a listing in the *Handi-Tourisme* brochure, plenty of restaurants are worth considering (if you can cope without needing the loo). Pavement terraces abound and most listed restaurants and brasseries on the squares will serve meals outdoors, many with excellent heated terraces in the winter or spring. The Pelican opposite Gare Lille Flandres even has Wi-Fi! Les Trois Brasseurs (see page 86) serves meals outside – and you are just across the road from the station with its 'facilities'. A handful of out-of-town eateries are included in the official listings but, again, a phone call will tell just how accessible a restaurant, café or club may be. Sometimes there is just the one step. As ever, be warned: no matter how easy it is to get in to an establishment in Vieux Lille, the street itself may still be the problem.

NIGHTLIFE

Underground cafés and cellar bars bring their own problems. Theatres and nightclubs often have a side entrance – as always, call in advance. The opera house promises seating for guests with all mobility restrictions at all performances (subject to availability) and has audio-described options for the visually impaired. The main Théâtre du Nord on Grand' Place is also accessible, with a lift from the ground floor. A lift from street level and reserved seating are available at the Nouveau Siècle concert hall. The Gymnase and Verrière theatres in Lille are officially totally accessible. Most of the central multiplex cinemas around the rue Béthune are easy to use – just check the situation for the individual screen you have in mind before handing over your cash.

MUSEUMS

New spaces, Maisons Folies and recent conversions are accessible. Older museums bring their own problems, but a phone call will usually result in assistance in viewing part of a collection at least. The planetarium, Forum Mitterand and Musée du Souvenir in Villeneuve d'Ascq, Manufacture des Flandres in Roubaix, Domaine Mandarine Napoléon in Seclin and the dolls museum in Wambrechies are all considered fully accessible.

▼ *Angels or demons? The Lille 3000 ramblas on rue Faidherbe.*

Practicalities

TOURIST OFFICE

Lille's tourist office is housed in the magnificent remains of the ducal Palais Rihour. The ground floor of the building has a friendly welcome desk with multilingual staff who can offer advice on sightseeing and excursions, and help with hotel bookings. Stacks of free leaflets and brochures may seem bewildering, but pick up the following essentials: a good fold-out city map, an up-to-date shopping plan and guide, and the latest issue of *Sortir*, the essential listings magazine. A range of specialist guidebooks is sold here, and this is the check-in point for those taking advantage of the all-inclusive city pass and hotel deal (see page 52). You may buy public transport passes from the information desk. Various guided walking tours of the city may be booked here and depart from the building. The hour-long minibus tour of Lille (strongly recommended) also departs from outside the main entrance. Prices and information are given on page 47.

A new guided tour option allows visitors to create their own itinerary, with a soundtrack delivered via their own mobile phones. Historical commentary, extracts from radio interviews and documentaries are available in French or English at the Palais Rihour, Grand' Place, place du Théâtre, rue de la Grande Chaussée, rue Esquermoise, Hospice Comtesse and Notre Dame de la Treille. Simply dial AlloVisit on ☎00 33 1 72 93 95 05 then 008 000 for Lille. Pick up a map-card from the tourist office for full details. Calls cost 34 cents per minute. Otherwise download all seven free four-minute mp3 files to your ipod from the ZeVisit website (⌂ www.zevisit.com/Partenaire-LIL-US.html) and keep them with you.

Lille tourist office <u>GP</u> Palais Rihour, pl Rihour, 59002 ☎03 59 57 94 00
einfo@lilletourism.com ⌂www.lilletourism.com [234 E4 & 236 B6]
⊙ Mon–Sat 09.30–18.30, Sun & holidays 10.00–12.00 & 14.00–17.00
🚇*Rihour* **e**** Métro 2 to Gare Lille Flandres, then line 1 to Rihour.*
Additional information desks at Lille Europe station & Lille Lesquin Airport are open during peak season.

Comité Départemental du Tourisme Nord 6 rue Gauthier de Châtillon, 59013 ✆03 20 57 59 59 ✉resa@cdt-nord.fr ⌂www.cdt-nord.fr. For information on tourism & travel in the department of Nord (including themed package breaks organised by the *Loisirs Accueil* short-break specialists). The above address is for postal enquiries only. The walk-in reception area is no longer open to the public.

Comité Départemental du Tourisme Pas de Calais La Trésorie, Wimille, 62930 Wimereux ✆03 21 10 34 60 ✉promotion@pas-de-calais.com ⌂www.pas-de-calais.com. For information on tourism & travel in the neighbouring department of Pas de Calais (including *Loisirs Accueil*).

Comité Régional du Tourisme Nord-Pas de Calais 4 pl Mendès France, 59028 ✆03 20 14 57 57 ⌂www.tourisme-nordpasdecalais.fr. For information on the region Nord-Pas de Calais.

CONSULATES

British Consulate 11 sq du Tilleul, 59800 ✆03 20 12 82 72

Canadian Consulate 30 av Emile Zola, 59000 ✆03 20 14 05 78

Other nationals should contact their embassy or consulate in Paris:

American Consulate 2 rue St-Florentin, 75001 ✆01 43 12 22 22

Australian Embassy 4 rue Jean-Rey, 75015 ✆01 40 59 33 00

Irish Consulate 4 rue Rude, 75016 ✆01 44 17 67 00

New Zealand Embassy 7ter rue Léonard de Vinci, 75016 ✆01 45 01 43 43

BANKS & MONEY MATTERS

The euro
See page 28.

Banks
Branches are all around town, with most major French banks to be found along rue Nationale. Generally open Monday–Friday 10.00–17.00 (some close 12.00–14.00); some branches will open Saturday 10.00–13.00; some

may close Monday. Banks close earlier than usual on the eve of holidays. Cash can be obtained out of hours at ATM machines (*distributeurs automatiques de billets*), widely available around town (there are even four within 100 yards of place Lion d'Or in the old town). Most ATM machines will accept Visa and MasterCard, and debit cards on the Cirrus and Maestro schemes.

Currency exchange

Available at most banks and post offices. Bureau de change counters may also be found in department stores, railway stations, airports and near tourist sites. Caution: even though exchange rates are fixed, commission rates are flexible. They must therefore be clearly indicated.

Credit cards

Visa and MasterCard are widely accepted, and American Express and Diners may also be used in many tourist and business areas. There is often a minimum purchase requirement of around €10. Depending on the type of card, you may withdraw up to €400 at automatic teller machines and banks. French credit cards contain a computer chip (*puce*), and users may be asked to key in a private PIN number during transactions. The magnetic strips on old-style credit cards from other countries sometimes fail to be read by the local swipe machines. Should this be the case, ask for your card number to be typed in manually.

Should you lose your card, you must notify the issuing bank as soon as possible to block fraudulent charges. Keep a note of your credit card number and call the appropriate customer service number:

American Express ☎01 47 77 70 00 (customer service) or 01 47 77 72 00 (lost or stolen cards)

Diners Club ☎08 20 82 05 36 (customer service) or 08 10 31 41 59 (lost or stolen cards)

Eurocard-MasterCard ☎08 00 90 13 87

Visa ☎08 00 90 11 79

Travellers' cheques

Whether in euros or international currencies, these may be converted in banks, exchange outlets and selected post offices. You are insured in case of loss or theft.

VAT & tax refunds

France charges value-added tax, VAT (or TVA in French), at 19.6% on most purchases. Food and drink, public transport and books are taxed at just 5.5% and newspapers, as well as goods from pharmacies, at the even lower rate of 2.1%. Non-EU residents over the age of 15 and staying less than six months in Europe can get a refund of the TVA on purchases amounting to more than €175 at any single store. Budget a reduction of 16.38% of the purchase amount, and add half an hour on to your shopping time to take advantage of the deal. Galeries Lafayette and Printemps department stores each have a department which specialises in handling this. The store staff have to complete a VAT refund form, which you then give to customs (within three months of date of purchase) when leaving France or the last EU country you visit. Therefore, you will need to add half an hour to your check-in time and have your purchases handy for inspection. Customs will stamp the form, which must then be mailed back to the shop within six months of the date of purchase. Refunds are usually simply credited back to your credit card account. A bit of a palaver, but have you *seen* those French wedding dresses, and that tableware? It's worth it!

Tips & service

Restaurant bills are obliged to include service charges (15%). However, it is traditional to round up the total in restaurants and bars, leaving small change behind. Hotel porters should be tipped €2–5, and chambermaids left an appropriate gratuity. Tip taxi drivers 10–15% of the fare. Hairdressers should be left 15%. Cloakroom attendants should be given €1. Public toilet attendants usually expect around 50 cents. In cinemas and theatres, tip the usherette 50 cents.

COMMUNICATIONS

Internet

Discover internet access points at key métro stations for picking up emails and surfing on the move: three at Lille Flandres, three at République–Beaux Arts, another three at Roubaix-Téléport and one at Tourcoing Centre. Most hotels and even B&B establishments provide internet connections or Wi-Fi for travellers (check at the time of booking); otherwise Lille has been slow to offer large city-centre internet facilities, though the post office opposite the opera offers them (see page 42). For any new cybercafés, check with one of the tourist offices. Remember that

French keyboards differ slightly from UK layout, so type slowly and carefully! All branches of McDonalds offer free Wi-fi.

Espace Web: Cyber-Laverie S 14 rue Desrousseaux, 59000 ☎ 03 20 85 07 73 **e** snq@espace-web.net ⌂ www.espace-web.net ⊘ Mon–Sat 08.00–19.30, Sun 11.00–19.00 [235 G6] 🚇 *Mairie de Lille* **e*** *Métro 2 to Mairie de Lille, cross square Laurent.* I love this idea, it is just so student town: cybercafé & launderette in one. Admire the art on the walls, wash your smalls & check up on your emails during the spin cycle. Broadband at €3 per hour.

Atlanteam MK 93 rue Solférino, 59000 ☎ 03 20 10 05 15 **e** lille@atlanteam.com ⊘ Mon–Sat 10.30–00.00, Sun 14.00–22.00 [234 C4] 🚇 *République–Beaux Arts* **e*** *Bus 12 from Gare Lille Flandres to Colbert.* Popular with a young crowd. Prices start at €1 for 15 minutes, then €3 an hour, but loads of deals offer free time online – you can even take out a subscription to cover a short break in Lille. Gaming sessions from 4 hours non-stop at €10 should be booked in advance.

Media

Press

UK daily papers are widely available, as is the *International Herald Tribune*.

La Voix du Nord Outside Paris, the French prefer to get their news from regional rather than national papers. This local daily paper gives the essential lowdown on everything happening in the region, with good national & international news coverage as well. Once an underground news-sheet published by the local Resistance, it has become the key news source for the region, publishing editions for each town in the north of France from its distinctive office on Grand' Place (see page 188). Read it over breakfast at your hotel, or sitting in a central café or bar to look cool as you check up on listings & entertainment news. The online edition is worth checking out before you leave at ⌂ www.lavoixdunord.fr. There are also several daily tabloid freesheets. Pick them up outside the stations for good arts coverage.

Le Figaro Popular middle-market national daily.

Le Monde The national daily paper of record.

Libération This left-wing tabloid has never lost its cool image with students & intellectuals.

Nord Éclair Local weekly.

Sortir Grab a free copy of the weekly listings magazine for Lille & the wider region. Published each Wednesday & available at hotel receptions, most bars & the tourist office.

Radio

Local news can be heard on 94.7FM and the university campus station on 106.6FM. Lille is also within the transmission area for BBC Radio 4 on 198LW.

TV

Local news and weather updates can be found on France 3. Tune into France 2 in the morning for the *Télé Matin* news and arts programme. Weather reports are on at around 06.55, 07.25, 07.55 and shortly before 08.40. French TV on mainstream channels offers reality *Big Brother*-type shows or endless discussion programmes featuring people in brightly lit studios wearing strong primary colours. I was once traumatised by an hour-long debate on the psychology of underwear – this at 21.00 on the leading commercial station. TFI, France 2 and to a lesser extent France 3 churn out lots of this stuff, but have good one-hour evening news broadcasts from 19.00. As for daytime TV, forget it! Once upon a time, before deregulation, there were stimulating daytime shows, such as *Continentales*, Alex Taylor's round-up of news bulletins from around Europe. Now expect shopping infomercials and cartoons. Channel 5 hands over in the evenings to the bilingual French and German arts channel Arté, which is well worth watching. M6 is pop vids and imported US series dubbed into French, and Canal Plus is a subscriber cable channel mainly showing movies, often in their original language. Some hotels offer cable or satellite TV, which usually means CNN or the BBC World news channel.

Post offices

At the post office you may buy stamps, post letters and parcels, make phone calls, send faxes and receive your mail *poste restante*. The branch at boulevard Carnot [235 F3 & 236 D5] offers internet access and you can probably even still use the *Minitel* (a trailblazing forerunner to the internet, now a quaint old-fashioned box of tricks that gives free access to directory enquiry services), and buy pre-franked envelopes. A great way to get rid of fiddly small change is to use the vending machines selling stamps. Many post offices accept payment by Visa and MasterCard. Stamps may also be purchased from tobacconists, kiosks and bars displaying the red cigar *tabac* symbol. Letterboxes are painted yellow. Post offices are generally open from 08.00 to 18.30 on weekdays and from 08.00 to 12.00 on Saturdays.

Telephones

Not all public phones are the same. According to where they're located, they will accept different forms of payment. Phones onboard Eurostar and other trains require MasterCard or Visa. Call boxes in some restaurants and bars may accept coins, whilst most public telephones require a phone card (*télécarte*) available from post offices, railways stations, tobacconists and news kiosks. Calls from hotels are invariably more expensive. Ask at reception for their rates per unit, and length of each unit: some hotels charge in units of 15 seconds! Post offices offer fax services. Internet cafés may offer web phone services.

Dialling

When calling France from outside the country, use the country code (33) and omit the first 0 of the listed number. To call international numbers from France, dial 00 then the country code and number (omitting the first 0). To call within France, dial the ten-digit telephone number. For operator-assisted dialling, key in 00+33+country code.

Country codes

Australia	61	**Ireland**	353
Belgium	32	**New Zealand**	64
Canada	1	**United Kingdom**	44
France	33	**USA**	1

Discounted rates

Discounts of 20–50% apply to domestic and European calls made 19.00–08.00 weekdays, Saturday 12.00 24.00 and all day Sunday. Discounts on calls to the US and Canada apply 19.00–13.00 weekdays and all day weekends.

Mobile phones

Most mobile phones will be able to use France Telecom's Orange or rival networks. Contact your service provider before leaving in order to set up or cancel international roaming. Pay-as-you-go simcards to use in your own unlocked mobile phone cost around €15 from supermarkets. If you are staying in France for a while, then consider buying a pay-as-you-go phone, complete with simcard, from €39.

Useful telephone numbers

Emergency services in English (police, fire, ambulance)	112
Ambulance	15
Car pound	03 20 50 90 14
Duty doctor	03 20 73 57 57
Fire	18
Hospital & medical emergencies	03 20 44 59 62
Lost property	03 20 50 55 99
Operator	12
Police (emergency)	17
Police (all other matters)	03 20 62 47 47
SOS (English-language crisis line)	01 47 23 80 80
Tourist information (anywhere in France)	3265
Weather (France)	08 36 68 02 75

WORSHIP

A full list of churches and other places of worship may be obtained from the tourist office (see page 37).

(Anglican) Christ Church S rue Lydéric, 59800 ✆ 03 28 52 66 36 [235 F7] *e** *Bus 13 from Gare Lille Flandres to Hôtel de Ville, cross Porte de Paris to rue Lydéric.*

(Muslim) Grande Mosquée de Lille 59 rue de Marquillies, 59000 ✆ 03 20 53 02 65 *e** *Métro 1 to Porte d'Arras, then bus 50 to Verne. Walk back along rue de Marquillies.*

(Jewish) Synagogue MK 5 rue Angellier, 59800 ✆ 03 20 52 41 59 [234 E7] *e** *Bus 13 from Gare Lille Flandres to Jeanne d'Arc. Walk up rue Jeanne d'Arc to rue Angellier.*

(Roman Catholic) Basilique Cathédrale Notre Dame de la Treille VL [235 F2 & 236 C3]. See page 187, & other churches listed on pages 186–8.

Local
Transport

METRO, TRAMS & BUSES

A superb automated métro system ties in with the tramways and buses. The unmanned VAL métro is completely automated, and runs on two ever-expanding lines crossing central Lille and serving the suburbs and metropolitan area. Central métro platforms are sealed off from the tracks by sliding glass doors that open when the train comes to a standstill. En route to the suburbs, the trains swoop and soar from underground tunnels to futuristic tracks high above the countryside and motorways. Try to sit at the very front for the true fairground-attraction experience.

Métro lines in France do not have names: they are numbered and platforms indicated by the terminus. Thus Line One will be marked either 4 Cantons or CHRB Calmette, and Line Two CH Dron or St Philibert.

Twin tramways run out to Roubaix and Tourcoing, passing the pretty Parc Barbieux and, on sunny days, provide a pleasant alternative to the underground. Métro and tram services run from 05.15 to midnight (from 06.20 at weekends).

The city bus network covers the areas of the old town that no métro could possibly reach, since so much of Lille is built on land reclaimed from canals and waterways. From the principal bus stops at place des Buisses, alongside Gare Lille Flandres, services fan out to the outlying districts, even crossing the Belgian border. Buses generally run from around 05.30 until 20.30.

The Citadine bus route is a circuit taking in the principal boulevards, the Citadelle, Zenith and both railway stations in a continuous loop sweeping around the city. It runs from around 05.30 until 21.30.

In the evening, the late bus network meanders through the town centre, Vieux Lille and out to the satellite towns half-hourly from approx 21.30 until 00.30. Most routes out of town leave the place des Buisses and some depart from place de la République.

Line 4 will get you back from Vieux Lille after dinner. Buses go midweek every 20 minutes until 22.30 then half hourly til 00.30,

Saturdays every 20 minutes until 23.30 then half hourly til 00.30, and Sundays hourly from 22.30–00.30.

Pick up a transport map from stations and tourist offices.

Public transport information can be found at: ☏ 08 20 42 40 40 and 🖰 www.transpole.fr. The website has an excellent journey planner; click on *Itineraires* to research a journey.

Tickets

One ticket costs around €1.30 and allows you to travel in one direction, changing from métro to tram to bus if necessary without buying another ticket. Carnets of ten tickets are better value at €10.60, and one-day *Pass Journée* tickets are available offering unlimited travel for around €3.60. There are also a couple of lesser-known bargains to consider: the *Pass Soirée* for travel after 19.00 is just €1.60. And if you are taking only short trips of less than three métro stops, such as the Wazemmes market, get the less-than-half-price *Ticket Zap* at just 65 cents each or 10 for €6. Should you intend to stay around the Grand' Place and Vieux Lille, the chances are you will not use much public transport, since the métro does not serve the old town (although buses manage to reach a surprising number of streets there). In that case you may do better buying just the occasional ticket. Should your plans involve trips out to Roubaix, Tourcoing or Villeneuve d'Ascq, or a few cross-town trips to and from the markets, a carnet between friends or a day card would be better value.

During the two days of the Braderie (see page 12) a special *Pass Braderie* gives unlimited travel on public transport across the metropolitan area for €4.60. A similar deal is offered from noon until the last bus, tram or métro on National Music Day (21 June).

The *City Pass* allows you to travel on all trams, métro and bus services, and provides unlimited access to major museums and attractions in Lille and the neighbouring towns, including the Planetarium and distillery tour. It also offers discounts on many concert, theatre, opera and ballet tickets. The pass costs €18 for one day, €30 for two days or €45 for three days, and may be bought at any local tourist office or by calling ☏ 03 59 57 94 00.

Buy regular tickets from bus drivers, kiosks and vending machines at métro stations, tram stops and bus depots – not forgetting to frank them in the brightly coloured stamping machines at the entrance to the station, the platform and onboard the tram or bus. Single tickets, day passes and the city pass can also be obtained from tourist offices. If you are staying in Lille for a while, or are a student at the university, there are many

331 or 314
Haute Bone

alternative discount options to discover. See the Transpole website
(🖰 www.transpole.fr) for details.

Lost property

If you have lost an umbrella, walking stick, wallet, sunglasses or domestic
pet on any bus, tram or métro, telephone ☎ 03 20 81 43 43.

TOUR BUS

An excellent way to see the sights in the shortest possible time is to take
the one-hour minibus city tour. Buses leave every hour from outside the
tourist office on place Rihour. The multilingual audio-visual commentary
is first rate. Tickets cost €10 (children and unemployed €8; free for
children under 6 and holders of the City Pass) from the tourist office. It is
wheelchair accessible.

AIRPORT TRANSFER

A shuttle-bus service links Lille Lesquin Airport (8km out of town) with
the main Lille Europe TGV and Eurostar station, a few steps away from
the main bus station at place des Buisses. The service runs hourly
Monday–Friday   05.00–20.00,   Saturday   05.00–18.00,   Sunday
07.00–22.00. The single fare is €5, return €8, with reductions of around
30% for passengers aged under 25 or groups of three or more travellers.
Buses leave from the stop outside the arrivals hall. Telephone ☎ 03 20 90
79 79 for departure times.

Trains link central Lille to both Paris Charles de Gaulle airport (the
TGV train takes 51 minutes) and Brussels Airport (Thalys train in 38
minutes).

TAXIS

Taxis may be found at clearly marked ranks and, if you are very lucky,
hailed in the street. The main ranks are outside the two railway stations,
Lille Europe (☎ 03 20 06 64 00 [235 J3]) and Lille Flandres (☎ 03 20 06
06 06 [235 G4]). Remember: when you book a taxi, the meter starts
ticking from the moment of your call, not from the time and place you
board the cab.

CAR HIRE

Most international car-rental agencies have desks at Lille Europe station and the airport, and offer special discounts to the various airlines and rail companies. However, it is often cheaper to rent a car from one of the smaller companies in town. Rent a Car (**S** 113 rue du Molinel ↳ 03 20 40 20 20 [235 F5]), five minutes' walk from the Gare Lille Flandres, has very low rates for one-or two-day rentals. Online bargains can often be found at ⌨ www.auto-europe.co.uk.

Avis ↳ (station) 03 20 51 12 31; (airport) 03 20 87 59 56
⌨ www.avis.com

Budget ↳ (station) 03 28 36 50 40 ⌨ www.budget.fr

Europcar ↳ (station) 03 20 06 01 46; (airport) 03 20 90 45 45
⌨ www.europcar.com

Hertz ↳ (station) 03 28 36 25 90; (airport) 03 20 49 67 89
⌨ www.hertz.com

Parking

Lille boasts 9,000 secure parking spaces in huge underground and multi-storey car parks tucked around the central area. Check with the tourist office for current rates as prices vary from site to site – from €1.30 to €2.10 per hour. Most car parks close at 01.00; however, the Euralille car park remains open 24/7. When shopping at Euralille, leave the supermarket trawl until last, since Carrefour checkout staff will stamp your ticket for free or reduced-rate parking. Night owls take note that if you are planning an evening on the town, best value may be found at the Rihour-Printemps and Nouveau Siècle car parks, which sometimes offer a special rate of €1.50 from 19.00 to 01.00 – check with the tourist office. If you must park in the street, seek out the nearest parking meter and display the ticket on your car dashboard. If you stay out of town and use the public transport system, park for free at Porte des Postes, CHR Calmette, St Philibert and 4 Cantons. In Lille, the car parks at Champs de Mars (just by the Citadelle) and Porte de Valenciennes cost just €1.60 for 3 hours or €3 for the whole day and include free bus transfers to any stop on the Citadine routes.

Parking information ↳ 03 28 36 86 86

CYCLING

Hire a bike at one of the many pick-up-and-drop-off points by railway stations. You will usually be asked to leave a returnable deposit of around €300, which can be organised by credit card. Ask at the tourist office for maps of cycle routes around Lille. For itineraries outside the city, see page 212.

Vélopole Bases may be found at 4 Cantons, CHRD Calmette, Les Prés, St Philibert & Tourcoing Centre métro stations, as well as Armentières mainline railway station ⊙ Mon–Sat 06.00–00.00 (except Tourcoing Mon–Fri 07.30–18.45, Sat 07.30–13.00, & Armentières which has extended weekday & additional Sun opening); book bikes online at the Transpole site ⊕ www.transpole.fr. On the outskirts of the city, hire a bike from Vélopole. From €1.50 for 1 hour to €15 for a week, pick up a bike at any designated station & drop it off at any other Vélopole branch. If you hold a valid métro ticket or travel pass, enjoy discount rates of €1 for 1 hour, €5 for a day, €6 for a 3-day weekend or €11 for a week. Baby seats, helmets & panniers also available, & free information on cycle routes in & out of town.

Ch'ti Vélo S 10 av Willy Brandt, 59000 ☎ 03 28 53 07 49 ⊕ www.chti-velo.fr ⊙ Mon–Fri 09.00–12.00 & 13.00–17.00 [235 H4] 🚉 Gare Lille Flandres **e**⋆ Métro or walk to Gare Lille Flandres. At the side entrance to Lille Flandres station, by the Tripostale, this is the local commuters' bike hire desk. Closed at weekends, but if you are staying from Fri through to Mon, the weekend deal is good value, & you can drop the bike off on your way to catch the Eurostar home. A range of hire options, season tickets, etc are available. €1 an hour, €5 for a day, €7 for the weekend. Book bikes online.

▼ The greener taxi rank – rickshaws now join bikes and segways as the alternative public transport options for getting around the city centre.

Local transport Cycling

Bike taxi

CycloVille ☏ 06 24 16 08 18. Rickshaw taxi service in the city centre.
€1 pick up charge + €1 per km & per person (2 people max).

E-BIKE & SEGWAY HIRE

Transpole <u>VL</u> Oxygene station at the Champ de Mars, 59000 ⊙ Mon–Sat
08.00–20.00, Sun 14.00–18.00 [234 D1] *e* Bus Citadines 2 to Jardin Vauban,
cross the Pont de la Citadelle & walk to Champs de Mars car park l;* <u>S</u> Relais
Oxygene, Pl des Buisses, 59000 ⊙ Mon–Fri 07.30–18.30 [235 G4] 🚃 *Gare Lille
Flandres e* Métro or walk to Gare Lille Flandres.*
Electric bikes & Segways for hire. The latter is the sci-fi way to travel.
Sway backwards or forwards to steer whilst standing on what looks like a
garden roller pretending to be a hovercraft. Shoppers note that there is a
Segway parking zone at the Tanneurs shopping mall (page 146). Half-day
hire for an e-bike is €7 (€5.50 for Transpole ticket or pass holders), €10
(€8) for a day or €20 (€16) for 3-day weekend. Segways €15 (€12)
half-day, €20 (€18) day, €40 (€35) weekend.

Accommodation

In a city where hospitality comes as standard, stories of northern welcomes are legendary. I only regret that one off-beat gem closed its doors just too early to be included in my Bradt guides: a B&B run by a former *madame* who, after years of service to the garrison, had ultimately transferred her attentions from the bed to the breakfast. Friends told me that many men who had visited the establishment as soldiers in their youth, and partaken fully of the fleshly delights on offer, had returned in later years with their families for a more orthodox *accueil*. Nonetheless, there are still plenty of conventional treats to be discovered in and around Lille, from the home-baked *petit déjeuner* brioche in a family home to a luxurious bedroom in a distillery devoted to the memory of Napoleon.

Chambre d'hôte is a particularly Gallic twist on bed and breakfast and, as well as our choice of the most welcoming and unusual homes (see pages 63–6), it is always worth checking out the latest B&B lists issued by the tourist offices. Self-catering is well worth considering if you are planning a longer stay. In the countryside outside Lille, consider the charms of a *gîte*; otherwise rent a studio or one-bedroom apartment at an *aparthotel* in the town centre. Remember that supermarkets and even some restaurants will often deliver and that Lille has some great markets for fresh food if you fancy recreating restaurant masterworks with a two-ring hob and a microwave!

Mobility-restricted guests should be aware that some of the older hotels, especially around the old Flandres station do not have lift access from the ground floor to the bedrooms – so always check when booking if you have a problem with stairs (see page 34).

Should you go for the city-centre hotel option, take a tip from me. Unless you are staying in one of the larger hotels with a grand breakfast-buffet selection – in which case you should eat heartily and just opt for a baguette and cheese for a lunchtime picnic – forego the standard hotel breakfast, usually costing €5–10 on top of the room rate. Instead, make your way to the main Paul bakery, on the corner of rue de Paris and the place du

▲ *A room with the best view in Lille: the Coupole Suite at the Hotel Carlton – at festival time, lord it over the city squares.*

Théâtre. In the magnificently tiled and draped surroundings of this fabulous shop (see page 115), enjoy an excellent *petit déjeuner* of fresh-baked bread, homemade jams, and superb coffee or tea, or sinfully sensational hot chocolate – all for around €4. Other good breakfast options include Le Pain Quotidien (see page 119) and the lobby of the Hermitage Gantois (page 54).

BON WEEKEND – BON PRIX

Loyal readers of this guide who mourn the passing of the excellent 2-for-1 Bon Weekend hotel deals may take heart. The Tourist Office still runs a series of packages for weekenders. The most practical is the Freedom of Lille deal. From €59 per person it includes one night's hotel accommodation and a two-day City Pass for free entry to museums and public transport. During the Christmas Market season, a €39 deal includes a night's hotel accommodation, the city tour bus trip, a turn on the ferris wheel and a glass of mulled wine. A three-day version is available for the September Braderie weekend.

Lille Tourist Office GP Pl Rihour, 59002 ✆03 59 57 94 00
⊘ Mon–Sat 09.30–18.30, Sun & holidays 10.00–12.00 & 14.00–17.00 [235 E4 & 236 B6]

CITY CENTRE

Hotels

Alliance VL 17 quai de Wault, 59800 ℂ 03 20 30 62 62
e alliancelille@alliance-hospitality.com ⏚ www.alliance-lille.com [234 D2]
e Bus 12 from Gare Lille Flandres to Foch. Walk through the park to the pond.
The hotel is on the right bank.

The highest-profile hotel in the city may be found just behind the recently renovated gardens of the place Foch, in a quiet waterside street a short walk from the Citadelle. On the banks of a dock built in the mercantile age of Charles the Bold, the high walls of the Couvent de Minimes are testament to four centuries of change. The usual 4-star perks of big buffet b/fasts in the morning, AC in the summer, & minibars & muzak all year round. Service is courteous & efficient & all is as one would expect of an establishment of this quality. To be honest, had it not once been a monastery, I'd enjoy the place a good deal more. But the fact that the old cloister of this listed 17th-century building has been smothered in glass & chrome & muzzled by an atrium & mezzanine piano bar gives the core of what might have been a charming & tasteful conversion the air of an airport hotel. Thus the gentle strains of George Gershwin are generally muted by my murderous thoughts towards the architect or corporate philistines who conceived & executed the project. Perhaps I am being unfair or unduly sensitive. After all, the current incarnation has greater dignity than the last. When the religious order was disbanded by the Revolution, the Couvent de Minimes saw service as a uniform warehouse to the garrison across the water. If you concentrate hard enough, you may still see some of the original charm, not least the sophisticated brick vaulting from the craftsmen who built the monastery back in 1622. Most of the major hotel guides wax lyrical about the place, & the Lille business community swears by it. Some bedrooms are well-equipped &

L'Hermitage Gantois S 224 rue de Paris, 59800 ℂ 03 20 85 30 30
e contact@hotelhermitagegantois.com
🖰 www.hotelhermitagegantois.com [235 F6]
🚇 *Mairie de Lille* **e*** *Métro 2 to Mairie de Lille.*
Walk westwards along av du Président Kennedy
then turn left on to rue de Paris.

Lille's only 4-star *luxe* hotel is more than just a
place to rest your weary head, it is a veritable
spa for the soul. One of the best-kept secrets in
the city, it's an unmissable site in its own right & architecturally a
consummation devoutly to be wished. Until recently, most visitors saw 224
rue de Paris as little but an imposing 15th-century gable on the walk from
central Lille to the Porte de Paris remnant of the original city walls (see
page 182). To locals, it always had a special place in their hearts as the
Hospice Gantois, a hospital & old people's home, its courtyard a peaceful
haven & escape from the bustle of everyday life. The institution was
founded in 1462 as the St John the Baptist Hospice by wealthy merchant
Jean de la Cambe, better known as Jean Gantois. His other main claim to
philanthropic fame was in establishing a rest home for retired prostitutes,
but his legacy of health care for the poor (irrespective of their lifestyles)
continued until 1995 when the hospice, a listed building since 1923, finally
closed its doors. This cluster of religious & secular buildings has been
united by architect Hubert Maes into an exciting celebration of one of the

comfortable, the live jazz evenings *tres décontracté*, & the restaurant in
the glazed courtyard is well respected by discerning locals. The hotel
room rate rises from around €215–399 & *demi-pension* deals are also
available. Wi-Fi. $$$$$

Carlton GP 3 rue de Paris, 59026 ℂ 03 20 13 33 13 or toll free 0800
181591 (UK), 800 888 4747 (USA & Canada) e contact@carltonlille.com
🖰 www.carltonlille.com [235 F3 & 236 C6] 🚇 *Gare Lille Flandres* **e*** *Bus 12*
from Gare Lille Flandres to Théâtre. Or walk along av le Corbusier & right into rue
Faidherbe.
A provincial grand hotel of the old school, with the usual 4-star comforts
liberally dispensed. Though the Alliance has the higher profile in the
package-tour brochures, the Carlton has an enviable location, one of the
key corner sites in the very centre of town, a chime away from the belfry
of the Chambre de Commerce. With Louis XV-influenced rooms from

few survivors of the long-demolished St Sauveur quarter. The imaginative revival of the street façades gives not a clue to the thrilling marriage within: contemporary design ties the knot with a respect for history, with beamed ceilings, panelled walls & smart tiled floors. The former dormitories & wards make way for 67 bedrooms & suites, clustered around 4 courtyards. Rooms are nicely equipped & bathrooms well-proportioned. Even if you can't afford to stay the night or go for the full €18 b/fast, remember that the central atrium bar is open to everyone. Flop in a comfy sofa & gaze heavenward through glass at the architectural harmonies or relax in the sauna. Among the eclectic treasures housed within the hotel are sundry vintage medical instruments (including a 1926 X-ray machine) & the body of the hospice's founder, buried in the chapel. Tuesday mornings see tours of the building (a bonus since the listed building used to open to the public only 2 days a year), but you may sneak peeks at the courtyards, chapel & other gems of the ground floor when you take the coffee & croissant bar b/fast at €9 or similarly priced afternoon tea. A lively New World wine list at around €5 a glass is the perfect way to toast the general manager Danielle Gey, whose wit & perception in hand-picking an excellent staff show that this lady from Biarritz is blessed with the typically *Lillois* wisdom to unite old walls with young minds. One trick of discreet revisionism makes me chuckle: the principal ballroom has been renamed the Salle des Hospices, the original title being considered unsuitable for the hospitality industry. Since Jean Gantois's day it has been better known locally as the Salle des Malades! Rooms €204–425. Wi-Fi. $$$$$

€150 & suites soaring skywards price-wise, before booking it is always worth asking for any weekend promotions that may easily halve the bill. An experience at any price is a stay in the panoramic rooftop cupola duplex suite, actually inside a turret dome, with arguably the best view of any building in town, overlooking the squares, the Vieille Bourse, the opera house & the first cobbled alleys of Vieux Lille. Wide picture windows on one level, quaint round windows on the other, & plasma TV should you ever tire of looking out on the city. A spa bath en suite adds to the feeling of luxury & romance – no need to mix with the lower castes in the hotel's main sauna. Mind you, we are talking €1,280 per night here. The public areas may seem slightly stuffy, but this is what the French consider British & therefore the height of sophistication. If b/fast at €16 is not included in the deal, then the home-baked delights *chez* Paul (see page 115) are just yards away. Private parking available. Wi-Fi. $$$$

Crowne Plaza <u>S</u> 335 bd de Leeds, 59777 ☎ 03 20 42 46 46
🖰 www.crowneplaza.com [235 J3] 🚇 *Gare Lille Europe* *e* Upstairs through the
exit & cross the road.*

Yes, it is one of those conference-type hotels, but it is the best of the
breed, stands slap on top of the Eurostar station & has superbly patient,
efficient & helpful staff; & if you are in town for business & can't run to
the absolute luxury of the 4-star alternatives & prefer a room more
practical than quaint, you can be in the shower within 3 mins of the train
pulling into the Gare Europe. Good views over the city from the top
floors & the multilingual front desk can even answer your queries in
Serbo-Croat. Valet parking available too. Rooms are €195, suites €480,
with b/fast adding an extra €16 to the bill. $$$$

Le Royal (Mercure Lille Centre) <u>GP</u> 2 bd Carnot, 59800 ☎ 03 20
14 71 47 e H0802@accor-hotels.com 🖰 www.accorhotels.com [235 F3 &
236 D5] 🚇 *Gare Lille Flandres* *e* Bus 12 from Gare Lille Flandres to Théâtre,
then walk behind the Opéra.*

A facelift for this dear old diva loitering behind the stage door of the
opera house. Just as the Opéra herself was rejuvenated for 2004, so this
until recently somewhat faded, slightly worn chain hotel, with its friendly
provincial welcome, has been spruced up in time for the renaissance of
this long-ignored corner of the city beside the place du Théâtre. With
good-sized bedrooms & spacious en-suite bathrooms, this acquisition of
the Accor group with its smart new look is no longer the forgotten hotel
of Lille. These days more often listed as the Mercure Lille Centre, thanks
to a corporate lack of imagination, it is still known locally by its original
name, Le Royal. Perfectly poised at the junction of the old & new towns,
a short walk from the station & handy for the fun of a night on the town
& a day at the heart of the city. Bright, AC rooms with smoke alarms,
huge windows, Wi-Fi & cable TV, €103–185. $$$–$$$$

Art Déco Romarin 110 av de la République, 59110, La Madeleine
☎ 03 20 14 81 81 e hotel-art-decoromarin@wanadoo.fr
🖰 www.hotelartdecoromarin.com.

Although La Madeleine is technically outside central Lille, the hotel is a
lot closer to the Eurostar station than many of the alternatives officially
designated as town-centre establishments. A relative newcomer to the
scene, this is smart, modern, & with more than a nod towards the art
deco style of its name. The reception area, with its helpful & charming
staff, is dominated by a coloured-glass ceiling, & the bedrooms are neat
& stylish. Internet access & radio are welcome additions to the

ubiquitous cable TV & pay-per-view movies. The hotel is just 5 mins'
walk from Lille Europe station (turn left onto the boulevard Pasteur &
right into av de la République), & stands next to the tramlines linking
Lille with Roubaix & Tourcoing. A free shuttle-bus service runs between
the hotel & the Grand' Place (stopping at the station on request)
07.15–10.00 & 18.00–23.00. Rooms €110–130. $$$

De la Treille **VL** 7/9 pl Louise de Bettignies, 59800 ✆ 03 20 55 45 46
e hoteldelatreille@free.fr ⏱ www.hoteldelatreille.com [235 F2 & 236 D3]
e* Bus 3, 6 or 9 from Gare Lille Flandres to Lion d'Or.
Don't come here looking for the quaint olde-worlde delights of old Lille.
Not unless you intend to spend your stay looking out of the windows.
Vintage character is hardly the keynote; instead tour operators' brochures
favour it for its location, as this internationally smart hotel lies in the
very heart of the old-town bustle. The famous cathedral Notre Dame de
la Treille is just behind the hotel, & across the way, through a doorway
by a craft shop, is the unexpected treasure of the Hospice Comtesse. The
hotel's entrance & reception area are welcoming, despite the contrast
with some of the oldest buildings in the oldest quarter of town. The
bedrooms – smart, inoffensive & clean, with marble bathrooms – are by
contrast lacking in the centuries-old charisma that any room looking
towards the rue de Gand & down on the place du Lion d'Or really
deserves. Rooms, with satellite TV, €105; b/fast €10 extra. Wi-Fi. $$$

De la Paix **GP** 46bis rue de Paris, 59800 ✆ 03 20 54 63 93
e hotelpaixlille@aol.com ⏱ www.hotel-la-paix.com [235 F4 & 236 C6]
🚌 Rihour *e* Av le Corbusier & right into rue Faidherbe, then left on rue des Ponts
de Comines to rue de Paris, or bus 12 to Théâtre.*
Another family-run gem, this time just around the corner from the
Grand' Place. Rooms here are devoted to great artists, & rather than
merely boasting a few cheap prints in the bedrooms & lobbies, the walls
are covered with neatly framed posters from great exhibitions around the
world. You may share your room with Van Gogh, Lautrec or Magritte, or
perhaps you might spend time getting to know a less-vaunted talent. Of
course, the hotel provides great inspiration to visit the many museums &
galleries in & around town. Larger rooms, at €112, have a lounge area
with soft furnishings for flopping after shopping, & each floor of the
hotel boasts a residents' lounge by the lift, where one may admire the in-
house exhibitions. Extremely helpful staff on duty day & night, & a
room rate around the €90 mark, make this a firm favourite. To be honest
the only possible reason for the hotel remaining in the 2-star category is

the modest size of the bathrooms, with surely the teeniest tubs in town. Since this is one of the closest hotels to Paul's bakery, the establishment has upped its game when it comes to b/fast, with an à la carte option as well as the croissant, bread & jam standard deal. Wi-Fi. $$

Grand Hôtel Bellevue GP 5 rue Jean Roisin, 59800 ℃ 03 20 57 45 64 e grand.hotel.bellevue@wanadoo.fr ⏱ www.grandhotelbellevue.com [235 E4 & 236 B6] 🚊 *Rihour e* Métro 2 to Gare Lille Flandres then line 1 to Rihour.*

Never mind the postal address, this hotel has double-glazed rooms on the Grand' Place itself, giving a thrilling goodnight view of a city at play. No mere onlooker, however, the hotel has long played an active role in the city's party moments. Since the evening that the young Mozart played in one of the building's original salons (the 9-year-old prodigy stayed here for 4 weeks with his father Leopold when he was taken ill en route from England to the Netherlands), the address has enjoyed much dabbling in the arts. A function room occasionally doubles as a theatre & b/fast is served in the Vivaldi room, whatever the season. The reception area adds a hint of a flourish to the décor, & the Windsor piano bar is the place for w/end cocktails. The marbled en-suite facilities add a certain indulgence to prices that are comfortably lower 3-star (€120–185). A complimentary daily newspaper & Wi-Fi. $$

Kanai GP 10 rue de Béthune, 59000 Lille ℃ 03 20 57 14 78 ⏱ www.hotelkanai.com [235 F4 & 236 C7] 🚊 *Rihour e* Métro to Rihour, then walk along rue Vieille Comédie to the corner of rue de Béthune.*

Same management as the late-opening brasseries by the métro station up the road & well known to night owls, this centrally located 2-star hotel in a noisy district has clean, modest-sized rooms smartly tinged with mauves & fresh, sharply designed shower rooms. Above the shops in the bustling pedestrianised zone & with no lifts to take you up 2 or 3 flights of stairs to bed, the place is nonetheless popular with a younger crowd & presided over by very welcoming & efficient reception staff. Most rooms are around €75 at w/ends, up to €100 weekdays & higher during festivals & major events. The very smallest rooms are under €70 at w/ends. If the Wi-Fi in the reception area & broadband & flat screen TV in the rooms is not your thing, you can always borrow a book from the shelves in the lobby. $$

Brueghel **S** 3–5 parvis St Maurice, 59000
📞 03 20 06 06 69 **e** hotel.brueghel@nordnet.fr
🖰 www.hotel-brueghel.com [235 F4 & 236 D7]
🚉 *Gare Lille Flandres* **e*** *Av le Corbusier to Gare Lille Flandres, left into rue de Priez & walk round the church.*

The least-known & most charming of the central hotels, this little gem is very much a word-of-mouth favourite. Tucked away in a quiet pedestrianised street between the old Garc Flandres & the shops of the rue de Paris, the hotel faces the recently scrubbed & shining church of St Maurice, which hosts some excellent classical concerts & organ recitals every summer Sunday afternoon. Overflowing window boxes announce the hospitality guaranteed within. Inside the cosy reception area, an authentic 1920s cage lift takes guests Noah-fashion, 2-by-2, to the bedrooms. Each year another floor is carefully restored. With impeccable taste, the rooms have been styled to combine minimalism with elegance & comfort. Natural coir carpets, wrought-iron mirrors, picture frames from salvaged wood, classic bathrooms – all proof that a budget hotel need not lack artistic inspiration. If you are planning to spend any considerable time in your room, do pack some slippers, since coir is lovely on the eye but less so on the soles of the feet (you can usually pick up a pair of slippers for under €4 at Tati around the corner, see page 152). Only the very smallest rooms miss the sophisticated touch, but with rates at €67–120, comfort & a warm welcome will not break any bank & it is genuine value for money. You may want to forego the lift just once to look at the excellent collection of paintings, prints & posters on each landing. Pick up a leaflet advertising the hotel's luxurious sister establishment, Le Château de Mazan in Provence, the former home of the Marquis de Sade (just imagine the room service). **S**

Chagnot **S** 24 pl de la Gare, 59800 📞 03 20 74 11 87
e contact@chagnot.com 🖰 www.chagnot.com [235 G4 & 236 E7] 🚉 *Gare Lille Flandres* **e*** *Av le Corbusier to Gare Lille Flandres & pl de la Gare.*
Helpful service & surprisingly comfortable & quiet (if bland & compact) rooms at the side of the Gare Flandres & above the fabulous Trois Brasseurs. The slowest lift in Christendom serves an astonishing 75 bedrooms, but be warned, as with so many of the hotels around the stations, the elevator does not go all the way down to the ground floor, so there's still one flight of stairs to negotiate. Reception & rooms are

stocked with local entertainment guides for visitors & the location provides for a quick getaway if you have an early train in the morning. Unexpectedly, for the price, the hotel can offer ethernet cables for the laptop. Rates from around €60 not including the uninspiring b/fast. I prefer to have a quick coffee at the Rallye bar next door then amble into town for hot chocolate & fresh bread by the Grand' Place. $

Flandre-Angleterre S 15 pl de la Gare, 59800 ℓ 03 20 06 04 12
e hotel-flandre-angleterre@wanadoo.fr ⑪ www.hotel-flandre-angleterre.fr
[235 G4 & 236 E7] 🚆 Gare Lille Flandres e* Av le Corbusier to Gare Lille
Flandres & pl de la Gare.
OK, so the hotel is hidden behind an infinite number of gaudy restaurant signs promising frites with everything! This is an unpretentious, old-fashioned railway station hotel. The current owners offer a family-style welcome to the simple yet spotlessly clean rooms. Soundproofed against late-night revellers catching the last train to Brussels & all place names Flemish. Rooms €56–70. $

Grand GP 51 rue Faidherbe, 59800 ℓ 03 20 06 31 57
e contact@legrandhotel.com ⑪ www.legrandhotel.com [235 G4 & 236 E6]
🚆 Grand' Place e* Follow signs to the Gare Lille Flandres, then bear right on to
rue Faidherbe.
Clean, modestly priced hotel on the recently restyled main thoroughfare from the stations to the squares. Each storey is decorated in a slightly different utilitarian style & rooms are bright if a teensy bit tight on space, which is fine if you intend to spend most of your time out exploring the town & saving the extra money for a special meal. Satellite TV, free Wi-Fi & soundproofed windows come as standard. Pay a little extra for the *chambre grand confort* with more room to manoeuvre & a nice big bathtub. Cheery & welcoming reception staff. Rooms €64–80. $

Lille Europe S Av le Corbusier, 59777 ℓ 03 28 36 76 76
e infos@hotel-lille-europe.com ⑪ www.hotel-lille-europe.com [235 H4]
🚆 Lille Europe e* Av le Corbusier to Euralille.
A suitably anonymous modern hotel in a suitably anonymous modern building, the *hôtel de la gare de nos jours* has charming, helpful staff, lots of identikit rooms & a buffet b/fast in a fully glazed 1st-floor salon. The hotel is part of the Euralille tower-block shopping & business complex. The plus point for overnighters & travellers with heavy luggage or plans to strip bare the shelves of the en-suite shopping mall is

its location, close to the TGV Eurostar station. But let's face it, with the Grand' Place & old town just 5 mins away, this is unlikely to be a first choice for visitors seeking the charm of old Flanders. Rooms €74–90. After a period experimenting with pay-as-you-go internet options, the hotel now offers broadband to all guests at the 1st-floor business centre, with views over the bustling city. $

Self-catering

Suitehotel Lille Europe S Bd de Turin, 59000 ✆ 03 20 74 70 70
e H5240@accor.com ⌂ www.suitehotel.com [235 J3] 🚊 *Gare Lille Europe*
e* *Cross bd de Turin from the station.*
A brilliant new concept by the Accor chain, this *apparthotel* opposite the Credit Lyonnais tower on the edge of town is a reinvention of the concept of hotel rooms. An L-shaped space, with bedroom & bathroom at 90 degrees to the living space, the room may be divided by sliding screens. An extra divan by the table/workstation allows a friend to crash for the night. Wi-Fi & ethernet connection are part of the multimedia kit which includes TV with movies & music on demand, free domestic phone calls within France & a computer keyboard for harvesting emails from the telly. Fridge, microwave & kettle in each room, & chill cabinets in the reception area stock salads, soups, desserts & ready meals. You may also dial out to order dinner from a score of restaurants Lille-wide, ranging from oriental & Italian takeaway to gastronomic addresses such as Clément Marot (see page 98). The extras are what make this place special. Free massage on Thursday evenings, nutritionally balanced b/fasts & the option of borrowing a bike, a Smart car or a digital camera from reception. Budget €120–150 per night. $$$

Citadines Lille Centre S 83 av Willy Brandt, 59777 ✆ 03 28 36 75 00
e lillecentre@citadines.com ⌂ www.citadines.com [235 H4] 🚊 *Gare Lille Flandres* e* *Av le Corbusier to Euralille. Left into av Willy Brandt.*
In the Euralille building, this central self-catering option offers extremely competitively priced modern studios & larger apartments with well-equipped kitchenettes & extra facilities, from buffet b/fasts (€8) to an in-house laundrette – wash, dry, & detergent for €10. Studios from around €98–145 per night, reductions for weekly bookings. A slightly higher rate is charged for those requiring the full hotel package, with daily maid service. Otherwise, pay the basic price & use the dishwasher, vacuum cleaner & ironing board provided. Security is pretty good, with

the front doors locked & guests given private entry codes whenever the main desk is unmanned. Very helpful staff at reception, & basement parking among the bonuses. Internet connection in rooms, Wi-Fi in reception area. $$$

Cosy's Lille Vauban Residence 69–71 bd Vauban ✆ 03 28 82 24 24 ⏴ www.cosys-residences.com/fr/lille [234 B3] *e* Citadine bus 2 from Lille Europe to Lille Solférino, then walk along bd Vauban to number 69.*
Close to the parks & the Citadelle, yet still an easy walk down the Solfé to nightlife. Flats sleep 1–5 people. Studios in summer from under €60, but regular rates from just over €90–180. $$$

Citéa Lille Vauban <u>VL</u> 17 rue Colson, 59000 ✆ 03 20 15 43 00 e lille.vauban@citea.com ⏴ www.citea.com [234 B4] *e* Bus Citadine 2 to Lille Solférino, walk south on bd Vauban then first left into rue Colson, & the address is on your right.*
I needed a little persuasion to return to this address. When, many years ago, the place was simply student digs, I spent the longest of long weekends here, first abandoning the bed for the floor & finally rushing out to Tati to buy my own fresh bed linen. Now my demons are laid to rest, the place is under new management, decency prevails & this is an excellent value, clean & welcoming self-catering option. Behind what looks like a basic apartment block in this side street above the Solférino linking the rue Nationale & the bd Vauban, is a warren of pathways linking a chain of buildings, all home to studios & 1-bed apartments. Some accommodation is still reserved for the university, other flats designed for visitors. Good-sized rooms, kitchenettes with microwave, hob & fridge, & sliding doors to the bedroom in larger units. A ground floor bar serves optional b/fasts & here the student residents mingle with visitors. Friendly reception staff, an underground car park & internet in the apartments. Ideally situated for night owls as the place is around 10–15 mins' walk home from the restaurants of the old town & the bars of the Solfé. The distance from the station (around 15 mins by bus to the stop around the corner) keeps the price surprisingly low. Rooms from €68–90 per night. $

Sejours et Affaires <u>S</u> 271 av Willy Brandt, 59777 ✆ 03 28 04 75 51 e lille.europe@séjours-affaires.fr ⏴ www.sejours-affaires.fr [235 H5] 🚆 *Gare Lille Flandres e* Av le Corbusier to Euralille. Left into av Willy Brandt.*
Don't be seduced by the franglais implication of the name; this is not a love nest, as much as a collection of self-contained studio & 1-bed flats,

aimed at the budget end of the business travel market, with a fair smattering of student digs as well. Less of an hotel style complex than the neighbouring Citadines, this slightly pared-down version has its key collection during working hours from a busy office rather than a traditional reception desk. Small but well-equipped apartments in the Euralille Towers. There is a b/fast option in the mezzanine bar. Situated right next door to the Carrefour entrance to the shopping mall (by the green pharmacy sign), it is very convenient for bringing in your own food & drink. Internet connection available. Budget €54–110 per night. $

Youth hostel

Auberge de Jeunesse S 12 rue Malpart, 59000 📞 03 20 57 08 94
e lille@fuaj.org 🖰 www.fuaj.org ⊘ daily 07.00–11.00 & 15.00–01.00
Feb–mid-Dec [235 F6] 🚇 Mairie de Lille e* Métro line 2 to Mairie de Lille, walk west along av Kennedy, turn left on to rue de Paris & right into rue Malpart.
The best-value accommodation in Lille, if you don't mind sharing a room & have a membership card from a recognised national Youth Hostelling Association. Rooms sleep 3–6 people & cost €13pp per night. $

Bed & breakfast

Local tourist offices (see page 37) have updated lists of B&B establishments.

Maison Carrée 29 rue Bonte Pollet, 59000 📞 03 20 93 60 42
e hassina@lamaisoncarree.fr 🖰 www.lamaisoncarree.fr [234 A4]
🚇 Cormontaigne e* Métro 2 to Cormontaigne, walk north on bd Montebello, left on rue de la Bassée then 2nd right to rue Bonte Pollet.
Ultimate *luxe*, designer-chic, €160-plus per night B&B, the last word in interiors, cool. Once visited, never forgotten. Those are the headlines. The reality is that an unassuming house on the corner of a street a good 15 mins further than any visitor might expect to stray from the centre turns out to be one of the most memorable guesthouses in France, combining the rarely entwined qualities of cutting-edge style with a warm & homely welcome. Already no stranger to the pages of the glossier lifestyle magazines, this fabulous house, rescued from demolition by its current owners, Monsieur & Madame Philippe, is well worth the schlep from the heart of Lille. Each room is decorated to the nines with breathtakingly good taste, retaining as many original architectural features as possible to offset against in-room luxuries as

▲ *The Jeanclos 'barbed wire' doors of Notre Dame de la Treille.*

diverse as silver-plated chairs & high-tech massaging electric beds, antiquarian heraldic prints & plasma screens, DVD & hi-fi. I love the vast en-suite hydro-bathrooms that could comfortably accommodate several generations of several families at the same time (although possibly in separate time zones!). From retro to Zen, there is a room or suite to appeal to every taste. B/fast is served in the principal dining room around a huge table with vast quantities of mouthwatering *viennoiseries*, home-made jams & delicious fruit juice. Secure parking available for guests taking the larger rooms. The gardens are as charming as the house, & the pool could seduce you from Lille for the entire weekend. I have included the public transport directions in the listing but if you are splashing out on this sort of luxury, spoil yourself & take a cab into town. $$$$

Ou Dorment les Fées MK 106 rue des Meunieres ☎ 03 20 38 39 98 **e** mc.coustenoble@wanadoo.fr [234 C8] 🚊 *Porte d'Arras* **e*** *Citadines 1 to Lille-Meunieres, walk east along bd Victor Hugo & turn left on to rue des Meunieres.* 'Where the fairies sleep' is a grand mansion offering a suitably large-scale welcome, slightly off the main tourist map in the residential district around Wazemmes. Managing to bestride the chasm between imposing & comfortable, this taste of the fine life remains homely. The spacious salons on the ground floor lead out to the delightful garden, with a table by the ornamental pond. Just the one guest room (a dbl) in what is still very much a family house. It is bright, with a marble washstand & a modern 4-poster bed. Possibility of internet access. Budget around €100–120. $$$

Péniche Lille Flottante VL

Square du Ramponneau/Champ de Mars ☎ 03 20 07 92 38
e bienvenue@lilleflottante.com
🖰 www.lilleflottante.com [234 C2]
e* Citadine 2 to Lille Champ de Mars & walk to the waterfront.

Excuse the pun (the name is a play on '*ile flottante*', a dessert of meringue & custard served in almost every French restaurant) – in a university town which once had a jazz club called Anglo-Saxo on the corner of the rue Angleterre, wordplay rather comes as standard. This is the most original B&B in town, a barge moored on the canal by the Citadelle. Don't expect standard bargee comforts, as this houseboat is much more *luxe* than the average working vessel. The 2 bedrooms are bright nautical white & blue with comfy dbl beds, slippers & bathrobes as standard. Power shower to wake you up in the morning & a nice deck with teak tables & tubs of plants for a leisurely b/fast as the rest of the city goes to work. The leafy mooring even has its own parking space. Wi-Fi. Budget around €120. $$$

La Maison du Jardin Vauban VL 6 rue Desmazières, 59000
☎ 03 20 54 74 05 e contact@jardinvauban.com 🖰 www.jardinvauban.com
[234 B3] *e* Citadine 2 to Lille Jardin Vauban.*
Eclectic & confidently stylish, where else would you find carousel horses looming behind traditional leather armchairs in the salon? This maison bourgeoise by the eponymous park is a B&B with a certain style. Fairground memorabilia, from puppets to an organ, nestle amongst more conventional furnishings in the living rooms. The 2 bedrooms offer their own brand of pampering – from the home cinema & king-sized dbl bed in the *Chambre Chocolat* (a conventional dbl bed & flat screen TV in the more modestly priced *Chambre Mauve*) – & the tree-filled city garden has a teak deck for b/fast looking out over the lawn. An oriental twist to the Victorian setting comes with the optional extras. A full Thai dinner is the table d'hôte suggestion for €30, & a 90-minute Thai massage may also be booked. Wi-Fi. Rooms €70–100. $$

Chez B&B MK 78 rue Caumartin, 59000 ☎ 03 61 50 16 42
e chezBandB@wanadoo.fr [234 C8] 🚊 *République–Beaux Arts e* Métro 2 to Gare Lille Flandres, changing to line 1 to République. Take rue Nicolas Leblanc, cross pl Lebon to rue de Fleurus then turn left on to rue Caumartin.*

I have already begun to kick myself for including this special address in my guide to the Eurostar cities, since it had always been a secret previously shared only with family & friends. I have enjoyed the hospitality of B&B, Bernard & Béatrice Quillerou, since the days that they lived in a quiet street outside the city walls & their two young sons contributed to the same polite & charming welcome. After moving to their current home, a 5-min walk or 10-min stroll from the Palais des Beaux Arts, they continued to offer bed & b/fast *en famille*. The welcome is heartfelt, & Béatrice speaks flawless English. The guest accommodation is tastefully furnished & homely, & whenever I speak to Béatrice I hear of the latest *coup de décor*. B/fast is taken with the family & might include home-made brioches & breads. Stay a minimum of 2 nights, & explore the many restaurants nearby. Rooms cost €45 or €60 per night. A great location for pottering around away from the shopping crowds; tranquil, yet still within easy reach of lively bars & restaurants. Minimum 2-night stay. $

LILLE METROPOLE

Domaine Mandarine Napoléon 204 rue de Burgault, 59113 Seclin
✆ 03 20 32 54 93 *e** Métro 2 to Lille Porte des Postes, then bus 55 to Burgault.
Something different for the weekend? Try self-catering with an emperor, spending the night in a distillery & museum. No longer available for casual visitors alas, but if you are planning a family party, wedding or other such bacchanalia in the Domaine's function rooms, here's an imperial treat to consider. 10 mins outside town at exit 19 of the A1 is the new home of the Mandarine Napoléon distillery, with its splendid grounds & private museum dedicated to Napoleon himself (see page 203). Not everyone gets to visit the old manor house at the centre of the farm. Exquisitely decorated & furnished, from the *trompe l'oeil* tent of the entrance hall to the elegant dining room, the beautifully & individually styled bedrooms & the honesty bar, where guests are trusted to pour their own drinks & settle their bills. Not a hotel as such, more a hugely upmarket *gîte* or *chambre d'hôte*. The catch is that nowadays you have to hire the function room at the distillery as well, so if you are planning a seminar or maybe a wedding, then grab the best accommodation for miles around as part of the deal. B/fast is laid out in the kitchen each morning & the enormous fridge may be stocked with steaks, eggs & vegetables should guests wish to cook a late supper for themselves. The room rate is around €200, b/fast €10, with payment for any other food & drink settled privately on departure. Advance reservation is imperative. $$$

L'Howarderie 1 rue des Fusillés, 59320 Emmerin ☏ 03 20 10 31 00
e howarderie@howarderie.com ⌂ www.howarderie.com ☺ closed Christmas
to New Year **e*** *Métro 2 to Gare Lille Flandres then line 1 to the terminus CHR
B Calmette. Bus 324 or 335 to Emmerin Mairie; hotel is signposted from the bus
stop. 2 mins' walk towards the church.*

This old Flemish farmhouse is a favourite with romantic weekenders
choosing to stay on the outskirts & making occasional forays into town.
The 17th-century buildings have been sensitively renovated to provide
welcome comforts in the spacious rooms with their distinctive, red-brick,
vaulted ceilings. The furnishings may be sympathetically suited to the
architectural period, but the comforts are 21st century: internet, cable TV
& marble bathrooms as standard. The hotel buildings are clustered
around a cobbled courtyard which in season is positively ablaze with
potted plants. Restaurant on site & friendly staff. A genuine rural find
just 6 miles from the centre of Lille. Rooms & suites €120–230. $$$

▼ *Door at Eglise St Maurice.*

Accommodation Lille Métropole

AND NOT FORGETTING ...

As well as the very individual charms of the hotels reviewed in the
guide, the international hotel chains are well represented in town and
across the metropolitan area. The Accor group alone (Sofitel, Novotel,
Mercure, Ibis etc) has nearly 2,000 rooms in the district. This is just a
selection of those branches in the central areas; there are plenty more to
choose from on the corporate websites of the hotel groups
(🕾 www.accorhotels.com 🕾 www.kyriad.com 🕾 www.envergure.com).

All Seasons
172 rue de Paris, 59000 ✆ 03 20 30 00 54

Campanile
Lille Sud rue Jean Charles Borda, 59000 ✆ 03 20 53 30 55

Comfort Hotel
Opéra 28 rue Anatole France, 59800 ✆ 03 20 57 14 24

Holiday Inn Express
75 bis rue Léon Gambetta, 59000 ✆ 03 20 42 90 90

Ibis
Lille Gares 29 av Charles St-Venant, 59800 ✆ 03 28 36 30 40
Hôtel de Ville 172 rue de Paris, 59800 ✆ 03 20 30 00 54
Opéra 21 rue Lepelletier, 59800 ✆ 03 20 06 21 95
Roubaix 37 bd Gl Leclerc, 59100 Roubaix ✆ 03 20 45 00 00
Tourcoing Centre du Gl de Gaulle, rue Carnot, 59200 Tourcoing
✆ 03 20 26 29 58
Villeneuve d'Ascq rue des Victoires, 59650 Villeneuve d'Ascq
✆ 03 20 91 81 50

Kyriad
Lille Centre 21 pl des Reignaux, 59800 ✆ 03 28 36 51 18

Novotel
Lille Centre 116 rue de l'Hôpital Militaire, 59800 ✆ 03 28 38 53 53
Lille Flandres 49 rue de Tournai, 59800 ✆ 03 28 38 67 00

Several other budget hotels can be found in the streets around Gare Lille
Flandres station. The tourist office publishes a list of all registered hotels
in and around town, and offers a booking service.

Eating
& Drinking

Food and drink matter in Lille. The best argument of the day is deciding where to eat – a tavern serving savoury tarts with fresh-brewed beers; an old-fashioned traditional brasserie; gastronomic elegance with starched linens and eloquent menus to set the pulse racing; or a moody jazz café by the city walls.

There are so many flavours to be discovered that one mealtime is simply not enough. From one table to the next, you may segue from that which makes Lille French and that which sets it so very much apart. Regional specialities are a happy blend of the Flemish and northern French styles. Dishes may feature the cheeses of Mont des Cats and Maroilles, *genièvre* juniper gin, the famous Blanche de Lille white beer and other local brews, all tickled with local wisdom to transform the simplest of ingredients into something special.

Waterzoi, on many a menu, is a stew usually of freshwater carp, tench and pike; rabbit may be prepared with prunes; winter warmers include the *hochepot* stew of meats and market-garden vegetables, and the inevitable *carbonnade à la Flamande* stewed in beer, onions and brown sugar. Year-round favourite *potjevlesch* is a white-meat terrine, usually of chicken and rabbit. If all is reminiscent of Belgian comfort food, remember that Lille's borders have shifted almost with the tides.

Even more Belgian is that most traditional of budget meals, a pot of mussels served with a heap of chips. *Moules-frites* are an institution here, the single menu served during the Braderie (see page 12), when the piles of shells outside the restaurants are the most photographed icon of the season. Sausage lovers should seek out the *Cambrai andouillette*, rated as amongst the best in France.

To round off the meal, modern chefs make ice cream and sorbet with local flavourings: *fleur-de-bière*, gin and the ubiquitous *chicorée*. Traditional desserts include *tarte au sucre* and a local variation of bread-and-butter pudding known as *pain perdu*.

Eating & drinking

69

▲ *Dish of the day or timeless classics, check out the* ardoise *for the freshest deals.*

Easy to forget, with all these local flavours, that Lille is in France. Fortunately, almost every other region is represented with a restaurant or five to offer the flavours that lure most visitors across the Channel in the first place. Plenty of Breton *crêperies* to ward off summer snack attacks, and a browse through the following pages should guide you to specialities of Bordeaux and the southwest, and Lyon and the southeast. So, great steaks, *confit de canard*, truffles and *foie gras* are never too far away. Never forget that Lille is still a port, the third most important river port in France, and it is very close to the big fishing fleets of the Channel. The freshest fish is on every menu: Dover sole and cod amongst the local catches; tuna, salmon and sea bass amongst every chef's party pieces.

If all is reminiscent of Belgian comfort food, remember that Lille's borders have shifted almost with the tides.

What to drink: might I suggest a beer (see page 113)? Lille is a great brewing region, with at least two brasserie restaurants serving draught created in-house. It would be a waste to order a standard multinational brand when the breweries around Lille create such memorable ales as the local Ch'ti, La Goudale and Trois Monts. A traditional lager is known as a *bière blonde*. Be guided by your waiter or barman and go with the seasonal specialities: in March, order the Bière de Mars, for one month only, a sprightly and heady affair; at Christmas, the Bière de Noël is a treat; at any time, but unbeaten as a summer cooler and quencher, the cloudy white Blanche de Lille, served with a slice of lemon, is simply heavenly.

Genièvre, a Dutch-style juniper gin, is distilled in and around the city (see *Wambrechies*, page 209) and is a popular chaser, flavouring or mid-meal *trou* (to be gulped in one to clear the digestive system for more food). The base of many a house cocktail, it was once popular 'with the ladies' as a *Chuche Mourette*, blended, like a kir, with *crème de cassis*.

BUDGETING

I lingered long, mused much and pondered hard over how to categorise the restaurants of Lille. Unlike hotels, it is not really fair to classify the eateries of the town by price, since a good value set-menu lunch at even a famous gastronomic restaurant can often cost less than grazing à la carte in a bistro. So do not be hidebound by the restrictions of these listings – since should you fancy just a main course at a pricier restaurant, it may still work out cheaper than three courses at a mid-range restaurant. Nonetheless, the listings ahead also feature a reality check with the rates for a free-range food fest.

Almost every restaurant will offer a special lunchtime deal at under €20 per person, with most having a two- or three-course suggestion for around €12–18. Be warned: the lowest-priced menu is usually served only at lunchtimes, so if you fancy good food and are worried about how far your euros will stretch, go for a big meal in the middle of the day and aim for something lighter in the evening.

Brasseries are ideal for those who would rather just have one course instead of the pricier menu, and make a lively option for kicking off or rounding off an evening on the town. Check out the bar and café options at midday for a filling sandwich or *plat du jour*.

WHERE TO EAT

Bistro, brasserie or fine-dining room: to be fair, they are all restaurants. I have highlighted those that offer traditional bistro and brasserie fare or style, or that offer a typical Lillois, Flemish or French atmosphere. The other restaurants listed may be trendier or more traditional, but each establishment offers something different. So do browse through the reviews in all categories before deciding where to lunch or dine. Lille's wine bars and *estaminets* are also well worth thinking about. And consider the Maisons Folies (see pages 189–92) in town and around the region for the opportunity to break bread with the artists of Lille and beyond. For typical opening hours, see page XVIII.

BISTROS & *ESTAMINETS*

Le Barbu d'Anvers GP 1 bis rue Saint Étienne 59000 ☎03 20 55 11 68 ⊘closed Sun [236 B5 (66)] 🚇*Rihour e* Métro 2 to Gare Lille Flandres then line 1 to Rihour. Rue Roisin into rue de Pas then right into rue St Etienne.* Tipped off about this welcome arrival on the scene, I made my way to the arched gateway tucked behind the squares back in January 2005, just weeks after the upmarket *estaminet* made its debut for the year-end party season. Directly opposite the crowd-pleasing Compostelle & hidden behind a high wall, the Barbu presents classic Lillois fare to an appreciative blend of after-work colleagues, uni friends & quieter couples & manages deftly to be both *estaminet* & restaurant according to appetite. For the lighter eater, the menu proposes a selection of soups 'to eat' or 'to drink' & standard dishes are tickled into a playful mood with a dash of something extra. With the duck-&-prune-based starter, the local *genièvre* gin from Wambrechies (see page 209) made a welcome appearance &, when I first visited, the reliable marinated herring had a clove-&-cinnamon-scented hint of Christmas spice to it. By 2009, fusion had made its inevitable mark on an essentially Flemish table, so a starter platter had Indian spiced smoked salmon with grilled dill gambas. But the local combos still rule the roost, namely Trois Monts beer in a gingerbread *carbonnade* & slow-cooked chicken with *spéculoos* biscuit sauce. You might not easily find a traditional *moules-frîtes* on every visit, but a contemporary gastro tweaking of the classics won't be too far away & a bistrot standby *steak tartare* will set you back €16. Midweek lunch menus hover around the €20 mark & the evening set price meal is €39. Otherwise budget lavishly for food & indulge in the wine list, featuring the ubiquitous Chinon, fast becoming the city's house red. $$$

Bistrot des Toquées Les Toquées de la Cuisine, 110 quai Géry Legrand, 59000 ☎03 20 00 12 46 ⊙www.bistrotdestoquees.com ⊘Mon–Fri lunch, Thu–Fri eve [234 A4 (1)] 🚇*Bois Blancs e* Métro 2 to Bois Blancs then walk* *the length of the av Dormoy, bearing left onto av Butin & turning right on to the quai Géry Legrand.*

This is a pleasing little oddity. The bistro is part of a waterfront cookery school a good half-hour from the stations & more than a walk from the centre. Budget around €30. However, it could be the ideal choice if you couple the meal with the gift of a mini *cours de cuisine* for the wannabe chef in your life. For €55 you may study one particular dish for 2–3 hours, & learn how to prepare it with tips from the experts. $$$$

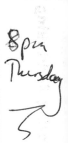

La Ducasse **MK** 95 rue Solférino, 59800
📞 03 20 57 34 10 [234 C5 (18)] 🚇 *République–Beaux Arts* ℯ* Bus 12 from Gare Lille Flandres to Eglise Sacré Coeur. Rue Solférino to pl des Halles Centrales.

Just another corner bistro with an accordionist leading a singalong of Saturday night standards. Perhaps, yet the atmosphere is second to none: the simple local stews & platters hit the spot, the beer & wine flow freely & the local crowd are the nicest people you could ever meet. Students passing through Lille for 2 or 3 years may choose the newest addresses along the road, but those living in apartments in the streets between the boulevards drop in here to sup with friends & neighbours rather than cook for themselves. The menu is unashamedly Flemish, & the local beers pulled from the pump. After an arduous day recording our BBC feature *Allez Lille*, my colleagues & I chose this corner for an anonymous, off-duty collapse. Hearing our English conversation, a local birthday party at the next table sent us over a bottle of wine & invited us to join them for coffee. A coin or two in the ancient pianola, & the honky-tonk piano-roll music whirred into action. Thankfully producer Jerome Weatherald had a spare recorder in his pocket & was able to capture a few moments of that magical mood on tape. We ended the programme with a hint of our wonderful evening at the Ducasse, & shared the true spirit of Lille in a way mere words might never have managed. Have a *hochepot* or *waterzoi*, a chunk of steak & a hefty slice of *tarte*, pour a large drink, sing along to a *chanson* from the golden age, & feel the glow for yourself. I returned a year later to celebrate the launch of the Beaujolais nouveau. A bottle of wine was left on our table to tempt us to try it. You might each have change from a €20 note at lunchtime & budget around €25–35 in the evenings, including a tipple or two … $$$

Estaminet Gantois See *Restaurant Hermitage Gantois*, page 94.
$$$

St André 37 rue St André, 59000 ☎ 03 20 06 94 37 ⊘closed Sun [234 D1
(22)] *e* Bus 6 from Gare Lille Flandres to Conservatoire. Walk along rue St André.*
Clean, bright, contemporary look on the corner of rue Voltaire, this is an
Italianate bistro take on gastro pub grub. Winter warmers include
welcome comfort food: mushrooms on toast followed by a cottage pie or
confit de canard as well as the more predictable lasagne & tiramisu
standards – legacy of its former identity as the corner trattoria La Nostra
Italia. The ever-changing daily menu is chalked up on the *ardoise*.
Budget €30 or so. $$$

Café Manu <u>VL</u> 5 pl du Concert, 59000 ☎ 03 20 74 11 40 ⊘closed Sun
eve & Mon [236 C2 (87)] *e* Bus 3, 6 or 9 from Gare Lille Flandres to Lion d'Or.
Then follow rue de la Monnaie.*
Any chef who relays broadcasts from his kitchen to a flat screen in the
dining room could never be accused of lacking in self-confidence. So
Emmanuel Cauchy has made his mark at various addresses in & around
the city. His latest showcase is earthy & real, & proof that substance will
always triumph over style. Slap bang opposite the *conservatoire*, across
the thinking foodie's market square at place du Concert, the former A
Côté des Arts is now renamed Café Manu with full-length windows for
2-way people watching.
   Within all is wood, real wood: rough timber, old railway sleepers,
rescued beams & salvaged chairs & tables, all designed to warm the
heart of an artisan or woodsman. Food on these tables is ripe & ready
crowd-pleasing stuff for the well turned-out crowd in the know, who
may have spent the last half hour weighing up the relative merits of five
varieties of *chicon* from market gardens. The décor is marked by
dripping wax & old *Ruinart* champagne bottles, but don't be fooled:
there is nothing old fashioned & lazy about the cooking. Whilst
contemporary summery vinaigrettes may season light & imaginative
approaches to bream & seafood (the fresh catch laid on beds of
perfectly pitched basmati), come the season when the air outside grows
chilly & sharp, a late autumn/early winter menu is laden with the time-
tested promise of proper lamb stews. Each forkful inspires a happy sigh.
For lunchtimes budget €17–21, evenings à la carte nearer €30. $$

Chez La Vieille <u>VL</u> 60 rue de Gand, 59000 ☎ 03 28 36 40 06
⊘closed Sun & Mon [236 E2 (90)] *e* Bus 3, 6 or 9 from Gare Lille Flandres to
Lion d'Or. Cross pl Louise de Bettignies to rue de Gand.*
Franck Delobelle may not be a grandmother, but his welcome is as warm
as the old wooden tables & hop-decked beams of this cheery Flemish

dining room. From the crockery on the shelves above the seats to the traditional wooden toys & games in the window, La Vieille is very much in the tradition of homely conviviality that marks out this popular estaminet from the master hosts of Cassel (see *t'Rijsel* below, & the newest successor on page 80) as the real McCoy rather than the fashionable reinvention that is the latest urban-rustic retro fad. Here the food is of exclusively seasonal regional standards – warm stews in winter & tasty flans in summer – all prepared to old country recipes & tasting as though stirred by a granddaughter under the watchful eyes of a matriarch. The menu comes in at €18.50. $$

Estaminet de la Royale VL 37 rue Royale, 59000 ✆ 03 20 42 10 11
⊘ closed eves (except Fri), Sun & holidays [236 A3 (34)] *e** *Métro 2 to Gare Lille Flandres then line 1 to Rihour. Cross Grand' Place to rue Esquermoise into rue Royale.*
Despite the rustic mirrors & milk-churn décor, this is the genuine article: a real *estaminet* neighbourhood bar in a centuries-old building in Vieux Lille, where a simple good, old-fashioned, home-cooked lunch is on offer at midday. *Rognons de veau* or a simple poultry dish might grace the €18 menu. Food is served only until 14.30, but you are welcome to drink with the chatty locals into the early evening. $$

Estaminet t'Rijsel VL 25 rue de Gand, 59800 ✆ 03 20 15 01 59
⊘ closed Sun, Mon & much of Aug [236 E2 (91)] *e** *Bus 3, 6 or 9 from Gare Lille Flandres to Lion d'Or. Cross pl Louise de Bettignies to rue de Gand.*
Rijsel is the Flemish name for Lille, so no surprise to find a warm corner of old Flanders in this relative newcomer to the restaurant scene. Jean-Luc Lacante, whose *estaminet* t'Kasteel-Hof in nearby Cassel is a long-time favourite with those who explore the countryside, brought his trademark combination of wit, style & homeliness to town at the turn of the millennium. Expect all the regional specialities here, from *potjevlesch* to sugar flans, on menus printed in old school-exercise books. Late one cold winter's morning, my parents & I stopped by for a hearty bowl of home-made soup, & very welcome we were made, even if the kitchen was not yet officially open. Budget comfortably around €20, & around €13 for lunch. Check out, too, Chez La Vieille, the sister *estaminet* across the way at number 60 & the newest *estaminet*, Au Vieux de la Vieille, off rue de la Monnaie (see page 80). $$

Gospel Café MK 78 rue Gambetta, 59000 ✆ 03 20 07 39 64
⌂ www.myspace.com/gospelcafe ⊘ Mon–Thu 11.30–18.00, Fri–Sat 11.30–22.30, Sun 11.30–17.00 [234 C6 (12)] ⌷ *République–Beaux Arts*

e* *Métro 2 to Gare Lille Flandres, then line 1 to République–Beaux Arts. Walk down rue Gambetta, the restaurant is on your left.*

Oh happy day. The spices grab you by the eyes & heart, & lure you into this cheery Caribbean influenced eaterie, café & occasional nightspot. Bright bold colours, Obama T-shirts & a morning-after-carnival atmosphere greeted us as we arrived for lunch a few days after the inauguration in Washington. Madame Boyunga welcomes vistors with spicy, ricey soul food & comforting creole savours of the south, making for lively lunches. Late-afternoon chocolate fixes are the perfect reward for hardcore shopping across the square. Closed most evenings, except the weekends, when live gospel music takes to the floor on the first & third Saturday of the month. Great on Sunday too, when brunch is served until 16.00 after a Wazemmes market moochfest. $$

La Houblonnière GP 42 pl Général de Gaulle, 59000 ℡ 03 20 74 54 34 [236 C6 (62)] 🚊 *Rihour* *e** *Bus 12 from Gare Lille Flandres to de Gaulle. Or walk av le Corbusier & right into rue Faidherbe then left to Grand' Place.*

You might be forgiven for thinking that the Grand' Place was lined with restaurant tables where one could sip & sup the day away simply people-watching. In truth, apart from the occasional café & a McDonald's, most of the restaurants are to be found in the street that links Grand' Place with the place Rihour, the main square itself being given over to grand buildings & the goddess. However, the Coq Hardi (see page 81) & its neighbour La Houblonnière offer that rare treat; rows of tables out on the square with the view over Lille's favourite meeting place. Admittedly tables are rather close to the traffic, but, hey, you are eating & drinking in the heart of the city. Don't spend a fortune – €20 should see you all right for the full 3 courses. Go for traditional foods such as *rillettes*, *andouillette*, a chunky *tartare* of smoked & raw salmon or the ubiquitous cheese dishes, *tarte aux maroilles* or *Welsh*. Not gastronomy, just hearty stomach fillers halfway through a day's hardcore walking or before an evening's serious partying. Dine upstairs to enjoy the witty artwork. $$

Le Passe-Porc MK 155 rue Solférino, 59000 ℡ 03 20 42 83 93 ⊙ daily for lunch & Fri eve; closed Aug [234 D6 (11)] 🚊 *République–Beaux Arts* *e** *Métro 2 to Gare Lille Flandres, then line 1 to République–Beaux Arts. Then follow the rue Inkerman to rue Solférino.*

Appropriately located across the street from a cluster of butchers' vans, this is a country market town bistro on market day. Old-fashioned (as opposed to knowingly retro) velvet & brown décor & honest earthy fare. In a street where style is on the up, here is a rare survivor of the bloodline that still exists only around the old market & slaughterhouse quarters on the edge of Paris or deep in what is now designated *La France Profonde*. The French, unlike their queasy neighbours *trans-manche* who take provenance of farmyard fodder no further than cellophane & polystyrene, love their meats for being meat, & a restaurant that makes free with the word abattoir is certain to find favour with hardcore carnivores. Signs in the window proudly announce the speciality (tripe) & the locally brewed La Goudale to be served with the meal. In reality the bottles that pass over the counter are as likely to be champagne or rich reds from the ever-changing wine list selected from the traditional wine regions of Bordeaux & Burgundy. My porcophile friends cannot recommend too highly. $$

La Petite Cour **VL** 17 rue du Curé St Etienne, 59000 ☎ 03 20 51 52 81 ☺ closed Sun & Mon [236 B4 (74)] *e** *Bus 12 from Gare Lille Flandres to de Gaulle. Walk under the Alcide arch to the debris St Etienne then left into the rue du Curé St Etienne.*

Very busy café in a courtyard with basic seating & tables. If proof were ever needed that the average age in Lille is 25 then just look around. Popular with families during the day & with students at night. Service may be brusque but the food is fine – no classic moments – & generous. I could have re-enacted the forest scene from *Sleeping Beauty* just hacking my way through a never-ending *salade niçoise*. A smoked fish platter was a bit tough, but *steak haché & frites* proved more reliable. If your appetite is not up to the occasion, the staff will happily split a main course & offer 2 plates. The inner dining area is suitably eclectic, designed to look like a courtyard, but the real open-air court is a happy suntrap for a light lunch. The outside loo leaves little to the imagination. Pay €24 for a 2-course menu with a glass of wine; otherwise budget closer to €30 in the evenings. Plat de jour lunches from under €15. $$

Le Pot Beaujolais **GP** 26 rue de Paris, 59000 ☎ 03 20 57 38 38 🖰 www.lepotbeaujolais.com ☺ closed Sun & Mon eve [236 C6 (56)] 🚇 Rihour *e** *Av le Corbusier & right into rue Faidherbe, then left on rue des Ponts de Comines to rue de Paris, or bus 12 to Théâtre.*

Le Beaujolais ancien est arrivé! Most restaurants in town remember Beaujolais only when the nouveau wine is released in autumn. In this tiny little bistro on the rue de Paris, the spirit of the most traditional of regions is reflected year round in the brown wood & check-cloth décor & most of all in the menu. Outside traditional mealtimes a selection of terrines & tartines are available at all times for those who fancy staving off the hunger pangs with the taste of old Lyon. A modest outlay will buy an alternative to a conventional sandwich, this time layered with *chèvre* & smoked duck breast. But at lunchtime & in the evening, tuck your napkin under your chin, take a deep breath, allow your waistline room to expand & get stuck in to the menu. This place is serious about its steaks, & the meat is treated with as much respect as wine here, even to the listing of the butcher's name on the menu. *Onglet* or *entrecôte*, expect quality & do not even think of ordering the *côte de bœuf* if your vocabulary includes the French for 'well done' or even 'medium'. Classic comfort cooking means a steaming plate of *petit salé* with Puy lentils or *andouillette* sausage in a *mâconnaise* sauce. Don't ignore the wine list. The Beaujolais classic crus are all there – & can be taken away too – so enjoy a Moulin à Vent or a Brouilly with the meal. Squeeze inside or sit on the pavement terrace & consider spending around €24 a head. Midweek lunchtimes see a menu at €16 for 2 courses, & a dish of the day at around €12. Keep an eye on this stretch of the rue de Paris. For years it has been the least interesting of the roads south of Grand' Place, but bars & restaurants are taking over from tired shops. Could be on the up. $$

Tuck your napkin under your chin, take a deep breath and allow your waistline room to expand.

Le Square d'Aramis <u>VL</u> 52 rue Basse, 59000 ☎ 03 20 74 16 17
☺ closed Mon eve, Sun & Aug [236 B4 (77)] *e* Bus 3, 6 or 9 from Gare Lille Flandres to Lion d'Or. Rue des Chats Bossus into rue Basse.*

Big portions & no illusions of grandeur in a bustling, bistro-style café that gets packed with families at lunchtimes & youngsters in the evenings. Value for money is the lure. The menu, *midi et soir*, is €22. Whatever you choose, the service is informal, with starters big enough to eat as a main course, & local dishes full of flavour. My first food memory of the place is of a *saumon cru* marinated in *bière de garde* that proved pretty darned yummy & *andouillette-frites* was ever the popular choice. A house speciality is a brace of reinterpretations of that old stager the *steak tartare*. You'll find the raw beef classic being mixed in a dozen brasseries across Lille, but only here will you be offered the €15 dish either Thai or Mexican style! The budget-conscious tend to opt for the sizeable *salade de poulet* with feta, fruit & a sesame dressing or the pasta of the day from the small but wide-ranging menus. $$

Au Tord-Boyaux <u>MK</u> 11 pl Nouvelle Aventure, 59000 ☎ 03 20 57 73 67
☺ closed Sun eve [234 A6 (4)] 🚇 *Gambetta* *e* Métro 2 to Gare Lille Flandres &*

then Line 1 to Gambetta. Cross rue du Marché until you get to the market.

If you find yourself in this chummy little bar-bistro in the heart of Wazemmes, then raise a glass to your fellow travellers & readers George and Violet O'Neill. For it was the O'Neills who stumbled upon this place on the very last weekend of Lille 2004. Having partied long & hard, with a well-thumbed copy of this book as trusty guide, they decided to spend the last morning of their stay at Wazemmes (see page 164), & thus they found themselves taking pot luck at market cafés & restaurants in search of a good sit down & sustenance. I was not surprised to hear of their experience, since a few months earlier I had received just such a warm welcome in the quarter. However, since people rarely believe me when I wax lyrical on the open, cheery *accueil* the Wazemmes community continues to extend to strangers, I let George take up the tale: 'Intending to just try some of the local beers we took a seat at one of the long tables. We were served with a dish of titbits which were added to by people from other tables. One man went into the Market Hall & came back with a bag of food. He & his wife proceeded to eat the contents & shared them with the rest of us. None of the staff found this unusual. People came & went to & from the market. A couple near us ordered from the blackboard & were eventually served steaks. We ordered the same & a bottle of Beaujolais nouveau then sat back & enjoyed the ambience of this charming little place. The food arrived, obviously cooked to order; it was delicious. A guitarist also arrived & played while we ate – mostly songs unknown to us but not to the rest of the customers who sang along with gusto.' I hate to say 'I told you so', so I'll content myself with suggesting that you budget around €20 & just go with the flow in one of the friendliest corners of town. $$

▼ *As the Braderie continues, the pile of mussel shells rises outside the Brasserie les Moules.*

Au Vieux de la Vieille

VL 2 rue des Vieux Murs, 59000 ℃ 03 20 13 81 64 ☉ Mon-Sat 10.00–22.30 [236 C3 (82)] *e* Bus 3, 6 or 9 from Gare Lille Flandres to Lion d'Or. From rue de la Monnaie turn left into rue au Peterinck.*

First the *estaminet* t'Rijsel, then came Chez la Vieille & now, inevitably, the Vieux de la Vieille: these glimpses of Flanders past in the present are the perfect antidote to the cutting-edge trendiness that never quite takes over the city. No matter how close fingers come to the pulse of the present, hearts & souls are always closest to the past. Since the boys from Cassel first brought their simple, honest country-style café concept to the big city around a decade or so ago, the sharp style of the rue de Gand has introduced a fresh generation of Lillois to the simplest pleasures known by their parents & grandparents when this part of France was still ignored by sophisticated society & was left to its own devices. An *estaminet* was originally a bar in a corner of someone's front room, where neighbours might drop in for a beer for an hour or two before bedtime.

The t'Kasteel-Hof in the rural hinterland between the coast & Belgian border retains that feel of makeshift hospitality, & in the rue de Gand the success of the 2 city branches, each with its own style, has been heartening. Such is the popularity of these simple bistros, whilst smarter premises change hands like dancers in a reel, that this third *estaminet-café* has opened at the point where the rue Peterinck unbuckles its belts & expands into almost a square in that straggle of workshops, studios & quaint counters meandering from rue de la Monnaie to the cathedral. This traditional café-bistro concept has old-style wooden games to play with while you linger over any of a couple of dozen artisan-brewed beers & the red-brick room itself is filled with drying hops & bric-a-brac from every granny's parlour. Pappy & Memère's influence is to be found on the homely *potjevlesch*-rich menus & in the spirit of their guests. Hospitality spills over from the bowls of Flemish soups & stews into the friendliness of the clientèle. If you can't find a table for two, certainly don't be surprised if a group of friends in a corner decide to squeeze closer together & invite you to sit with them. The menu deal for €20 includes 3 courses & a beer. $$

L'Arrière Pays **VL** 47 rue Basse, 59000 ☏03 20 13 80 07 [236 B4 (76)] *e* Bus 12 from Gare Lille Flandres to pl Général de Gaulle. Walk up rue Esquermoise & turn right into rue Basse.*

Lovely rooms (red-brick décor upstairs, classic style downstairs) are simple & modern, respecting the period of the building, which doubles as a local grocery shop selling terrines & oils. Pause to sample the traditional fare. €7 buys a wholesome tart. B/fast/brunch-style menus (€11/9.40) are popular at Sunday brunchtime. Budget €18 à la carte. $

Le Coq Hardi **GP** 44 pl Général de Gaulle, 59800 ☏03 20 55 21 08 [236 C6 (60)] *Rihour e* Bus 12 from Gare Lille Flandres to de Gaulle. Or walk av le Corbusier & right into rue Faidherbe then left to Grand' Place.*

An institution on the central square of Lille for donkey's years, the tables spreading out across the pavement are better known than the small restaurant behind them. In fact it was only when the winter weather grumbled ominously that I ventured to check out the restaurant itself. Small but perfectly busy, with service on 2 floors, the Coq Hardi is unashamedly basic rustic. Untreated wooden ceilings, sacks of baguettes inside the front door & a constant flow of customers keen on value-for-money lunching. Huge portions are the order of the day, whether *andouillette de Cambrai* with *frites* or a *tartare des deux saumons*, served ready-mixed or with the additional ingredients on the side. Most *plats* €7–12. In the sunshine take a big bowl of *moules* or a huge summer salad & lunch outdoors for well under €15, indulging in good old-fashioned people-watching at this key corner between the old town & the main square. $

Le Resto du Ch'ti 61 rue d'Isly, 59000 ☏03 20 00 85 73 ☺Mon–Sat lunch, Thu–Sat dinner, closed Sun [234 A4 (2)] *Cormontaigne e* Métro 2 to Cormontaigne.*

Bienvenue chez les Ch'tis, so the cinema posters had it for the best part of a year. The tradition here, just that bit further away from the centre than most visitors would think of travelling, is less of comedy, but of the honest northern welcome & value for money. Where else will you eat home-style cooking at these prices? Henri & Murielle Leclercq had long been mine hosts on rue St André. Now, away from the pricier centre of town they can serve classic braised chicory dishes, grandmotherly ladlings of rabbit with prunes & a hearty steaming *carbonnade*, each for under €10. *Cuisine de terroir* without paying the earth. $

Eating & drinking **Bistros & estaminets**

BRASSERIES

Brasserie André <u>GP</u> 71 rue de Béthune, 59800 ✆03 20 54 75 51
[236 B8 (45)] 🚇 République–Beaux Arts **e*** Métro 2 to Gare Lille Flandres then
line 1 to République–Beaux Arts. Cross pl Richebé to rue de Béthune.

This is where good *moules* go when they die. Sumptuous traditional
brasserie décor, with wonderful wooden-panelled arches & dark wooden
walls contrasting with white, starched napkins, tablecloths & aprons. Not
cheap by brasserie standards – your meal could set you back €50 – but
your lunch companions will be businessmen, bankers & people who
don't mind paying a tad over the odds for a classy setting for classic
favourites. For the non-mussel-eater, indulge in beefsteaks, lamb & the
like served in rich *bordelaise* fashion. The pavement terrace spills out on
to the main shopping area. $$$

*The waiter's apron stains are a veritable menu
for the illiterate.*

Le Meunier <u>S</u> 15–17 rue de Tournai, 59800 ✆03 28 04 04 90
🖑 http://contactmeunier.free.fr [235 G5 (31)] 🚇 Gare Lille Flandres **e*** Av Le
Corbusier, then left at Gare Lille Flandres.

Once upon a time every provincial French railway station had a stolid,
reliable railway restaurant serving basic meat, fish & chicken – standard
fare to while away the 2-hour delay between cross-country trains. At the
side of the old Flandres station, amid the *friteries* & burger bars, is to be
found one such old-fashioned *buffet de la gare*-style dining room, which
has been fuelling weary passengers since 1946. Canteen cutlery & heavy
white plates, & a respectable line in pâtés & *rillettes* are there to take
away as well as to eat in. Diners will be offered such fare as *tripes à la
mode de Caen, tête de veau or tournedos rossini* rather than the pan-fried
spring vegetables with steamed fruits in their coulis of pretension that
one might expect from more fashionable eateries. One eats here to
remember railway holidays chugging through a less sophisticated France
in less demanding times. Lots of choice on lots of set menus at €14–28.
$$$

La Baignoire <u>MK</u> 8 pl Béthune, 59000 ✆03 20 30 07 44 [234 E5 (29)]
🚇 République–Beaux Arts **e*** Line 2 to Gare Lille Flandres then line 1 to
République–Beaux Arts.

See the listing under *Bars*, page 114. $$

Brasserie Alcide GP 5 rue des
débris St Etienne, 59800 ✆ 03 20 12 06 95
[236 C5 (64)] 🚇 *Rihour* **e** *Bus 12 from
Gare Lille Flandres to de Gaulle. Or walk
along av le Corbusier & turn right into rue
Faidherbe then left to Grand' Place.*
Where better to indulge in a
carbonnade flamande than in this most
typical of brasseries? Alcide has been
found under the arch at the main square since the 1870s, & in shades of
red, black & white, it still hints at its original Napoleon III style despite
comtemporising its look, décor & cooking under *chef de cuisine*
Christophe Bonvalet. Oysters or a seasonal *feuilleté* of asparagus are a
prelude to succumbing to a main course of *moules-frites* or *carbonnade*,
heady with the *saveurs* of the brewery & laced with the scent of
tradition. Uncompromising brasserie fare survives the sophistication of
the place, so *tête de veau* & pigs' trotters still have pride of place
alongside the obligatory oysters at the beginning of the meal, sole is
served *meunière* & *crêpes suzette* will be flambéed with a flourish at the
end of the evening. Service is as solid & professional as you could hope
for. You can dine here for around €30, or push the boat out as far as you
like beyond that. A 2-course €19 menu is pretty good value for money at
the most basic level, but fixed-price meals rise to €45. $$

Brasserie de la Cloche GP 13 pl du Théâtre 59800 ✆ 03 20 55 35 34
[236 C6 (59)] 🚇 *Rihour* **e** *Bus 12 to Théâtre.*
Having had the square pretty much to itself, the Cloche is facing up to
new competition with the emergence from the shadows of a string of
bars & bistros around the revived & revitalised cultural hub by the Opera
House. My money says that nothing much will change here. The
restaurant on the Rang de Beauregard is known for its distinctive sign on
the wall, but even more so for its tables on the square itself, where
informal & friendly waiting staff serve unpretentious fare to an
undemanding public. So the waiter's apron stains are a veritable menu
for the illiterate, & the waitress's air hostess *maquillage* is rendered
human by the tattoo on her shoulder; all is convivial, & the portions are
the size that friends would serve you. Food is a bit of a hit-&-miss affair
– a leek tart had much of the string & card about its consistency – but a
fellow diner's *plat du jour* wafted the appetising aromas of home-cooked
meat & two veg, & the *salade bergère* was the cheesiest double-edged

Eating & drinking Brasseries

platter of comfort food you could hope to risk. You can get away with spending just €18. Best of all is the wine list, with more than a dozen interesting wines served by the glass. I predict the post (& intermission) concert & opera crowd will welcome the €15 late-night snack of smoked salmon & champagne. $$

Brasserie de la Paix GP 25 pl Rihour, 59800 ✆ 03 20 54 70 41
⌂ http://paix.restaurantsdelille.com ⊘closed Sun [236 B6 (49)] 🚇 Rihour
e* Métro 2 to Gare Lille Flandres then line 1 to Rihour.
Café society '20s & '30s-style lives on here; the décor, the welcome & the food are from the heyday of the French brasserie. Recent editions of the *Ch'ti* guide have waxed almost Proustian on the subject. Great platters of seafood, roast *canette de Challans* cooked with fresh figs, & a chicory *crème brûlée* are amongst the attractions. The period feel is strictly for diners inside the restaurant. Sit outside on the pavement & you can enjoy the very modern spectacle of shoppers trekking from boutique to boutique & commuters emerging from beneath the queasy custard-coloured waters on the pyramid fountain at Rihour métro station. Menus from €15 lunchtimes to €26 in the evenings. $$

La Chicorée GP 15 pl Rihour, 59000 ✆ 03 20 54 81 52 [236 B6 (50)]
🚇 Rihour *e* Métro 2 to Gare Lille Flandres then line 1 to Rihour.*
We have all found ourselves here at some stage of some late-night session. Open from 10.00 until dawn, the old reliable brasserie on the corner is the perfect standby when an evening has just flown by at the bar, café or jazz club & nobody is ready for bed yet. Part of the family stable of brasserie-style restaurants that cluster around the corner of the place Rihour, the décor is now latin block shades with strategically placed artworks. An all-day (until 22.30) menu of around €10–16 is a bit limited, & the full-blown à la carte should run to around €25. However, a steaming bowl of onion soup topped with a gruyère-covered *croûton* should fill you up & leave the wallet relatively unscathed. Since prices rise by around 20% after midnight, the waiters are perfectly happy to serve just a starter or 1-course refuelling option in the small hours. At sunrise the place is busy with night-shift workers, road sweepers & métro staff rounding off the night's work with a hefty steak & refreshing beer, as the rest of us follow our noses to the bakery for b/fast croissants & hot chocolate! $$

Aux Moules <u>GP</u> 34 rue de Béthune, 59000 ☎ 03 20 57 12 46 [236 B8 (46)] 🚉 *Rihour e* Métro 2 to Gare Lille Flandres then line 1 to Rihour. Rue de la Vieille Comédie leads to rue de Béthune.* No surprises here – the menu pays lip service to other tastes, but the speciality of the house is *moules*, either *marinières* or in beer, in big pots or small bowls, with or without *frites*. Mussels by name & mussels by the bucket load. When the establishment first opened its doors in 1930 the set menu was 4 francs; these days a *moules* meal will cost around €16. Famous for boasting the highest pile of mussel shells stacked up on the pavement outside the restaurant during the Braderie festivities each September, the place is dominated by a huge mural of the heyday of the *plat du jour*. Waiters are either young & chirpy or lifers who can recall prices in 'old' old money! Great for late lunches on Sunday afternoon, or mid-afternoon *crêpes* during a shopping excursion through the pedestrianised streets south of the place du Général de Gaulle. Leave room for the house rhubarb tart at lunchtime or the massive éclair for self-indulgence at any hour. $$

▼ *Indoor alternative to the street market – fresh veg in the Halles at Wazemmes.*

Les Trois Brasseurs <u>S</u> 22 pl de la Gare, 59800 ✆ 03 20 06 46 25 [236 E7 (97)] 🚋 *Gare Lille Flandres* ***e*** * *Av le Corbusier to Gare Lille Flandres & pl de la Gare.*

Flanders is famed for its beers – whatever you do you must try at least one of the region's distinctive flavours. Many local *artisanales* beers are made in the traditional method, & some larger breweries offer guided tours & tastings for the public. As for me, I stay in central Lille & always pay a visit to Les Trois Brasseurs opposite the old Lille Flandres station. The director of Pelforth – the commercial brewery behind the Pelican lagers favoured by Calais trippers – created this genuine brasserie. Monsieur Bonduel decided to get back to brewing basics, & we all have cause to be grateful to him. It was the welcome I found here that first drew me to Lille, & I will never cease to be thankful. The clientele ranges from solo business types at the bar to groups of friends, locals & visitors. The bar staff are rarely less than convivial, the waiters never less than harassed. In this always-packed bar-restaurant the only beers served are those brewed in copper vats on the premises. For €4.50 buy a *pallette* – a tasting tray of 4 small glasses of the various home brews, the *blonde, brune, ambrée* & *Blanche de Lille*, the refreshing bitter-sweet thirst quencher ideally served with a slice of lemon. This tasting tray is the best way to get to know the beers of Lille. March & Christmas see special seasonal beers added to the range. The menu is excellent northern home cooking: rabbit stews, roasts & the cholesterol-packed *Welsh*, a bowl of melted cheese, ham & beer with a slice of bread & chips. If you are feeling really adventurous, try the beer tart or beer sorbet! Set-menu deals are the best value at around €11, as are the house *flammekeuche*, & the daily special, such as marrowbone or a *carbonnade*, is always reasonably priced. A range of promotional combinations can be found on the blackboards or in the newspaper-style menus. Otherwise budget at €20 & you won't go far wrong. The restaurant next door serves the same food in a more traditional bistro setting, but I like to dine amongst the dark wood & bright copper of this convivial & very special brewery. The house beers may be bought to take home by the bottle or *tonnelet* (mini-barrel), a useful souvenir on a Sunday when the Euralille shops are closed. $$

RESTAURANTS

A l'Huîtrière **VL** 3 rue des Chats Bossus, 59000 ✆ 03 20 55 43 41 ✑ www.huitriere.fr ⊘closed Sun eve [236 C4 (80)] *e* Bus 3, 6 or 9 from Gare Lille Flandres to Lion d'Or.*

'Absolute perfection & faultless' was the verdict of my dinner guest; I just beamed in contentment & the glow of unalloyed pleasure. The short walk past the fresh fish counters, the classic mosaics, baskets of shells & wondrous confections *en gelée* & in bottles is dappled in a maritime twilight. Once in the narrow vestibule twixt the domains of the fishmonger & the *maître cuisinier*, a warm welcome from the fabulously efficient & courteous staff instantly sets the standard for the evening.

In the restaurant itself all is calm, all is bright. Light wood panels; lovely wool tapestry; table appointments charming, with white & navy Limoges service atop crisp white linen. Exquisite & discreet service is attentive with no hint of intimidation. The wonders from the kitchen never fail to stimulate nor enchant. I recall an entrée of wild Scottish salmon *mi-cru mi-cuit*, lovingly prepared, briefly roasted, pan-fried & seared in spices on the outside, yet succulent & raw within & laced with a fine horseradish dressing. *Trois petites royales* revealed themselves as truffled-up seductions of leek, cabbage & *petits pois*: simply superb. Though this is a fish restaurant, honourable mention must go to the *escalope de foie gras de canard* in a *pot-au-feu de nouveaux legumes*. The main course varies with the catch & the season, & according to the taste of the diner.

Our waiter regarded my companion's request for a variation on the menu suggestion as a challenge rather than an affront, & took a genuine delight in consulting with the kitchen to create the perfect dish to meet a customer's exacting tastes. John Dory roasted in its skin with asparagus *meunière* with *vinaigrette au beurre* was proof, if such were ever needed, that the sea is no poor relation to the pasture. The *sorbet à la fleur de bière* is the northern answer to a *trou normand* & clears the appetite for game.

Impeccable desserts – try *mi-gratin, misoufflé* of wild woodland strawberries – & pastries, chocolates & *petits fours* are simply heavenly. A wisely compiled wine list included a smooth & refined Chateau Moulin Riche 2ème cru Bordeaux St Julienne decanted in time for the main course. Budget a good €100 per head, or €138 for a seasonally truffled or lobstered 7-course gastronomic menu. 3-course business lunch at €45. New oyster bar for more modest munching. $$$$

Le Jardin du Cloître <u>VL</u> 17 quai de Wault, 59800 ☏ 03 20 30 62 62
[234 D2 (20)] *e* Bus 12 from Gare Lille Flandres to Foch. Walk through the park
to the pond. The restaurant is on the right bank.*
In the business-park perpendicular atrium of the Alliance Hotel is to be
found a restaurant that boasts professional service, a fine *filet mignon* in

N'Autre Monde <u>VL</u> 1 bis
rue du Curé St Etienne, 59800
☏ 03 20 15 01 31
🖰 www.nautremonde.com
⊘ closed Mon [236 B5 (71)]
🚇 Rihour *e* Bus 12 from Gare Lille
Flandres to de Gaulle, walk up rue
Esquermoise, then turn left.*
Would-be culinary stars take
note: a truly great chef does not
have to be 'clever'. A maestro
should be able to play his
ingredients without too many
theatrical flourishes. In this
comfortable squeeze of a dining
room between shopfronts a
stumble from Grand' Place into the old town, the waft & weave of nature
does the bidding of a young virtuoso for even the simplest dish on the
menu. David Bève's piece of cod that passeth all understanding was
sublime, divine & delicious: speared with a vanilla pod, on a bed of the
most basic garden produce. The stalwart of the greyer reaches of the
Atlantic proved as exotic as a conventionally nobler catch. The first lesson
of the day was that garden produce does not have to be red or shiny or
drizzled with oils & vinegars to be worth a second glance. The masterclass
in root veg was steamed only to an awakening: each of half-a-dozen winter
varieties, privily spiced, attained perfection in texture & taste.

North African spices fragrance the air, testament to the world food
philosophy of the place, always delightfully balanced so that the gentle
scent of later arrivals' tagine in no way distracts from the playful mirabelle
or pistachio lacings of your own final course. Desserts, in their turn, are
gorgeous, & the option of an extra cheese course is a no-brainer, given that
next door is the counter of *maître fromagier* Philippe Olivier – so the
provenance is impeccable. There are 9 coffees to choose from, all arabica.

Coffee is not exclusively shackled to the end of the meal: a frustrating the inevitable *blanche* & the ubiquitous piano player. This is where business people from TGV business towns north, south & east of Lille meet up to discuss business policy over a jolly decent business lunch. Menus €34–52. $$$$$

glance at a recent menu (frustration due to the fact that by the time I get back to Lille, the dish will have been overtaken by an even fresher innovation) offered a walnuted crumble of *sandre* served with endive braised in coffee. Mild consolation for missing out on some of the dishes is David Bève's online recipe page on the website. A neighbour of mine has downloaded the secrets of rabbit thighs with *fourme d'ambert* cheese & will one day pluck up the courage to cook the dish!

The menu changes almost with each new moon, & on the winter noon of my visit, the prime plate amongst my fellow diners was a wild boar risotto. You know the food is good when even business lunchers do the lovers' thing & pass forks across the table. This is not the exclusive province of expense account *divertissement*. Besides a smattering of *hommes d'affaires* were a couple of true couples, & plenty of ladies lunching *en fille*. A sharply coiffed man in black who knew the value of skincare lunched with a tousle-haired, bluff fellow in boots who knew the value of life.

The chairs may be dolls-house-princess baroque, but the subdued décor falls safely short of the operatic. The obligatory chandelier & solitary candelabrum do not outshine the regular lighting in the room, & spotlights are turned to photos of orchids hanging on pink walls. Not conventional Barbie-pink, but the rosy hue of an older & wiser Barbie, two marriages post-Ken & with a judicious appreciation of the muted palette being kinder to riper skin tones.

There is usually a lighter-priced vegetarian plate, modestly couched amid the more exotic dishes on the menu. Starters cost €16, mains from €13–30 & desserts a little over €10, so budget easily over €50 for a full scale immersion. Discover a midday limited menu baptism at under €20, exclusively woven from the daily specials, so that adventurous diners on a timid budget need not miss out on a taste of the future.

The innate sophistication & well-tuned instinct of the young chef & his partner Harry Baclet led to the 2009 Gault et Millau guide singling out Bève as a new '*jeune talent*' of France. A first trophy stands on a table by the door. Do not be surprised, by the time you read this, to find even more laurels & garlands. $$$$$

Le Sébastopol MK 1 pl Sébastopol, 59000 ☎ 03 20 57 05 05 🖰 www.restaurant-sebastopol.fr ⊘closed Sat lunch, Sun eve & mid-Aug [234 D6 (9)] 🚊 République–Beaux Arts *e* Métro 2 to Gare Lille Flandres, then line 1 to République–Beaux Arts. Rue Inkermann to pl Sébastopol.* When I first attempted to lunch at this distinguished ivy-covered building beside the wonderfully exaggerated Théâtre Sébastopol, a lone bastion of toque-&-napkin tradition in an area best known for excellent Asian restaurants, I had money in my pocket & an appetite to match. Alas, I had not booked & the dining rooms were packed. My second application proved more successful, but though the appetite was as sharp as ever, my wallet was showing signs of wear, so I opted for the lowest-priced lunch menu at €28. Take it from me, bargain pricing on the menu does not mean corners cut in the kitchen. A *clin d'oeil flamande* selection promised flavours of the region from first till last. Chef Jean-Luc Germond, who since my initial visit has at long last been recognised by the Michelin inspectors, concentrates on finding hidden flavours in fish & fowl, & the budget voyeur need not worry about missing out on his celebrated techniques just because sea bass & St Pierre swim in pricier streams on the bill of fare. After a piquant & lavish starter of succulent strips of raw fish marinated in *fleur de bière*, generously spiked with sea salt, the fisherman's friend turned his attention to *dos de cabillaud*, taking the humble if elusive cod from the chilly North Sea & throwing spells over it. So light is the delicious flaky fish & the feather bed of milky potatoes & *genièvre* gin that it all but defies the laws of physics, solid on the plate & melting like winter into spring on the tongue. What might have been sickly nursery-creamery sweet proved to have a stimulating bitter adult aftertaste. The same wit & talent for culinary paradox could be discerned in the dessert – which reflects the north of France's wonderful market gardens – a *feuilleté* of strawberries & rhubarb, the latter almost crisp to complement the softer fruit. The pâtisserie was excellent, as we had been led to expect from the 3 types of pastry offered with apéritifs & the *mise en bouche* revealed as a *croquillant des champignons* in the finest, crispest, lightest filo. The sweet berry coulis had a tangy near-jelly of sharper fruit. Friends & readers have since reported back on cannellonis of white leeks filled with *daube d'agneau* & lightly cooked duck with a lip-smacking flavour of pear & bergamot, all from this same lunch deal. The full gastronomic menu (which should require a napkin just for reading it) might feature such mouthwatering combos as *crépinette* of lamb's trotters with a vinaigrette of green lentils & juniper, or succulent red mullet fillets on a citrus-flavoured crisp fennel purée, & costs €60–80 depending on whether you opt for the choice that includes a half-bottle of vintage Bordeaux, & à la carte could set you back a good €100. The 7-dish *dégustation* 'Musée et Gourmandise', costing €68, is for seriously gastro-fiendish art lovers planning on being seriously late for the Goyas at the Beaux Arts up the road. A nice touch is the menu note that '*nos hôtes*' under the age of 12 may benefit from a specially created €15 junior gastronomic menu – judicious variants on themes from the main adult selection. Nicola Diment emailed me after a thrilling meal featuring scallops worthy of a paragraph in their own right, & such was her enthusiasm, I suggested the place to my parents for a very special anniversary lunch the following month. They, in their turn, strayed from a €52 set menu (with wine) & indulged themselves ` a la carte with carefree abandon & unuttered inner squeals of delight. Good to see the place has lost none of its magic. The old pre-war dining room is dressed in bright yellow with contemporary decorating techniques & art & sculptures from local galleries. Welcome is warm & genuine, with the chef keeping a close eye on the dining room whenever the swing doors afford a glance, rather than the uptight preening of certain other *maîtres cuisiniers*. Equally, the attentive & hospitable service does not come with the almost religious fervour one finds in many temples of cuisine. First-rate food, served well with good taste & no pretensions. Germond's online recipes are a rarity amongst such showcases – actually doable at home! $$$$$

L'Ecume des Mers GP 10
rue de Pas, 59800 ✆ 03 20 54 95 40
☺ closed Sun eve & most of Aug
[236 B5 (67)] ⛇ *Rihour* **e** *Métro 2
to Gare Lille Flandres then line 1 to
Rihour. Rue Roisin into rue de Pas.*
Refurbished in pleasure-port seaside blues & framed Poseidonesque mosaic, the newest aspect of the restaurant is the menu, the entire *carte* printed daily to reflect the catch of the day. There are a few non-fishy items on the menu, but one comes here to taste the sea. At L'Ecume des Mers, they do what they do & they do it well, & what they do is prepare freshly caught fish in the classic manner. Nothing too clever: a tartare of the oft-overlooked haddock with olive oil, raw sardine in a tarragon marinade, a cold monkfish *bouillabaisse* perhaps, as a change to the standards, but traditional favourites follow the seasons. On a grey day go for an *aïoli* of *morue* or a warming & filling *choucroute* with halibut, smoked haddock & salmon. When your credit card & whim decides to leap like a lustful salmon, push your financial boat out & order turbot or lobster. A mix of well-to-do couples & business foursomes choose to dine indoors; a younger element basks on the pavement terrace outside sharing platters of oysters from the iced counter, be they *fines claires* or *belons*. Eavesdroppers with a cultural bent might spot illustrious neighbour Jean-Claude Casadesus, director of the Orchèstre Nationale de Lille, in conversation with a world-renowned soloist. From every other table comes the reassuring clink-clank of *glaçons* in well-stocked ice buckets ringing against a crisp Chablis or a *demi* Pouilly-Fumé from the fairly priced wine list. Oh, & the worst-kept secret in town is that the reason the fish is so good here is that everything the kitchen knows it learned from L'Huîtrière (see page 87). Here, it is Antoine & Elvire who uphold the good name of the legendary Proye family. Menus €18 at lunchtime & €26 midweek evenings, otherwise make sure you've a good €50 or more in your pocket or on your credit limit. $$$$

Le Fossile <u>GP</u> 60 rue St Etienne, 59000 ☎ 03 20 54 29 82
⌂ www.lefossile.com ⊘ closed Sat & Sun [236 A6 (41)] 🚇 Rihour *e** Métro 2
to Gare Lille Flandres then line 1 to Rihour. Rue Roisin into rue de Pas & left along
rue St Etienne.

Many years ago, I knew a restaurant in Paris that never bothered with
menus. They had only ever served one dish as long as anyone could recall
& it was that or nothing! I was reminded of the old place when I came to
revisit La Coquille, a favourite address of many readers of this guide, the
dining room sandwiched between the Nouveau Siècle building & the
back entrance to the Novotel. Alas, that last relic of the realm of the
barnyard – very much the country of clucking & grain – had shut its
doors for the last time & in its place stood Le Fossile – a newcomer to the
city, but a restaurant with its own 35-year pedigree in Alsace & a worthy
successor to the previous tenants of this fine old red-brick building.

The reminiscences were ignited by the house speciality, or perhaps that
should read the house obsession. Steak is served here. Steak or steak is
the choice on the menu. Unlike the Parisian table of sepia-tinted memory,
there is an option. Either go for *onglet* (the house cut) in any of 3 guises,
or choose a *filet* steak (more of which follows). A friend of mine whose
carnivore credentials would satisfy both Darwin & Tennyson salivated at
a repast red in tooth & claw, & pronounced the house speciality of *onglet
a l'echalotte* triumphant. The beef may also be served with mushrooms or
unfussed. The *filet* is presented in all the classic formats, *maître d'hôtel* or
with Roquefort cheese, mushrooms, cognac, pepper & a choice of wild
mushroom sauces. Mind you, after 22.30, these alternatives are dropped
from the menu, as is the only other main course dish, *tournedos rossini*.
As you might expect, the wine list has practically adopted Bordeaux
citizenship, & our recent snuffling through the pages yielded a 2000
Chateau Beau Site *cru bourgeois exception* St Estèphe at €46 & a 2002
Margaux for €35. The various steak main courses straddle the €20
boundary & the starters (very *escargot, très canard*, seriously *foie gras*)
range from €8–16. Desserts are equally classical at around the €7 mark,
but only a true trencherman will get that far. Still my wimpy *côterie* has
not discovered the 'secret' pudding, the identity only revealed at the table.
When pushing the boat out & loosening the belt buckle, do indulge in a
glass of armagnac. I only know one other eaterie with anywhere near
such a selection of *digestifs* & that is to be found over 700 miles south of
Lille! The Fossile armagnac archive ranges from 1885 to 1996 & features
in the *Guinness Book of Records*. $$$$

Eating & drinking Restaurants

Oui Fooding <u>GP</u> 13 rue des Bouchers ☎ 03 20 38 52 67 ⊘closed Sun & Mon [236 A4 (39)] 🚇 *Rihour* *e* Métro 2 to Gare Lille Flandres then line 1 to Rihour. Pass the tourist office then right into rue de l'Hôpital Militaire, cross place de l'Arsenal to rue des Bouchers.*

In an 18th-century vaulted cellar, a laid-back crowd sip from Monsieur Jacques's impressive wine list & sup on imaginative seasonal dishes. The atmosphere was created with no *Gitanes*-rich fug of smoke, as ciggies were banned here long before the current European ban came in; all the better to appreciate the fine flavours. Less troglodytic types may prefer the main room, with full-length windows & a hint of spindly greenery taking advantage of the natural light to grab a fix of photosynthesis as the rest of us enjoy the €10 *plat du jour*. *Fooding* is one of those new French hybrid noun-verbs that can depress a lexicographer at 20 paces, but the phrase begins to make sense when you take time to roam through the chef's imagination. Fresh ideas join the menu every month – perhaps pastis & star anise added to the traditional garlic butter for the *escargots* (simple genius) or making the €16 burger from minced veal & serrano ham. There is usually a vegetarian pasta option for each course (be it a wild mushroom & artichoke ravioli or that old standby lasagne) so 'carnivoyeurs' may be as happy as their chums diving into a *tête de veau* (fooding style) *à l'orange*! Budget a good €40 per head, plus wine. $$$$

La Petite Cave <u>VL</u> 80 rue St André, 59000 ☎ 03 20 06 60 66 ⊘ daily from 12.30 & 20.30 [234 D1 (21)] *e* Bus 3 or 6 from Gare Lille Flandres to Magasi.*

See page 131 for more on this cellar restaurant cabaret where diners are serenaded with good old-fashioned *chansons*. $$$$

Hermitage Gantois & Estaminet Gantois <u>S</u> 224 rue de Paris, 59000 ☎ 03 20 85 30 30 [235 F6 (30)] 🚇 *Mairie de Lille* *e* Métro 2 to Mairie de Lille. Walk westwards along av du Président Kennedy then turn left on to rue de Paris.*

Chef Sébastien Blanchet presides over the showcase restaurant of the magnificently renovated Hermitage Gantois (see page 54) as well as its sister Estaminet Gantois next door (entrance in rue Malpart), so you can be sure of the same sharp eyes supervising the shared kitchen whether you want to spend more than €40 in the one or less than half the amount in the other. In the flagship dining room (itself as much an occasion as a location as the rest of the gloriously refurbished building), part with €45 for the 3-course menu or €35 for just 2 dishes. Lille's fervour for fish is well served by Monsieur Blanchet with a starter of mango-enlivened perch fillets that demonstrate a flirtatious talent for matchmaking, followed by a classically & simply presented turbot. Alternatively, a braised *jarret de veau* emphasises the simplicity of prime ingredients treated with respect. Desserts head towards the comfort-food route with scintillating *clafoutis* & traditional *tatins* given good menu space & plenty of attention from pastry chefs with the lightest of touches. All this, & a sympathetically selected wine list. Next door at the Estaminet Gantois, the bill of fare reflects the history of the working-class quarter home of this great 4-star *luxe* hotel. *Rillettes* & terrines, *flamiche au maroilles*, *hochepot* & the spoils of *la chasse* are offered at €13 for a main course, €19 for 2 courses or €26 for 3 including coffee. $$$$ & $$$ respectively.

L'Assiette du Marché VL 61 rue de la Monnaie, 59000 ℃03 20 06 83 61 ⊘ closed Sat lunch, Mon lunch, Sun & holidays [236 C2 (84)] *e* Bus 3, 6 or 9 from Gare Lille Flandres to Lion d'Or.*
Venture away from the cobbled streets around the Musée de l'Hospice Comtesse into the sedate courtyard of a townhouse that was once upon a time Louis XIV's royal mint in the city & the building that gave the street its name. In our time, the *maison particulière* has a more modern tradition as a restaurant & the newest incumbent is yet another scion of the Proye family who hold court at the celebrated *Huîtrière* (see page 87). The cuisine chez Thomas Proye is something of an *assiette* from many *marchés* with talents & tricks culled from all 6 corners of France. If the regional or fashionable food terminology is too obscure, just ask your waiter to interpret. The *carte* wryly acknowledges the ephemeral nature of trendy menu-speak. Nothing obscure about the ingredients: hearty halibut roasted with mustard & a Valenciennes *jarret* in beer were on the weekly menu when first we checked the place out. Flavours may not always have lived up to the excellent presentation on an initial visit, but on encouragement from some readers (mailbag has been evenly split on this one) we tried again & relished a starter of camembert with black cherries & dessert of pan-fried pineapple & ginger *millefeuille*, the goal of fusion now comfortably attained. As for the wine list, it is a true *tour de France*. Pay €16 for 2 courses or €20 for 3. Grazing free-range nudged the bill towards €30 a head before we started on the wine. $$$

Aux Lillois 84 façade de l'Esplanade ℃ 03 20 55 64 82
⌂ www.auxlillois.com ⊘ closed Sat lunch, Mon eve & Sun [234 D1 (23)] *e* Bus 6 from Gare Lille Flandres to Lille Esplanade.*
You may remember this site as the former L'Esplanade, but a relatively

new regime has taken on the old restaurant by the Citadelle. With a menu at €21 for 2 courses & €28 for 3, the sweet-toothed might decide that it is worth considering dessert over starter if planning a light lunch or supper as the pâtisseries, like the breads, are made in house. Food is knowingly global, so the ubiquitous gazpacho comes with serrano toasties & the beef carpaccio has a Thai twist. Downstairs, serious wine lovers can choose from 120 labels in the ground floor *bar à vin*. $$$

Le Bistroquet <u>MK</u> 44 rue de Puébla, 59000 ☏03 20 42 03 47 ⊘closed Sun, Mon eve & Sat lunch [234 C5 (16)] ⛬ *République–Beaux Arts* *e** *Bus 12 from Gare Lille Flandres to Eglise Sacré Coeur. Rue Solférino to pl des Halles Centrales. Left to rue de Puébla.*

Don't let the rather strange green-trellised ceiling or the tourist-taverna-style mirrored tiles put you off. Despite its garish décor, the Bistroquet is what it sounds like, a reliable source of savoury sustenance! The bistro theme is less *flamand* than *montagnard* & *Savoie* flair, with dishes such as the classic cheese fondue or a much-appreciated *raclette* or *tartiflette*. The welcome is genuine & effusive, the ambience holiday happy – but not touristy – & the food just fine. Spend around €28 per person, or opt for a budget lunch, dish of the day, wine & coffee for €15. $$$

In Bocca Al Lupo <u>VL</u> 1 rue des Vieux Murs, 59800 ☏03 20 06 39 98 ⏥www.in-bocca-al-lupo.com ☺Tue–Sun lunch, Thu–Sat eve [236 B3 (81)] *e** *Bus 3, 6 or 9 from Gare Lille Flandres to Lion d'Or. From rue de la Monnaie turn left into rue Peterinck.*

Opposite the celebrated Italian deli-palace La Bottega (see page 158) stands its Latin sister. And where else would the trendy place aux Oignons crowd choose to lunch? Seriously fashionable, no linens, just shiny tabletops, polished floors & comfy chairs, the atmosphere suffused with orange & inky hues. Somehow this contemporary city-centre look manages to straddle the very Flemish traditions of the quarter & the reassuringly conservative classic Italian flavours from *antipasti* to *dolci*. No anachronistic modern twists here, just *scaloppa alla Milanese* & *saltimbocca* to please the most critical *nonna* in the business. No set menu, but a budget of around €25–30 per healthy appetite should suffice. $$$

La Cave aux Fioles **VL** 39 rue de Gand, 59800 ☎03 20 55 18 43 ⌂ www.lacaveauxfioles.com ⊘closed Sat lunch, Sun & holidays [236 E2 (92)] *e* Bus 3, 6 or 9 from Gare Lille Flandres to Lion d'Or. Cross pl Louise de Bettignies to rue de Gand.*

Eccentric, eclectic & the warmest welcome in town. Happiness comes à la carte at the top of the dear old rue de Gand. Whenever I close my eyes & think of eating out in Lille, it is La Cave aux Fioles that springs to mind, & judging from my postbag since first writing about the place, many readers feel the same. Follow the cobbles to the far end of the old town to the honey glow from the windows of a warm & friendly dining room. What looks like the front door to the restaurant remains resolutely locked, but enter the unmarked door to the side of the windows, & pass through a narrow & dark entrance hall lined with posters from legendary Lille festivals past to reach the central covered courtyard between 2 houses. All around are the husks of 17th & 18th-century homes, paneless casement windows opening out to the brick, stone & cobbled court. Inside, tables are scattered through the various rooms, candlelight enhances the brickwork, & the trad jazz sounds mellow the scene even further. In winter a roaring fire concentrates the cosiness even more, but whatever the season, the true warmth comes from the welcoming & hospitable staff: from the barmen who serve the house cocktail *Fiole d'Amour* (grapefruit, gin & grenadine), to the waitresses who patiently wait as you agonise over choices. The house *foie gras de canard* comes with a surprise tipple, but the fresh mushrooms stuffed with roquefort sound fabulous. Then again, what about a soup of mussels with leeks? Will tonight be the night for the local *waterzoi d'homard* or should one indulge in strips of goose magret dripping with a honey sauce? Whichever dish wins, the garnish & vegetable accompaniment varies '*selon l'humour du chef*'! By dessert I have usually rediscovered decisiveness, & I forego such sirens as *gâteau au chocolat de la Tante Mazo* in favour of the remarkable *délicatesse du Nord* – the bitterest ice-cream I have ever tasted, blending chicory with *genièvre* gin. Although there are 20 tables here, such is the artful design that one never notices more than one's immediate neighbours & the sense of privacy is supreme. The full evening menu with cocktails & coffee comes to €35; lunch options from €15 are also available. If a day's shopping on the rickety paved streets has played havoc with your calf muscles, don't be daunted by the thought of the trek up the rue de Gand: the restaurant's private London taxi will collect you from your hotel. **$$$**

Eating & drinking Restaurants

Clément Marot GP 16 rue de Pas, 59000 ☏ 03 20 57 01 10 ⊘ closed
Sun & Mon eve [236 B5 (68)] 🚉 Rihour *e** Métro 2 to Gare Lille Flandres then
line 1 to Rihour. Rue Roisin into rue de Pas.

It took me 4 years of eating & treating in Lille before I found myself
crossing the threshold of Clément Marot's dining room near the upfront
terraces of his louder neighbours. I could hardly wait 4 weeks before
returning. Suffice to say, this is the type of restaurant we all hope to
stumble upon in our journeys across France. The main dining room is
somewhat post-war traditional in decorative style: commemorative plates
on a rack above panelled booths; heavy plate ice buckets & tureens on
well-polished surfaces; certificates alongside framed paintings of
favourite holiday spots; & a waitress in black skirt, white blouse & lace
apron hovering by the champagne magnums & long-stemmed cut
flowers. The other room next door is more modern & presumably
favoured by the business-lunch brigade. In the older room, I settled
down to wallow in traditional dishes & investigate the wine list. The
price of the *carte-menu* varies, depending on whether you choose a half
bottle of wine or Tattinger on ice. I quickly discovered that recipes as
described on the menu are not written on tablets of stone. A lively chat
with the waiter, chef or (if you are lucky) patron brings plenty of
alternative suggestions. The signature catch of *sandre* on the menu on
my first visit was intended to be prepared with sesame & a *coulis de
poivrons*. I needed little persuasion to agree to an alternative version
using Marot's hallmark flavour *chicorée*, a locally produced delicacy
from the sandy soil of coastal Flanders that the chef uses in dishes from
the main course to the *bavarois*. Inspiration! The smoky, coffee-like
flavour of the sauce complemented the fish's crisp topping of sesame
seed. I was equally glad to have been nudged away from my original
thoughts of a terrine starter in favour of a *salade de poisson en
escabèche*. This turned out to be a wonderfully old-fashioned &
fabulously sharp presentation of sardines marinated in the house
champagne vinegar (Marot eschews the balsamic), with a dash of lemon
juice & thyme on local leaves to provide a truly kicking salad. Local
produce is first choice wherever possible. Thus poultry comes from the
town of Licques where free-range turkeys dine on corn & grain to
become the north's answer to the legendary fowl of Bresse, & where,
once a year, before Christmas, the mayor & corporation, & *confrères de
la dinde*, march the town's flocks to one of the great gastronomic fairs of
the region. One such fowl may be found even on the €17.50 midday 2-
course menu – a trio of choices offered for each starter, main & dessert.

Remarkable value. If, like me, you cannot decide on a dessert, just let the chef-patron choose for you. I may well never eat another *crème brûlée* as long as I live. It was pure cream, which still breathed the air of the dairy, & was quite simply the best I have tasted this side of childhood. The welcome from all the restaurant team was second to none, & hospitality seems to be the key to this place's discreet success. The 'be our guest' approach even extends to the wine list. Rather than compromise with a half-bottle of a lesser vintage, we were encouraged to buy a full bottle with the assurance that, at the end of the meal, staff will wrap up the rest of the bottle to be enjoyed – as the wine list has it – at your own table in the comfort of your own home. Cold winter evenings are ideal for indulging oneself on the grander menus at €36–66, or throwing budget to the wind & going à la carte. $$$

Le Compostelle GP 4 rue St Etienne, 59800 ☎ 03 28 38 08 30
⌁ www.chateauxhotels.com/compostelle [236 B5 (69)] 🚇 Rihour *e** Métro 2 to Gare Lille Flandres then line 1 to Rihour. Rue Roisin into rue de Pas then right into rue St Etienne.

'Make yourself at home' is the unspoken invitation at this great big popular restaurant just beside the main square of Lille. The building (a staging post on the pilgrims' route to Santiago de Compostela) may date from the 16th century & boast the only Renaissance façade in Lille, but the refurbished décor is the very model of a modern appreciation of *temps perdus*. Alain Roussiez has glassed in the open courtyard & created a warren of colourful dining rooms on each floor. The bar & the Blue Room are my favourites, being packed with real bookcases – not stuffed with imposing leather-bound tomes, but well-thumbed paperbacks stacked & piled at random. The urge to browse & dip when waiting for friends is irresistible. Other salons are Provençal pink & theatrical yellow. As to the kitchen: serviceable fare with an ambitious blend of regional & national dishes; little to offend the palate. Sometimes I've found nothing so exciting as to distract me from my conversation. At others, flavour & texture have won through. Menus at €23–43, but what to choose? My advice would be to stick to the *cuisine du nord*: a cold North Sea *hochepot* of fish, then the *noix de veau* prepared with melted Maroilles cheese. A refreshing sorbet made from the *genièvre* gin from nearby Houlle makes for a sparky finale to an occasionally lacklustre meal. $$$

Les Faits Divers VL 44 rue de Gand, 59000 ☎ 03 20 21 03 63
☉closed Sat lunch & Sun [236 E2 (93)] *e** Bus 3, 6 or 9 from Gare Lille Flandres to Lion d'Or. Cross pl Louise de Bettignies to rue de Gand.

Young & buzzing, bright & lively. Wise regulars book early, because by mid-evening there is not a table to be had. Pretty imaginative fare served by staff who are on the ball & on the move. A vegetable burger or smoked salmon rolled with chickpeas could be the opening act to a main of rabbit, kangaroo or caramelised quail fillet. Not always the obvious choice for a romantic *diner à deux* for older couples, but fun for the young & certainly the ideal venue for relaxing amongst friends. Menus at €20–26 plucked from the à la carte list, which is also the budget for a pleasant bottle of wine. If you have not booked at the weekend, then arrive before 20.30 to be in with a chance. $$$

L'Intrigue 44 rue de la Halle, 59800 ✆03 20 74 28 60 🖰 www.restaurant-lintrigue.fr ⊘closed Sun [234 D1 (24)] *e** Bus 6 to Conservatoire. From rue St André, turn right into rue de la Halle & the restaurant is opposite the Halle au Sucre at the junction with rue des Archives.

Intrigue is well named: darkened windows from the street, a first dining room smart & neat for a respectable public display of acquaintance, & the back room where even lunching businessmen look as though they might be having an affair. Here is low lighting, a huge parody of the sort of clock that might have been designed for trysting &, on all sides, secret staircases & arches in the brickwork to suggest forbidden rendezvous after coffee. Only the wipe-clean vinyl tablecloths in this room bring an unwelcome quasi-sordid addition to the mock-furtive feel. With a €16 midday menu & à la carte at double that, this intrigue is certainly not the exclusive preserve of sugar daddies & their gold diggers. As befits an address where the inappropriate partnership is practically the *liaison d'etre*, the menu is no *marriage blanc* of inappropriate & doomed flavours – instead we encounter unexpected & unlikely bedfellows ripe with ulterior motives, & throbbing with unexpected passions: peanut & *foie gras crème brûlée*, mussels with lemon grass & coconut milk, sweet & sour steak, & even the North Sea's resident paragon cod here cross-dresses in banana leaves.

Staider options imply respectability. The hamburger with non-startling rosemary potatoes & guinea fowl with sage are probity *sur plat*. But maybe they are not quite as naive as they seem. The tuna *à la plancha* with salsa & cereal turned out to be a connivance of north Africa, Latin

Meert **VL** 27 rue Esquermoise, 59800 ☎ 03 20 57 07 44 ☉ lunch only Mon–Sat [236 B5 (65)] 🚇 *Rihour* **e*** *Bus 12 from Gare Lille Flandres to de Gaulle.* Best known as the pâtisserie to the great & the good, the grandest tea-shop in the north of France (see page 118) now has a restaurant behind the exquisite shopfront & the dainty *salon de thé*. Of course, as visitors to the Piscine gallery in Roubaix already knew, the house is no stranger to proper catering, so the arrival of a dining room around the courtyard at the back of the building was probably inevitable. Here, budget is not the issue, as you are as likely to part with just over €20 on a main

America & a dash of what classic crooners used to call 'Old Italee'!

Since almost all my fellow diners this Monday noon had already opted for the tuna, I followed suit & was not disappointed. The side dish of creamed mashed polenta arrived first, with the main platter just a discreet moment or two later. If the mangetouts belied their promise & were too overcooked to be considered anything other than garnish, the fish itself was perfection, practically *à l'unilaterale*. The top was sprinkled with whole grain, flash-cooked to nearly a crisp, whilst the core & underside were moist, tender & so rare as to be collectable. Served on a bed of lightly parmesaned salad leaves with the side bowl of salsa. I was still fragile from a wonderful Saturday night some 36 hours earlier, & therefore was not as young as I might have been so I forwent wine, but neighbours quaffed the fruits of Languedoc with evident satisfaction.

Since I was that day merely putting a tentative toe into the waters of fine living, I listened to the litany of *desserts du jour* – a recital of original thought – & opted for the *écume d'agrumes*, since I thought it sounded fruity & guessed it might be a kinder oasis amongst so many grand chocolate ideals. Then the French dictionary of my subconscious threw up the translation of *écume* as froth & I was filled with dread that the most ghastly gift Britain has forced upon the world of cuisine these past few years might be presented to me – the hated 'foam' that trendy chefs like to inflict upon their acolytes, as pointless & unwelcome as frogspawn at a picnic.

But frabjous day, this chef has no tawdry chemistry set & what was presented was a scrumptious airy cream suffused with tangy citrus fruits – sublime, delicious, light; a triumph of flavour over substance, a dream. I toddled out from the contrived low-lit discretion of Intrigue into the bright, sunny Lille afternoon feeling deliciously guilty & content. $$$

Eating & drinking Restaurants

course should you choose suckling pig cooked in straw, a traditional shepherds pie or even a grey burgundy truffle risotto! But coming in under that €20 barrier is Lille's take on a Brit standard & entitled (in English) 'Double Fish & Chips', here presented with skate & a langoustine risotto. You might also get away with paying even less for a true Caesar salad. The simplest omelette is probably the truest test of a kitchen. No suspense here, trust me, it passed! No set menu, so budget around €35–40 per person. Delightful, charming & genuinely welcoming staff, as chic & special as the place itself. Dine upstairs or downstairs at courtyard level. Midweek evenings, an alternative bar-snack style menu of platters is offered, from 19.00. $$$

Orange Bleue **VL** 30 rue Lepelletier 59800 ☎ 03 20 55 04 70 ⊙closed Sun [236 C4 (75)] *e* Bus 12 from Gare Lille Flandres to de Gaulle. Walk under the Alcide arch to the debris St-Etienne & continue to the rue Lepelletier.*
I am so glad that I took a short cut along the rue Lepelletier on the eve of signing off a previous update of the book, or else I might have missed out on the smart, efficient & welcome treat that is this popular eaterie just a matter of yards from the Grand' Place. Here, in a large airy dining room with enough space twixt tables for plenty of bulky carrier bags – proving it to be popular among the serious shopping set at lunchtime – celebratory portions are enjoyed with a sneak peek down into the spotless kitchens of the basement. Swift & friendly waiting staff whiz-glide through the room, managing the extraordinary feat of dashing from one end of the restaurant to another without anyone else feeling in the least bit hurried. Food-wise, expect to be assailed by savoury flavours, whether you take the Orange menu (served at all times except Saturday evening) of tapenade, pasta & dessert for €18, or graze à la carte for around €10 more. My *croquante* of haddock *à l'anneth* offered gossamer-fine leaves of filo, dill & smoked haddock that hit more culinary g-spots than you might expect. Pasta & salad options are served in huge quantities as are all the main courses. Cheese does not wait for the end of the meal here, appearing (as *maroilles*) inside chicken in a gingerbread sauce, & (in *chèvre* guise) as stuffing to a saffron-teased salmon dish. Red meat carpaccios are generously presented & late risers looking for a kick-start to the remains of their day might even forego the *plat principal* & opt for a starter & dessert in the name of a tardy brunch. Don't bother with the wine list – do as the locals & go for the seasonal suggestion chalked around the room. Inevitably a red Chinon was available for the low €20s a bottle, with around half the bottle price for a jug & perhaps €4 a glass. No need to rush off after licking the platter

clean: no matter how busy, the staff encourage lingering with a good choice of *digestifs* from *fleur de bière* to calvados, to keep the feelgood factor nice & high. $$$

Origan **VL** 58 bd Carnot, 59000 ☎03 20 13 08 88 ⊘closed Sun [235 G3 (32)] 🚊 *Gare Lille Flandres* **e*** *Cross the Parc Matisse to the bd Carnot.*
An inexpensive luncherie so painfully trendy & so sharp that you'd cut yourself if you fell upon this place by accident. At Origan, the fusion concept goes far beyond the plate. New York studio-style skylights burnish an endless row of shiny black tables with individual linen runners, & to keep the place exclusively packed with the young & fit, the painted grey doorstep is obviously inspired by the north face of the Eiger. You can guess just how New European the smart guys at the next table will be merely by reading the menu: open sandwiches of *foie gras* with Granny Smith carpaccio & chopped hazelnut & glass of white port (1 kid ye not) have optional side orders of either a *légume du jour* crumble, tomato confit salad or gratin of penne with *gran padano*. Admit it, you can already picture their homes!

But don't mock, people this hip won't be fobbed off with anything but the best when it comes to actually eating, so food is prepared with flair & talent & served with style, & flavours certainly live up to the gilded frieze that runs the length of the restaurant, an enumeration of fine herbs scrawled across panels & mirrors alike. The monochrome of the décor serves to highlight the vibrant hues on the plates. Since this is already a hit with the busy & beautiful lunch crowd, most food is the sort of thing you might enjoy whilst keeping your finger on the pulse & your eye on the ball, & is itself a euro-combo of mezze & tapas. The hyper-fusion theme continues through the proper main courses. Lunch menus & sandwich-based snacking at well under €20, à la carte budgets around €35. $$$

Les Remparts **VL** Logis de la Porte de Gand, rue de Gand, 59800 ☎03 20 06 74 74 🖱www.terrassedesremparts.fr [235 H1 (33)] **e*** *Bus 3, 6 or 9 from Gare Lille Flandres to Lion d'Or. Cross pl Louise de Bettignies to rue de Gand.*
Easy to find your way to & from this, the final restaurant on the rue de Gand gastronomic thoroughfare: it is a listed landmark & marked on all the maps. Housed in the original 1620 fortifications of the old town constructed during the Spanish invasion, there can be no more dramatic setting for a restaurateur with a knack for the flamboyant & romantic gesture. My first experience of the restaurant had been pretty

disappointing – a bland lunch served in a stuffy overheated function room on the day President Chirac opened the Palais des Beaux Arts. Even when chums began nagging me to give the restaurant a second chance, saying that the cuisine had enjoyed a thorough overhaul, I was not inclined to return. When, however, a sudden summer downpour found me stranded at the foot of the steps leading to the restaurant that straddles the main road, I decided to dry out & try out the new-look Terrasse. The place was packed to capacity, the outside terrace on the fortification being *hors de combat* owing to the weather. Charming staff managed to find us a table amid the eccentric décor, which resembled the private dream life of a hyperactive department-store window dresser. We made ourselves at home amongst wooden sunflowers beneath huge polystyrene rabbits hibernating on mock grass & outsized daisies on the rafters overhead. Then, under new management, the design grew trendier, the bunnies replaced by discreet sheep. Now, with another proprietor Bruno Suppa, the higher standards of food remain. *Riz de veau*, reliable steaks, subtle grilled fish & smart presentation are very much the thing, with €40 per head a probable budget. To be honest, most people come here for the location, but in recent seasons, more have returned for the food. One tip for the new proprietors: since the restaurant is one of the few with a working lift from the street to the dining room, it might be worth considering finding a way to give access to disabled diners, since the elevator stops several stairs before the level of the dining room. $$$

La Table de Vivien 55 rue St André, 59000 ☏ 03 20 39 51 69
⌂ www.latabledevivien.fr ☺ Tue–Fri lunch, Tue & Thu-Sat eve [234 D1 (25)]
e* *Bus 6 from Gare Lille Flandres to Conservatoire then walk the rue St André.*
This is food for consenting adults, testified to by the glances of complicit pleasure across the room when a solitary diner at a distant table takes the first mouthful of a dish that you yourself enjoyed one course earlier. Appreciation as at a concert, just as one aficionado recognises a stranger's thrill at a fugue – appropriate for a restaurant so close to the conservatoire. This gastronomic bonding was not evident from the first, as we were the earliest arrivals at the restaurant, & our aperitif was plonked rather than served, the manner so relaxed as to be disappointingly the wrong side of casual. Happily, service perked up as the restaurant filled with regular diners & professionalism rose to the level of the welcome. Things began to improve as soon as the food arrived. A mushroom *velouté* was a subtle distillation of *cèpes* into the lightest feather-creamed soup.

This was what we had come for. I'd been tipped off about Vivien Fleckenstein's arrival at this address just that bit further along the rue St André from the main cobble trail: trade whispers were becoming more audible & the foodie press had already begun to notice the chef. With a pedigree that trailed names including the Lyonnais lion Paul Bocuse, terms served in the kitchens of other Michelin veterans, & a local word-of-mouth reputation, his style was self-determined '*semi-gastromonique*' & reliant on produce both seasonal & local.

The *soupe de moules* was so well judged to be considered as wisdom in its own right, the quality of the ingredients never compromised, but gently manoeuvred into the savoury spotlight. A sudden sharp burst of spice to clean the palate was a precision stab of invigorating flavour that had been coyly hidden to allow the mussels their own moment of glory with their intrinsic taste unsmothered, but arriving almost as applause on the final sweep-clean of the plate. The chicken that was the dish of the day was moist & understated within a light, fresh & fruity jus. The *foie gras* element of the recipe was full-flavoured, though threatening to influence the palate away from the chicken. Perhaps a *foie gras* mousse might have been less obtrusive. Across the napkins, a salmon crumble was a return to the judiciousness that marked out the rest of the meal. As near to perfection in texture & taste, the *comté* cheese, more conventionally companion to a trout, was remarkably restrained for this scintillating highlight of our lunch. When it came to dessert, we agreed that the laurels went to the chunky, juicy *tarte aux pommes*, narrowly beating the *crème brûlée* in the comfort food stakes. The budget is around €35 pp. $$$

▼ *Indulge yourself with a decadent dessert . . .*

Tentation VL 34 bis rue des Bouchers, 59000 ✆ 03 20 15 29 39
🖰 www.restaurant-tentation.com ⊘ Tue–Sat [234 E3 (28)] 🚊 *Rihour* **e*** *Métro 2 to Gare Lille Flandres then line 1 to Rihour. Pass the tourist office then right into rue de l'Hôpital Militaire, cross place de l'Arsenal to rue des Bouchers.*
Just about the last street to qualify as Vieux Lille, the rue des Bouchers has been home to an eclectic range of fashionable eateries over the 15 years or so that I've been idling with intent in the quarter. Tentation, with its smart brick walls, smart artworks & far smarter habitués, is the newest home of Julien Descendos, a familiar figure on the local food scene. Welcome is spot on, friendly without being intrusive. The house cocktail is a wowser of raspberry (that northern stalwart) to perk up the tastebuds before the anticipated assault on preconceptions. Fruity flavours favour seafood, from the pineapple chutney with the gambas & chorizo brochette to the spicy, citric scallops. Otherwise discover a range of more classic pairings in goat's cheese with a *confiture d'oignons* & a *parmentier* of duck seasoned with armagnac. To be honest, on our autumnal visit we found that several dishes were probably a little ambitious. Competition amongst Lille's younger restaurateurs has never been fiercer, & this can lead a kitchen to attempt concepts perhaps a stride or so beyond its reach, but desserts are good & in the earlier courses we found that the more obvious stronger flavours were most successful. The *duo de thon* worked well, as did a redcurranty roasted camembert. We found that subtlety in blending some other themes certainly proved less effective. In future I'll most likely dawdle over the menu & see what the regulars have chosen, using facial reactions across the room as my guide. Lunch at €15 is probably the best value in the old town, with 2 courses, a drink & coffee included. Otherwise, the main €31 menu keeps the evening budget in check, but if you ever, as we were, are tempted to browse the full selection, you should manage to keep each guest's food bill beneath the €40 threshold. $$$

What Else MK 181 rue Solférino, 59000 ✆ 03 20 10 08 85
🖰 www.whatelse-restaurant.com ⊘ closed Mon night, Sat lunch & Sun [234 D6 (10)] 🚊 *République–Beaux Arts* **e*** *Métro 2 to Gare Lille Flandres, then line 1 to République–Beaux Arts. Then follow rue Inkerman & turn left onto Solférino.*
The south may have its midi blues & hues, but nowhere does glorious grey like Lille. A luminosity that defies the word dull, this is the *ciel du nord*, inspiration of songwriters & artists alike. On one of those monochrome hazy days, when the only sign of a horizon on the Solfé is the creamed, sepulchural spire of the silhouetted Sacre Coeur justifying the skyline, when the Michelin-starred Sébastopol restaurant across the way is *complet*

or just wrong, & you are bewildered by the array of alternative eateries at the crossroads of the pleasantly profane; on one of those days, you choose the most monochrome of restaurants for lunch. Black & white is the motif, from the ranks of grey, bulbous lamps on the shelves to the regimented line of tables & chairs. The uniformity is shattered almost as soon as your waiter returns with your first course – sliced & layered shafts & shards of brightly-coloured Mediterranean produce, or a perky slice of marrowbone with a drizzled jus. Roast lamb with crushed potatoes & a colourful splashing of *legumes* at an angle or a main course & desserts so ornate that even the hippest of diners has to make an effort not to ooh-ah! Privileged punters get to sit on sofas by the fireplace. Budget €30 & just a little bit more. Good value lunch menu at €15. $$$

Berliner VL 22 rue Royale, 59000 ℓ 03 20 39 38 54 [236 A3 (36)]
e* Bus 12 to de Gaulle, cross Grand' Place to rue Esquermoise & on to rue Royale.
Newish arrival on the scene, & I'd welcome comments from readers. I've not yet had a chance to try this, but trusted friends have told me that the food is interesting, the décor described to me as both streetwise & squat-style & the reinvention of the tapas concept is worth checking out. I'll be dropping in some time soon. $$

Les Charlottes en Ville GP 10 rue Faidherbe, 59800 ℓ 03 20 55 13 74 ↗ www.lescharlottesenville.com ⊙ daily 11.30–15.00 & eves from 19.00 [236 D6 (58)] ☒ Rihour *e* Bus 12 from Gare Lille Flandres to Théâtre. Or walk along av le Corbusier & right into rue Faidherbe.*
Thanks to readers & Lille 2004 revellers who hailed this place as a great spot for early lunching during festive weeks. This is no fast food Spud-U-Like but a proper restaurant in the centre of town where all platters are based around proper, chewy, thick-skinned jacket potatoes all named for regions of France, from the *foie gras* forests to the seafood ports. The execution is classy enough to rise above the simple concept & by 12.30 on a chilly February the place was packed as tall, thin waiters attended tables of good friends of all ages, middle-aged couples, elderly widows with gloves, families with picky kids & workmates all intending to eat well on huge plates of tatties served with meats, fish & dairy fillings on the side. Having arrived at 11.30, I could not face too much so I had *oeufs en cocotte* & salad with mine. Delicious, warming & it set me up to admire the fun of the place. What was once seriously camp faux-paysan baroque décor has been tamed into smart standard contemporary, but the camp flourish remains with the flamboyant view out towards the opera house. Pay €8–12 for 1 course or €18 à la carte. $$

Eating & drinking Restaurants

▲ *The waffles at Meert were a favourite of Charles de Gaulle.*

Clair de Lune **VL** 50 rue de Gand, 59000 ☏03 20 51 46 55 ⊘closed Sat lunch & Tue [236 E2 (94)] *e* Bus 3, 6 or 9 from Gare Lille Flandres to Lion d'Or. Cross pl Louise de Bettignies to rue de Gand.*
Earliest visits opened the eyes & mouths of my friends to the potential of *mignon* of pork in an arabica coffee sauce, halibut in cider, & a somewhat scrummy *oeuf cocotte* with smoked trout & leeks. Recent forays have only slightly reined in invention & concentrated on bringing to the fore the essential ingredients, whether a supreme of guinea fowl or that old standby, trout with almonds. Desserts continue to comfort. Bread & butter pudding is what *pain perdu* is all about, only the bread here is brioche & the spices heartily northern – & with that on the menu, who needs the ubiquitous tiramisu & crumbles – those *parvenu* puds that have all but elbowed France's native *tatins* into obscurity from Lille to Marseille. Though some have claimed the service to be brusque, I found nothing to complain about. Unpretentious staff did not bat an eyelid when I opted for a couple of starters one evening, having over-indulged elsewhere at lunchtime, & paid me the same courtesies as others pigging out on the €20 or €26 menus. Lunches from €12. $$

Le Flams **GP** 8 rue de Pas, 59000 ☏03 20 54 18 38
⌖ www.lesfaitsdivers.fr [236 B5 (70)] 🚇 Rihour *e* Métro 2 to Gare Lille Flandres then line 1 to Rihour. Rue Roisin into rue de Pas.*
Welcome to the home of the *flammekeuche* – that not-quite-pizza, not-quite-*crêpe* adopted speciality of the city. The fad has long left its Alsatian roots to become a social must here in Flanders. We are talking about a large, thin, dough base spread with either savoury or sweet toppings; the former based around cheeses, mushrooms & ham, the latter the blend of fruit, sweets & *eau de vie* toppings that one finds in any

crêperie. Cut out a square of your flam', roll it into a cigar shape & hold it with your fingers to munch over a chilled beer & a heated discussion about life, love & politics. Lunchtimes, the place is filled with office workers & shoppers taking advantage of the special deals (a savoury & a sweet *flammekeuche* with a 25cl glass of *bière blonde*) & menus starting at €11. Evenings, it's a regular student hangout, 50m from the Grand' Place, with groups of friends sharing a selection of flams, picnic style. After dark, budget €16 to feel replete. In good weather, step across the road to the summer terrace; in winter stay cosy indoors amongst the warm brickwork. Quick snack on the €6.50 menu express. $$

Omnia GP 9 rue Esquermoise, 59000 ✆03 20 57 55 66 ✆ www.omnia-restaurant.com [236 B5 (63)] 🚇*Rihour* *e** *Métro 2 to Gare Lille Flandres then line 1 to Rihour. Rue Roisin into rue de Pas.*

150 years ago, this was a dance hall, *café-concert*. Then, the dancing girls extended a welcome that was a little too enthusiastic for the morals of the day, so the place became a brasserie. The affectionate nature of the personnel continued to enhance the reputation. It closed down for a while, to reopen as an art cinema in the 1960s, then the programming nudged way beyond the frontiers of art, & it closed once again to reopen as the flamboyant brasserie Taverne de l'Ecu, with the old music-hall stage restored to house the vats for the home-brewed beers served on tap in house. New incarnation for Omnia has kept the beer but ditched the brasserie cuisine & the alternative entrance through the old theatre foyer on rue de Pas in favour of a rather garish 1980s hairdressing salon formica frontage & a main entrance that looks more like a modern homage to its dodgy nightclub past. Basically, food is regional & Italian, with a hint of the stir-fry & burger-flip. Not much on the menu for vegetarians, but carnivores can enjoy midweek lunch for €12 or go for the other menus at €20 upwards. A lively crowd is as rumbustious & enthusiastic as ever – quaffing domestic *blonde* & *ambrée* ales or more exotic beers from other continents, but ready to get heady on spirits, wines & trendier tipples. Another new management team & promise of theme nights brings this venue with an appetite for appetites into its latest incarnation. $$

La Patatière GP 31 rue Saint Etienne, 59000 ✆03 20 06 14 78 [236 A6 (42)] 🚇*Rihour* *e** *Métro 2 to Gare Lille Flandres then line 1 to Rihour. Rue Roisin into rue de Pas & left along rue St Etienne.*

After the success of Les Charlottes en Ville in its various incarnations (see page 107) jacket potatoes prove the filling fast-food rivals to *flams* as this city's carb rush of preference, both at lunchtime & before surrendering to nightlife. This bistro-styled venue opposite the car-park-concert-hall combo of the Nouveau Siècle building serves jacket potato platters from €12–16. Themes range from spicy veggie options to Landais homage to the country of *foie gras* & smoked duck. For those who want to cut back on the carbs, the platters are available without the potato, served as a salad. Just as the original restaurant names its plates after regions of France, so here you will find a mix of camembert apples & gingerbread as tribute to Normandy & cockles & mussels heralding Dunkerque. Expect international concepts as well, from Italy to Mexico: the triple-filling *dégustation* platter features curry from India & smoked fish from Norway. A full set menu, with coffee, for €16. $$

La Ritournelle MK 38 rue de Puébla, 59800 ✆ 03 20 57 91 51
☺ closed Sat lunch & Sun [234 C5 (14)] 🚊 *République–Beaux Arts* *e** *Métro 2 to Gare Lille Flandres then change to Line 1 to République–Beaux Arts. Walk up the bd de la Liberté & turn left onto rue Puébla.*
On a quiet street – if such a concept were possible around the eternal festival of eating, drinking, flirting, cruising, schmoozing & double parking that hums in neon & brown panels around the old market *Halles* – is a new team flourishing menus on the site of the former Albert II. On the site of ex-*wunderkind* Stéphane LePrince's former gastronomic kitsch homage to Belgian royalty, friendly staff prepare local standards & serve them with good humour. Actually it was a flurry of informative emails from readers who had trekked down here in search of its Bradt-listed predecessor & who stayed to graze contentedly on simple standards that alerted me to the changes. Happy to report that the old-fashioned dining room has retained much of its stylish panelling, offset by muted yellows, blues & greys – a truly civilised setting enhanced by an honestly lovely & friendly welcome just a stroll from the pulsating nightlife of Solférino. Lunchtime business types have marked the place as a favourite haunt. Menus begin at around €15. Budget an unrestrained dalliance at around €25 & enjoy. $$

WINE BARS

Aux Lillois 84 façade de l'Esplanade ✆ 03 20 55 64 82
🖰 www.auxlillois.com ☺ closed Sat lunch, Mon eve & Sun [234 D1 (23)]
e* *Bus 6 from Gare Lille Flandres to Lille Esplanade.*
120 wines to choose from at this wine bar by the Esplanade. Flat-rate menus at €21 for 2 courses & €28 for 3. $$$

Au Bout des Doigts <u>VL</u> 5 rue St Joseph, 59000 ✆ 03 20 74 55 95 ⊘ closed Mon eve [236 D2 (89)] *e** *Bus 3, 6 or 9 from Gare Lille Flandres to Lion d'Or. Cross pl Louise de Bettignies, turn left at the Kfé Mixt & then right into rue St-Joseph.*

Finger food is fun. If you like the *amusebouche* freebie appetisers that posh restaurants serve before the food you actually ordered, you'll love this place. It serves nothing else. Welcome to a world without cutlery; an unexpected hideaway in a relatively charming half-unspoilt street on the cusp of a party. Here, in the anticipation zone behind the Australian bar & the main courses of rue de Gand, is a wine bar with a fabulous line in nibbles. Pass some quaint white-stone red-brick cottages & turn into the uncompromisingly modern bar where wine is poured out at €4–15 a glass, bubbly at €10 & a pretty fair selection of bottles of vino to share start at €12. Let your eyes grow accustomed to the Barbie-playpen colour scheme, then peruse the menu of mouthfuls. Here be platters of canapés, ranging from the simply stuffed or spread on toast varieties to shot glasses & mini ramekins of culinary confections. The menu is helpfully divided into assortments of meat, fish, veggie, cheese or dessert options, which means that no one has to compromise & prices range from around €9 for a selection of 6 savouries to €30 or €40 for massive platters with several dozen *bouchées* to try. Simply appreciate & allow yourself to be enchanted by the sheer happiness of the concept & its execution. Start early in the evening before hitting the streets & opt for half a dozen snacks as a stomach liner, or wind up here later in the night & take €10–15 each in lieu of dinner. Budget around €20 a head including a glass of wine. $$

Les Compagnons de la Grappe <u>VL</u> 26 rue Lepelletier, 59800 ✆ 03 20 21 02 79 ⊘ closed Sun & Mon eve in Oct–May only [236 C5 (73)] *e** *Bus 12 from Gare Lille Flandres to de Gaulle. Walk under the Alcide arch to the débris St Etienne into rue Lepelletier.*

I stumbled across this summer terrace quite by chance: there is a gap in an alleyway, which opens out to reveal a wine bar with a delightful courtyard. Families & friends sit & chat under sunshades, sipping wines from some of the lesser-known vineyards of France. Platters of *charcuterie* & farmhouse cheeses are colourful & plentiful. The place positively hums with contentment. It's worth popping in to check on any special theme evenings or culinary events. No reservations taken, service

Eating & drinking Wine bars

can be a hit-&-miss affair & the opening hours of noon till midnight vary with the weather. In winter enjoy a glass of wine in front of a roaring fire. Budget €25 per person. $$

Au Gré du Vin <u>VL</u> 20 rue Peterinck, 59800 ☏ 03 20 55 42 51 **e** augreduvin@nordnet.fr ⊙ Tue–Sat 12.00–14.20, Sun 12.00–13.45 [236 C3 (83)] **e*** *Bus 3, 6 or 9 from Gare Lille Flandres to Lion d'Or. From rue de la Monnaie turn left into rue Peterinck: the shop is on your right.*
Go on, treat yourself. Have a nice glass of wine from the Languedoc at

CAFE SOCIETY

The dividing line between a bar and a café has blurred over the years. Generally one does a lot more sitting down in the latter and standing around in the former, and bars stay open later – usually until 01.00 or 02.00. You can enjoy a coffee in a bar and a beer in a café, so your choice really depends on where you feel most at home.

Cafés tend to be best for talking, and Lille has its regular venues for philosophising or swapping notes on this week's great read. Bars range from traditional locals to the seriously fashionable spots where your clothes say more about you than your neighbour can spell. For the hottest joints in town see pages 136–8, and don't forget that the coolest hangouts may not be what you expect. Who would imagine that the essential address in Vieux Lille would be the Café Oz (a pub better known to locals as 'L'Australian Bar')? Find it on the place Louise de Bettignies, at the corner of the rue de Gand and avenue de la Peuple Belge [236 D2 (88)]. And when televised sport is on the agenda you will be amazed at the crowds at the English, Irish, Scottish and Welsh pubs across the city.

The cooler the bar, the later it starts to get busy. Thus *estaminets* (traditional northern locals) and cafés will do a roaring daytime trade and wind down in the early evening, whilst the party places often unbolt the front door any time from 17.00 to 20.00, with some truly trendy establishments waiting until 22.00 to get started.

You will often find two sets of prices on display. In most cases the lower price applies to drinks served to those standing at, or leaning against, the bar, and the higher for waiter service at a table. In some trendier establishments, the second figure indicates a 10–20% price hike after 22.00 or midnight. In a neighbourhood bar, one orders a drink, enjoys it and pays on leaving. Busier, fashionable hangouts may expect probably the only place in town you'll taste a tangy Picpoul de Pinet with a cold collation. Lunchtimes only, this neat little wine shop – specialising in the oft-overlooked but ne'er-forgotten full-flavoured delights of Languedoc Roussillon – serves a simple platter of food with which to sample the Corbières, St Chinians, Fitous & Banyuls or the better-known bottles of the southwest. A good place to buy exotic specialities for picnics or presents: *aubergines languedociennes* or jars of salt flavoured with the spices & scents of the *garrigue* scrublands of the sultry south. Find change from €20. $$

payment at the time of ordering. If all this sounds stressful and complicated, don't worry. Settle down, have a drink and forget about it. There is never any pressure to move on once you have ordered your first tipple. A modest espresso can last an afternoon, if you've a mind to settle down on a comfortable terrace, and a glass of beer may be nursed as long as you like as the evening dissolves past the witching hour. Beers (see page 70) come in bottles or on draught (*à la pression*), served usually as a *demi* (25cl) in a tall glass. Each bar seems to have its own name for a larger half-litre measure, but if you fancy something close enough to a pint, ask for a *grande*. Beer is the best-value drink, wine often surprisingly expensive by the glass, and spirits decidedly shocking considering how cheap they can be in supermarkets. Soft drinks, or *sodas*, include Coca Light (Diet Coke), Orangina and occasionally the local fizzy violet-flavoured lemonade. And don't forget the mineral waters. A refreshing compromise is a lager shandy, known locally as a *panaché*.

▲ Boulangeries *are an excellent option for breakfast.*

BARS & CAFES, *CREPERIES* & TEA ROOMS

Nurse a coffee for an hour, have a beer with friends, a late-night light snack or mid-afternoon sugar rush. Traditional restaurants are not the answer: time to explore the infinite variety of bars, cafés, *salons du thé* and *crêperies* that provide sustenance before, between and beyond mealtimes.

La Baignoire <u>MK</u> 8 pl Béthune, 59000 ☎ 03 20 30 07 44 [234 E5 (29)] 🚇 *République–Beaux Arts* *e** *Line 2 to Gare Lille Flandres then Line 1 to République–Beaux Arts.*
Not the traditional image of a brasserie, & as much a fashionable watering hole & meeting place as a restaurant, this newcomer to the scene is a useful floppery after a 2-hour-plus stint at the Palais des Beaux Arts, just across the way, or midway through a shopping marathon in the pedestrian quarter. Galeries Lafayette's opening may have raised the average age of the clientele. Although this should by rights be listed with the brasseries on page 82, I prefer to think of this more as a place for a drink as you wait for friends & keep an eye open for fashion victims making the most of the staircase. If you have to eat here, expect standard fare with menus from €10–24. $$

Paul GP 8–12 rue de Paris, 59000 ☎03 20 78 20 78 [236 C6 (57)] 🚇 *Rihour* ✦* *Bus 12 from Gare Lille Flandres to Théâtre. Or walk av le Corbusier & right into rue Faidherbe, then left to the Vieille Bourse.*

Don't bother with breakfast in your hotel. Come to Paul for the best breakfast in town. Not the biggest, nor the most varied, but certainly the best. This corner-site bakery opposite the Vieille Bourse is the place to go for fresh croissants, just-baked bread & creamy, piping-hot chocolate first thing in the morning. The breakfast tray served on solid wooden tables against the blue-&-white tiled walls & heavy tapestries of the bread & cake shop is the perfect way to start the day. Find inspiration in the words of wisdom painted on the old wooden beams, or concentrate on the scrumptious homemade jams & crunchy, crusty baguettes. A range of breakfast options at around €2–6. I have good news for long-time fans: after a brief period of confusion, the curving wooden staircase once again leads to the famously bright & airy 1st-floor restaurant dining room. Those who recall the gentle climb to tasteful tables by the windows & washstands in mirrored washrooms can once more enjoy light snacks with unimpeachable views across the squares. Paul has now spawned scores of satellite bakeries & *viennoiserie* counters across Lille, throughout Paris, France & beyond, but this old corner shop between the Opéra & the main square remains something special. $$$

Les Trois Brasseurs See page 86. $$

Au Vieux de la Vieille See page 80. $$

BD Fugue VL 5 rue Royale, 59000 ☎03 20 15 11 47 🖥 www.bdfugue-lille.com ☉Tue–Sat 10.30–19.00 & Mon 14.00–19.00 [236 A4 (38)] ✦* *Bus 12 to de Gaulle, cross Grand' Place to rue Esquermoise & on to rue Royale.*
It had to happen. After the *café philo* & the *café littéraire*, here comes the café comic strip. The French love their BD – *bandes dessinées*, comic-strip artwork & novellas – just as much as the Japanese love theirs, & vast sections of any self-respecting bookshop are devoted to the form. So now comes a café where aficionados may chat & browse over an espresso. A friendly welcome is guaranteed in this bustling corner of the old town. $

Café Aux Arts VL 1 pl du Concert 59800 ✆ 03 20 21 13 22 [236 C2 (86)] *e** *Bus 3, 6 or 9 from Gare Lille Flandres to Lion d'Or. Then follow rue de la Monnaie.*

Sit on the strip of pavement terrace & watch the comings & goings of the conservatoire opposite & the rue de la Monnaie to your right. Nothing special, just the traditional cane chairs & smart blue awning you would appreciate after an hour or so sightseeing. Fine for a quick beer & break after the Hospice Comtesse & Vieux Lille window shopping. $

Le Café de Foy GP 6–8 pl Rihour, 59000 ✆ 03 20 54 22 91 [236 B6 (51)] 🚇 *Rihour e** *Line 2 to Gare Lille Flandres then line 1 to Rihour.*

Squeezed between the thrusting elbows of many a visitor-packed bistro & ice cream parlour, Foy is a popular choice for budget-conscious *plat du jour* lunchers, rendezvous-shifting friends or mere people-watchers. Most visitors know the packed terrace, but locals think of the 1st-floor room where Thursday night conversation goes beyond shopping stories & idle gossip. This is the *café philo* of the squares. If your French is up to it, take the plunge. $

Café Leffe GP 1–5 pl Rihour, 59800 ✆ 03 20 54 67 37 🖰 www.cafe-leffe-lille.com [236 C6 (52)] 🚇 *Rihour e** *Line 2 to Gare Lille Flandres then line 1 to Rihour.*

On the corner of Grand' Place & place Rihour, next to the theatre & on the threshold of the pedestrianised shopping zone, Leffe's tables prove irresistible to the laden & the early. A €10 midweek menu adds to its popularity during shopping hours. Fast service keeps the Belgian beer flowing at the dithering point of the evening as you debate whether to go to a show or a restaurant, stay & watch the match on the big screen, head off to a local club or hop on a train to Belgium. $

Envies de Saison GP 63 rue Nationale, 59000 ✆ 03 20 77 19 84 ⊙ Mon–Fri 08.00–18.00, Sat 10.00–18.00, closed Sun [236 A6 (44)] 🚇 *Rihour e** *Line 2 to Gare Lille Flandres then line 1 to Rihour then walk up rue Roisin & turn left on to rue Nationale.*

'Mouthwatering' may be a cliché, but 'drool' is not a word I like to use around food. Sandwiches that give a new dimension & purpose to aspirational salivating are served in this healthy little shop where cheeses blend with berries & honeys & herbs, grilled vegetables in toasted rolls taste like forbidden fruits, & salads & pastas in the chill cabinet are even more alluring than the chunks of *charcuterie* squeezed between slices of wonderful breads. Read the list of fillings chalked up daily to give goosebumps to your tastebuds, then agonise over how to spend your €5.

Grab a sandwich or order a herbal tea & take it upstairs for a light lunch or energy boost. A good takeaway section too, & here's a tip – 20% off all fresh food after 17.00. $

Le Galichon VL 24 rue Royale, 59000 ☎03 20 78 14 75 ⊘closed Sat eve & Sun [236 A3 (35)] *e** *Métro 2 to Gare Lille Flandres then line 1 to Rihour. Cross Grand' Place to rue Esquermoise into rue Royale.*
One consolation for the passing of the most charmingly named establishment in town (Le Caillou dans la Théière – the pebble in the teapot) is the fact of being able to enjoy scrumptious *crêpes & gallettes* when I've lunched well & can't quite face a 'proper' meal that evening. Light & lovely & none too pricey. Lunch menu at under €11 includes one savoury & one sweet pancake. $

Jardins de Julie & Lea GP 4 rue des Malfonds, 59000 ☎03 20 06 59 60 [236 B7 (48)] 🚊*Rihour e** *Métro 2 to Gare Lille Flandres then line 1 to Rihour. From rue de la Vieille Comedie, turn right into rue des Fosses & left into rue des Malfonds.*
Between the Galeries Lafayette & the Grand' Place is this little turning. An oasis amongst Italian restaurants & workaday brasseries is the tiniest of florists, with a tropical hut beach bar within & chairs outside for sipping & supping. Fabulous cocktails of fruit juices & edible flowers, & light snacking on salads & sandwiches. You can watch the transformation of the shop from abandoned opticians to 'Florabar'on YouTube! $

Khedive GP 7 pl Rihour, 59000 ☎03 20 54 37 82 [236 B6 (53)]
🚊*Rihour e** *Métro 2 to Gare Lille Flandres then line 1 to Rihour.*
In these health-conscious times, when smokers are expected to rend their garments & carry a bell, a politically incorrect *terrasse* for those who otherwise might be seen huddling on doorsteps & blocking the entrance to smoke-free railways stations & shopping malls (interestingly, the fug that garlands the portals of these new breathe-right sanctuaries is like a triple espresso shot of nicotine that could flay & slay an asthmatic at 40 paces), an address for those who still like a cigar & sigh for the sight of a humidor. On most café terraces, drinkers & diners may puff with impunity but here, next door to Leffe & in front of the Foy, is a place where tobaccophiles may walk tall & strut. A sign in the window invites visitors to explore a '*Cave aux Cigares*'. Snacks are served from 06.00

until midnight to satisfy the munchies & refuel those whose tastebuds have been shattered by a life on the weed & tolerant non-smokers alike, who fancy the shot of a refreshing glass of beer & a freshly made sandwich. The closed-in (in winter) *terrasse* attracts a lively mix of students & musicians from the nearby theatres & concert halls, shoppers & strangers, all squeezed around tables cluttered with ashtrays & beer glasses & army recruitment leaflets. Great for the Christmas markets when a big €3.50 glass of mulled wine is better than any scarf for an early evening warm-up. $

Maison du Moulin d'Or (Morel et Fils) GP 31–33 pl du

Théâtre, 59000 ☎ 03 20 55 00 10 [236 C6 (61)] *e* Bus 12 from Gare Lille Flandres to Théâtre.*

A pastel-blue legend of lingerie is reborn in arabica. In 1997, Morel et Fils, purveyors of ribbons, laces & corsetry since 1831, sadly closed the doors of their Maison du Moulin d'Or, surely the prettiest shop in Lille (see page 184). Now, with the familiar window displays, a terrace outside the Opéra, stripped floors, grand staircase & much original décor within, it is a welcome & welcoming café bar, still under the care of a 7th generation *fils* of the original Monsieur Morel. $

Meert VL 27 rue Esquermoise, 59800 ☎ 03 20 57 07 44 [236 B5 (65)] 🚇 *Rihour e* Bus 12 from Gare Lille Flandres to de Gaulle.* Charles de Gaulle himself would never have dreamt of saying '*Non*' to the celebrated *gaufrettes* – or filled waffle – that has graced many a palace & presidential biscuit barrel since this shop started trading in the 1760s. This unassuming house speciality of the chocolate-box quaint pâtisserie is a tiny miracle: a light, feathery, crispy wafer packed with a sugared explosion of flavour. The town's most famous son continued his regular order for the *gaufrettes* all his life, & ate them, so he wrote, 'with great pleasure'. The Belgian royal family gave their warrant to Monsieur Meert in 1849. The pretty cake shop, decorated in 1839 with mirrors, balconies & *Arabian Nights* exotica, is a feast for the eyes. The tea room behind the shop provides savoury lunchtime snacks & sumptuous afternoon teas, where a selection of cakes & a pot of tea should set you back around €6–12. Lemon meringue tarts are creamy delights; the *safari* a surprisingly heavy dose of fluffiness for hardcore chocolate addicts only. See also page 101. $

Le Pain Quotidien **GP** 35 bis pl Rihour, 59000 ☎03 20 42 88 70
☺daily 08.15–22.30, closed Mon eve [236 B6 (54)] 🚊*Rihour* *e** *Métro 2 to*
Gare Lille Flandres then line 1 to Rihour.

Readers of my *Bradt Guide to Eurostar Cities* will recognise the name &
décor of this café from its earlier Brussels incarnations. This cheerful
clone of the ideal brunchery pushes the same indulgence buttons as the
original. Imagine turning up mid-morning at a country farmhouse, just as
the farmer's wife is removing the day's baking from the oven. OK, so no
one wipes floury hands on an apron, but the welcome smells & tastes are
the same, whether you want a generous tartine of freshly baked bread,
butter & apricot jam or a slice of lemon tart. Yummy hot chocolate &
coffee take the chill off a December roam around the Christmas Market
opposite. Snack inexpensively or lavish €15 on a menu charged with
huge salads & sandwiches served at hefty family-sized tables in a wide,
airy room dominated by a massive dresser sporting hundreds of jars of
tempting preserves. Weekend brunches for €18. $

Le Palais de la Bière **S** 11 pl Gare 59800 ☎03 20 06 38 94 [236 E7
(96)] 🚊*Gare Lille Flandres* *e** *Métro 2 to Gare Lille Flandres – but you might as*
well walk.

Smart, modern, airy & bright bar contrasts with the greasy chips &
soggy beer-mat norm of station 'caffs'. Nice place for coffee & croissant
between stepping off the Eurostar & walking into town. $

La Pâté Brisée **VL** 65 rue de la Monnaie 59000 ☎03 20 74 29 00
[236 C2 (85)] *e** *Bus 3, 6 or 9 from Gare Lille Flandres to Lion d'Or.*
Looking for a light lunch in the old town? Then squeeze past the punters
queueing at the counter of this cheery pâtisserie across the way from the
Hospice Comtesse & find a seat in the cosy red-brick dining room. All
the sweet & savoury pastries you could buy to take home are served here
on marble-slab tables. I loved a Roquefort tart, but traditional quiche
lovers will fine plenty of variations on the theme to savour, chicken &
tarragon being something of a 'wow' with the regulars. My source for
this was the lady at the next table whose eyes were watering with the
effort of not talking with her mouth full, as she dabbed at the lightest
pastry crumbs at the southeastern corner of her lips in her eagerness to
advise me on my first journey though the menu. The fruit flan I chose
for dessert was so nice I clean forgot to make notes, but it blended the
sharpness & sweetness of late plums with a texture that melted off my
fork. Main courses are around €8 & there is a full menu for €15
including drinks. $

Rouge Cacao VL 25 rue Masurel, 59000 Lille ☎ 03 20 31 63 63 [236 B3 (79)] *e** *Bus 3, 6 or 9 from Gare Lille Flandres to Lion d'Or. Take rue de la Monnaie then first left to pl Gilleson; the café is on the parvis Notre Dame.*

No need to squint at our map to find the rue Masurel: this dual-purpose café & artist's outlet is slap opposite the main doorway of Notre Dame de la Treille. A burgundy & glass façade, topped with a teeny little wrought-iron balconette lets sunlight into the bright & nursery-coloured ground floor, with a slender staircase leading into a basement room. Here, you can enjoy an espresso for less than €2 & a chunk of tiramisu or gâteau for not much more before browsing the exhibition space to check out local brushstrokes & creativity. $

Les Secrets du Blé MK 47 rue de Puebla ☎ 03 20 57 57 57 ⊙ closed Sun [234 C5 (15)] 🚇 *République–Beaux Arts* *e** *Métro 2 to Gare Lille Flandres then change to Line 1 to République–Beaux Arts. Walk up the bd de la Liberté & turn left onto rue Puébla.*

Originally, I checked out this address near the party district in response to readers' cries for vegetarian dining options (see page 121), but this *crêperie* is a great stopping place for anyone exploring this side of town. Only vegans will be disappointed (after all, you can't make a crêpe without breaking eggs), but a good mix of savoury & sweet pancakes should assuage most appetites. $

Tous Les Jours Dimanche VL 13 rue Masurel, 59000 ☎ 03 28 36 05 92 ⊙ Mon–Sun 11.30–18.30 [236 B4 (78)] *e** *Bus 3, 6 or 9 from Gare Lille Flandres to Lion d'Or. Take rue de la Monnaie then first left to pl Gilleson & cross the parvis to rue Masurel.*

The dinky little streets around the cathedral constantly produce new delights & diversions, & this is a sweetie, an almost eccentric little tearoom & snack bar in a second-hand shop. So, should you really like the plate or the cutlery with your apple tart, the dish that your quiche was cooked in or the cup from which you are supping a mid-afternoon hot chocolate, ask for it to be added to your bill. It may well be for sale, along with the chair & picture above the table. Brunches at €19.50 served in winter months, afternoon snacks from around €5 & other light meals for €15. $

Au Fut et à Mesure MK 5 rue Faisan, 59800 ☎ 03 20 48 20 66 ⌨ www.aufutetamesure.com ⊙ 17.00–03.00 [234 C5 (17)] 🚇 *République–Beaux Arts* *e** *Bus Citadines 2 to Nationale, then walk west on rue Nationale, turning left into rue Faisan.*

This is so cool. No queues at the bar on match days, you can yell at *les bleus* to *allez* from the comfort of your seat & never miss a goal nor a top-up. Sport on the flat screen & beer on tap – literally. Your table has its own beer pump & with a smart card you serve yourself directly, whilst keeping a weather eye on your 'online' tab. Settle up at the end of the night. Brothers Benoît & Guillaume, with their friend Quentin, transformed an old office twixt the *Solfé* & the rue Nationale into the obligatory wood & steel look student-hangout bar & the place has been an instant hit with the locals.

Le Windsor GP 5 rue Jean Roisin, 59800 ☎ 03 20 57 45 64 [236 C6 (55)] ⚑ *Rihour* ℮* *Métro 2 to Gare Lille Flandres then line 1 to Rihour.*
The bar of the Grand Hôtel Bellevue (see page 58) presents the cocktail-hour rendezvous for those who would prefer to wait in discreet comfort surrounded by potted palms & gentle music than sit on the edge of a fountain in a busy square.

VEGETARIAN

I am constantly amazed at the European concept of vegetarian. When researching a Paris guide for the meatless and fancy free, I regularly encountered bacon served as standard on the vegetarian special and, on one occasion, a respected airline served all its passengers broccoli quiche – except for the single soul who had requested the vegetarian alternative, which turned out to be roast chicken and salad!

When I first began researching this guide, I struggled to find any exclusively vegetarian restaurants in the city and, apart from linking to specialist publications and websites, I merely nudged readers towards contemporary student-friendly places with a good range of salads. I have to admit to vegans being completely left out in the cold, but for those who eat eggs, the dreary standby of an omelette is always the unimaginative option. But Lille does boast an enviable range of ethnic restaurants (see pages 122–3). In my experience, cuisine from Mediterranean, Hindu or Muslim cultures is often far more likely to include interesting vegetarian options.

Since this book first came out, and during my various visits to the city during its regular yearly cycle or reinvention, I have actively sought decent veggie fare in the city and bombarded student groups with calls and emails in my hunt for good addresses. Here are my tips for a hearty spread.

Layalina MK 32 rue d'Artois, 59000 ☎ 03 20 42 85 58 [234 D8 (7)] ℮* *Bus 13 from Gare Lille Flandres to Artois.*
Although this could never be described as a meat-free zone, this

unexpected corner of the Mediterranean offers a simply massive spread of vegetarian mezze. Spend around €15. $

La Rizière MK 10–12 rue Jules Guesde ✆03 20 74 59 82 ⊘closed Mon, open Sun [234 A8 (5)] 🚇 Gambetta *e** Métro 2 to Gare Lille Flandres, then line 1 to Gambetta. Cross rue du Marché on to rue Sarazans; rue Jules Guesde is the3rd turning on your left.

The number one choice for local vegetarians. An Asian restaurant (actual ethnic delineation between various oriental cuisines blurs in France: most Chinese is Indochinese aka Vietnamese, with satay peanut sauces rife in curry houses), this offers the widest choice of proper meals for hungry veggies. The menu is imaginative with a good range of traditional 'duck-style' & 'beef-style' dishes that are 100% vegetarian,

BEYOND FRANCE

Of course, there is a lot more to dining out in Lille than exploring the diverse delights of French cuisine. With a good 500 restaurants in and around the city, you could discover many of the world's great national dishes. However, if you have made the trip to France and to Flanders, the chances are you have come in search of flavours French or Flemish. Thus the main listings and reviews on these pages concentrate on guiding you to the right table. Nonetheless, the multicultural charms of a modern French city are reflected on the plates of Lille, especially in the streets around the old station and along the rue Gambetta, place Sébastopol and Wazemmes. Lebanese, Tunisian, Algerian and Moroccan delights are to be found, with countless cafés and restaurants promising couscous, tabbouleh and tagines. Vietnamese and Chinese restaurants too, with the occasional promise of Caribbean flavours, add to the global menu for a Lille night out. Meze from Greece, paella from Spain and the inevitable trattoria or pizzeria on the corner keep the European flags flying in this food-fest of global diversity. The themed weekends of Lille 2004 reflected the gastronomic versatility of the city, with many events marrying food, flavours and sounds of other lands. When Lille went all Bollywood for the first Lille 3000 fest, Bombaysers de Lille, the city rediscovered its own excellent Indian restaurants. Eastern fusion concepts have begun to take over many traditional sites in the city centre. The rue de Paris, south of rue Molinel [235 F5-6], is a hotbed of start-up ethnic eateries: where else would you find a Lebanese pizzeria? Remember the simple rule when choosing restaurants unlisted in with sauces that are full of flavour (extremely rare in French veggie restaurants, which often believe the cruet to be a tool of the devil). Menus from €7.50 midweek lunch & €13. $

Otherwise, find meat-free options at the following addresses:

Au Bout des Doigts See page 111. Order a platter of meatless finger food at this fashionable hangout. $$

Les Charlottes en Ville (see page 107) & **La Patatière** (see page 109). Fun food & a variety of fillings at these jacket potato restaurants. $$

Les Flams See page 108. $$

---

any guidebook: go where the crowds are. And here are just a few recommendations:

Caribbean **La Canne à Sucre** MK 68 bd Victor Hugo ✆ 03 20 52 29 00 [234 D8 (8)]

Chinese **La Perle d'Orient** S 8 rue du Vieux Faubourg ✆ 03 20 31 28 18 [236 E6 (95)]

Fusion **Tiger Wok** GP 45 rue Tanneurs ✆ 03 20 14 91 60 [236 C8 (47)]. Offers an early evening plate of East-West tapas.

Indian **Aux Indes** GP 38 rue Thiers ✆ 03 20 21 02 66 [236 A4 (40)]

Japanese **Tokyo** GP 55 rue Nationale ✆ 03 20 12 98 88 [236 A6 (43)]

Kurdish **Yol** MK 140 rue Nationale ✆ 03 20 74 80 24 [234 C4 (19)]

Lebanese **Flandres Liban** MK 127 rue des Postes ✆ 03 20 57 28 69 [234 B8 (6)]

Moroccan **Soleil d'Agadir** VL 5 rue Princesse ✆ 03 20 31 49 71 [234 D1 (26)]

Polish **Le Pot au Feu** MK 449 rue Gambetta ✆ 03 20 54 14 70 [234 A4 (3)]

Réunion **Le Paille en Queue** GP 12 rue du Curé St-Etienne ✆ 03 20 13 89 49 [236 B5 (72)]

Spanish **Las Tapas** VL 116 rue St-André ✆ 03 20 06 96 59 [234 D1 (27)]

Thai **Le Marché Flottant** MK 38 rue Gambetta ✆ 03 20 13 07 87 [234 D5 (13)]

Vietnamese **Lac Hong** VL 12 rue Royale ✆ 03 20 06 01 03 [236 A3 (37)]

LES HALLES

MK Pl des Halles Centrales, rue Solférino, 59800 [234 B5–C5]
🚇 République–Beaux Arts 🚌* Bus 12 from Gare Lille Flandres to Eglise Sacré
Coeur. Rue Solférino to pl des Halles Centrales.

Wazemmes may be the daytime weekend capital, but another
marketplace, the former Les Halles wholesale district straddling the rues
Solférino and Masséna, is the centre of nightlife. Part student hangout,
part city of singles and part party-animal safari park, the restaurants, bars
and pavements are an electrifying life-force on Friday and Saturday
nights. The old covered market itself houses a run-down supermarket
that still manages to catch some of the party buzz and cheery chaos as
people stock up on last-minute supplies for rendezvous with friends in a
student bedsit before hitting the bars. Like any city's party zone, a
number of bars and restaurants open and close with the frequency of a
revolving door, but firm favourites survive each new influx of
undergraduate revellers.

Those who care about looking cool may or may not still hang out at
the Café La Plage and Le 16. Sporty types (read 'rugby club') make
noisy alpha-male sounds at L'Arms Park or pull their own pints at Au
Fut et à Mesure (see page 120). Eighties retro-heads prefer L'Ibiza, filled
with the sounds and tipples of the decade that taste may have bypassed,
but which haircare products annexed for all time. Students on a tight
budget bring their own atmosphere to the cheap and cheerful mood Chez
Gino, where a beer is just €2, whilst those willing to pay for imported
Cuban ambience enjoy tequila slammers at Le Latina Café. La Bûcherie,

Les Trois Brasseurs See page 86. The brasserie social snack of as
many savoury or sweet-topped *flams* as you can manage. $$

Envies de Saison See page 116. Best sandwiches in town. $

Secrets du Blé See page 120. Lille's *créperies* are excellent
compromises for snacking with friends. $

an institution in the quarter since the social dark ages, is a veritable meat-rack – lively dance floor, cruisy cocktail bar and the benchmark of the social scene – and the first point of contact for making new friends. Restaurants, on the other hand, are strictly for old acquaintances. The season's newest crop of dining rooms will provide a perfect hideaway for couples. Do not dismiss the area as merely the haunt of the green and trendy. There are more than a few bars, cafés and restaurants well worth a detour, both around the square and along the rues Gambetta and Puebla. This is one quarter where you should never rely on the printed word for a guarantee of fashion. Trends change fast here, so walk slow and watch where the locals go. Oh, and don't pronounce the full word when referring to Solférino. That is the mark of a stranger or wrinkly. It is Solfé!

Le 16 42–44 rue Masséna, 59800 ☎ 03 20 54 86 70

Au Fut et à Mesure 5 Rue Faisan, 59800 ☎ 03 20 48 20 66

L'Arms Park 136 rue Solférino, 59800 ☎ 03 20 38 63 74

Le Latina Café 42–44 rue Masséna, 59800 ☎ 03 20 07 14 81

La Bûcherie 32 rue Masséna, 59800 ☎ 03 20 30 66 06

Café La Plage 122 rue Solférino, 59800

Chez Gino 21 rue Masséna, 59800 ☎ 03 20 54 45 25

L'Ibiza 20 rue Masséna, 59800 ☎ 03 20 30 19 50

▲ *Cheese is just one of many culinary delights to be discovered at Wazemmes market*

Nightlife
& Entertainment

Lille famously boasts that Saturday night always offers a choice of a hundred alternative diversions – and it is no bragging exaggeration. This is a city that knows how to fill the hours of darkness. Quite apart from the diversity of bars and restaurants, from the *intime* and quirky rue de Gand to the city of singles that is rue Solférino, the variety of performances would not disgrace a national capital city. *Sortir*, the listings magazine, is published every Wednesday. Pick up a free copy at your hotel or the tourist office. The local newspaper *La Voix du Nord* also carries comprehensive entertainment information.

THEATRE

The Théâtre du Nord on Grand' Place is a very good place to start. Stuart Seide's artistic direction really put this stage on the national cultural agenda. Challenging and fresh approaches to world classics have led to groundbreaking productions of Beckett, Molière and of course Shakespeare – a *Romeo and Juliet* turned round the central schism by 90°, presenting the divide as less between Montague and Capulet than between the two generations. In a city where almost half the population is under the age of 25, that certainly created more than a murmur. The theatre's contribution to Lille 2004 was a programme featuring four works by Shakespeare while Pinter, Beckett *et al* are frequently to be seen.

Young theatre has its own voice at Le Grand Bleu, where programmes are essentially geared to the hip-hop rather than hip-replacement set. Other fringe and new-wave venues include the Théâtre de la Découverte à la Verrière and the Théâtre des Nuits Blanches. The Zem is the community theatre of Wazemmes and has a full programme of workshops. Conventional and comfortable family fare is served up at the Théâtre Sébastopol. Light comedies that would run on Shaftesbury Avenue, Broadway or the Grands Boulevards play here. The weekend bill may feature such old favourites as *Le Dîner des Cons* ('The Dinner Game') or concerts by TV crooners. International visitors perform at the up-front Le Prato and Villeneuve d'Ascq's Rose des Vents. During festivals, scores of other spaces, great and small, are called into service. The playhouses of other towns in the conurbation are also worth checking out since most venues are within half an hour of Grand' Place. After all, public transport in the Métropole continues until midnight. Do not dismiss the Maisons Folies (see pages 189–92) nor the new Gare Saint Sauveur. These have exciting and vibrant performance spaces, and have already been bagged by dance companies, musicians and experimental theatre groups. You'll find fringe theatre and comedy at other alternative venues. The Péniche du Pianiste (see page 130) and Moonlight Café (see page 135) are worth considering.

Theatres often close on Monday, but several offer Sunday matinées. Tickets for many productions may be bought on line (⌁ www.fnac.fr) or in person from FNAC's box office (see page 162). It is customary to tip the usherette between 50c and €1 when being shown your seat.

Le Grand Bleu 36 av Marx Dormoy, 59000 ✆ 03 20 09 88 44
⌁ www.legrandbleu.com [234 A4] 🚇 *Bois Blancs* *e** *Métro 2 to Bois Blancs, then walk along the avenue.*

Le Prato 6 allée de la Filature, 59000 ✆ 03 20 52 71 24 [234 D8]
🚇 *Porte de Douai* *e** *Métro 2 to Porte de Douai. From rue de Douai turn left into allée de la Filature.*

La Rose des Vents Scène Nationale bd Van Gogh, 59650 Villeneuve d'Ascq ✆ 03 20 61 96 90 🚇 *Pont de Bois* *e** *Métro 2 to Gare Lille Flandres then line 1 to Pont de Bois. Rue Vétérans to bd Van Gogh.*

Théâtre de la Découverte à la Verrière MK 28 rue Alphonse Mercier, 59800 ✆ 03 20 54 96 75 ⊙ closed Mon [234 B6] 🚇 *République–Beaux Arts* *e** *Bus 12 from Gare Lille Flandres to Eglise Sacré Coeur. Rue Solférino to pl des Halles Centrales, right on rue des Stations & right to rue Alphonse Mercier.*

Théâtre du Nord GP 4 pl du Général de Gaulle, 59000 ✆ 03 20 14 24 24 [234 E3 & 236 B6] 🚇 *Rihour* *e** *Bus 12 from Gare Lille Flandres to Théâtre.*

Théâtre Sébastopol MK Pl Sébastopol, 59000 ✆ 03 20 54 44 50 [234 C6] 🚇 *République–Beaux Arts* *e** *Métro 2 to Gare Lille Flandres changing to line 1 to République–Beaux Arts. Rue Inkerman leads to the theatre.*

Le ZEM Théâtre MK 38 rue d'Anvers, 59000 ✆ 03 20 54 13 44
⌁ http://zemtheatre.free.fr [234 C6] 🚇 *Gambetta* *e** *Métro 2 to Gare Lille Flandres then line 1 to Gambetta; walk up rue de Flandre & rue d'Anvers is the 5th turning on your left.*

CABARET & CASINO

For years, showbiz glamour and comedy were an essential part of Lille nightlife. As served with a flourish and a flounce at the late lamented Les Folies de Paris, where *La Cage Aux Folles* met Hollywood with the biggest cross-dressing floor show north of the capital – a pancake-pasted flurry of feathers, sequins and star lookalikes. Customers would be entertained, mocked and teased in camp patois by the revue's outrageous director Claude Thomas, then be transported to a world where every Celine, Marlene or Liza was a boy, and a stripping Michael Jackson was revealed to be a Y-chromosome-free zone. While no self-respecting Parisian is likely to admit to visiting the Paris cabarets, you would always find locals at the Folies. When the Folies closed for the last time, it seemed as though ostrich feathers were forever lost to Flanders. Now, however, the *royaume* of the showgirl is set for a revival with a new cabaret on the site and the advent, across town, of the new casino with the promise of weekly floor shows.

Au Bonheur des Dames 61 rue Achille Pinteaux, 59136 Wavrin
📞 03 20 58 55 53 🖰 www.aubonheurdesdames.fr
Full Monty-style evenings are provided Au Bonheur des Dames, some way out of town, for those who like their hen nights scented with squeals & baby oil. A celebration of depilated masculinity, from the sun-bed to the stage, it is proving a hit with office-party crowds who admire men who can still walk the walk after waxing the boxer line. More popular apparently than its predecessor in Lille itself, where the hunks lost a certain credibility by doubling as drag queens & dressing as Madonna before getting their more manly kit off for the girls. The most common complaint was that the boys' eyeliner used to detract from the full effect of the thongs, but how things have changed. An ad recruiting the 2009 vintage exhibitionists for the venue read: '*Nous recrutons pour les weekends 2 strip teasers, profil 18/25 ans, corps sportif et gueule d'ange. Envoyez votre candidature avec plusieurs photos...*'. Real angels don't wear mascara, not in this century. Menus €35 (for those who like their chicken on a plate) to €60 (for girls with a champagne lifestyle who prefer their beef hot & peppery).

Casino Barriere de Lille S 777 Pont de Flandre, 59777 📞 03 28 14 47 77 ⊘ daily 10.00–04.00 🚇 Lille Europe or Lille Grand Palais
The spanking new casino-hotel opening at the end of 2009 promises 150 rooms & suites & a purpose-built showroom theatre for 1,200 diners, a range of theme bars & a snack bar as well as the principal restaurant. But

▲ *Traditional street signs.*

the casino owners could not wait until the place was fully built before opening for business, & have already created a loyal clientele at a temporary venue across the parvis de Rotterdam, both in the gaming rooms & the popular Lilas Heaven restaurant – which proved quite a magnet for business lunchers from those major international firms with offices in the Euralille complex. Habitués used to a mere 9 gaming tables (blackjack, *roulette anglaise* & stud poker) & only 150 slot machines, as offered at the temporary address, will be in for a shock as the new casino spreads itself across 40,000 square metres of the city, which may not sound much, but works out at 10 acres for living high on the hog in smart suits whilst betting the farm on evens. The showroom will present around 3 live shows a week in the first season. Thursday night is scheduled for a 'mini-concert', Friday is a full variety show & Saturday's programme is for live music. The casino switchboard or tourist office will have up-to-date listings each week. If the very notion of a casino conjures up promises of full James Bond role-play, you may be only slightly disappointed, since whilst ties are appreciated on gentlemen, they are no longer *de rigueur*. Full evening dress may be out, but smart & stylish is still essential to get you through the door, thus trainers & T-shirts have no place even in a modern casino. If the old Folies punters make it through the door, we may see the dry martini being replaced by a *chuche mourette*, shaken not stirred (see page 70)! Even poker fantasies are PC: no smoking in the gaming rooms or show rooms, although stressed-out gamblers may adjourn to a dedicated fug-filled room for a wheeze, cough & ciggie break before returning to the tables. Not all casino employees work as croupiers or bouncers – the venue has its own resident addiction counsellor.

La Péniche du Pianiste **VL** Av Cuvier, (opposite Champ de Mars), 59000 ✆ 03 20 57 14 40 🖱 www.penichedupianiste.com [234 C2] *e* Bus 3 from Gare Lille Flandres to Esplanade.*
What began as a floating piano-bar on the Deûle is now something of a cult café-théâtre. Live music, sometimes alternative comedy, & an eclectic range of entertainment – see videos of previous shows &

updates on 3 months' worth of programming on the website. Admission prices for shows vary, but are usually around €10. The previous formula of a set menu has been relaxed & you can dine from €20–25 or just have a drink at the bar.

La Petite Cave VL 80 rue St André, 59000 ℡ 03 20 06 60 66 ⟨🖰⟩ www.lapetitecave.fr ⊘ daily from 12.30 & 20.30 [234 D1] *e** *Bus 3 or 6 from Gare Lille Flandres to Magasin.*

Originally tucked away along the rue Nationale, far from the paths of casual trippers, now firmly re-established in Vieux Lille, this low-key Lillois institution has long offered a recreation of a Montmartre *bouchon* filled with *chanson*. Discover *La Vie en Rose* – coloured brick in the vaulted cave itself that nightly echoes homage to the names & faces featured on golden age vintage EP & LP sleeves of Montand, Brel, Brassens, Trenet, Mistinguett, long-forgotten Eurovision starlets & of course, *La Môme,* Piaf herself. Singers perform to piano, guitar or accordion as they key into such a particularly French fast-track to the soul, the confessional torch-song & 3-minute 1-act tragedy that is strictly *chanson*; those essentially Parisian dance-hall & piano bar numbers providing our own private soundtracks to every trip to France. Since the passing of the much-lamented Folies de Paris across the av du Peuple Belge, this revue has developed a form & shape as an alternative entertainment & is less ad hoc than in the early days. Service is ever friendly & attentive, & the 3 set 4-course menus hover around the €50–70 mark (including drinks) & feature standards such as *châteaubriand,* oysters & *tarte aux pommes,* often with a Flemish twist. All is reminiscent of the nutritious, generous portions of homely, robust fare served by a preoccupied aunt & delivered with a generous helping of *nostalgie* from the ages of the Moulin Rouge to the era of Johnny Halliday.

Le Prestige Palace VL 52 av du Peuple Belge, 59000 ℡ 03 20 30 93 46 ⟨🖰⟩ www.leprestigepalace.com ⊘ Thu–Sat 19.30, Thu & Sun 12.30 [235 G1 & 236 D1] *e** *Bus 3, 6 or 9 from Gare Lille Flandres to Lion d'Or. Cross pl Louise de Bettignies & turn left.*

The *Cage aux Folles*-style anarchy of the transvestite revue that once held court here is gone. In its place is the traditional pancake-&-feathers revue that has been a staple entertainment ever since Hollywood invented France. Showgirls with their curves factored to the max, with sequins & plumes glistening & shimmering at every wiggle & strut, & hugely amplified voices sing in time to the teeth & tinsel being flashed on the stage. No one leaves without seeing a can-can! If you are going to

Nightlife & entertainment Cabaret & casino

stage a floor show, then trust an old stager to do it properly. Thierry Fééry is the director, producer & mastermind behind the Prestige Palace, & he is no stranger to Lille's entertainment scene, having been a former artistic director of the Théâtre Sébastopol across town. Not only that, but he arrives on the av du Peuple Belge having produced shows for Belgium's second greatest export to France, the actress & singer Annie Cordy. The show room is a big restaurant with all tables facing the stage. Dinner & show €53–80. Reservation essential.

CINEMA

Le *7ème* art thrives in and around Lille. June sees Lille hosting an international Independent Film Festival. One out-of-town multiplex, Kinépolis at Lomme, boasts 23 screens. However, you will not need to leave the centre of Lille, unless you wish to catch a festival screening of an obscure classic at Le Fresnoy in Tourcoing (see page 204), since everything else will be available around the pedestrian shopping streets surrounding rue de Béthune. The main selection is that offered at the 14-screen Ciné Cité UGC. Just along the pavement, the six *salles* of the Majestic specialise in original-language versions of international flicks, with subtitles rather than the dubbed versions screened elsewhere. Artier yet are the preferences at the Métropole near the station. At the far end of the rue de Béthune, the Palais des Beaux Arts has its own art house, La Garance. Further down the boulevard de la Liberté, the new Gare Saint Sauveur has its own 208-seat cinema. In addition to listings and reviews in *Sortir* magazine, a free guide is produced by the picture palaces of Lille, distributed in cinemas and tourist offices. Budget tip: midweek morning screenings, at 11.00, are often half price.

Ciné Cité UGC GP 40 rue de Béthune, 59000 ☎ 08 92 70 00 00
⌂ www.ugc.fr [234 E4 & 236 B8] 🚊 *Rihour* *e** *Métro 2 to Gare Lille Flandres then line 1 to Rihour. Rue de la Vieille Comédie leads to rue de Béthune.*

La Garance GP Palais des Beaux Arts, pl République, 59000 ☎ 03 20 15 92 20 [234 E6] 🚊 *République–Beaux Arts* *e** *Métro 2 to Gare Lille Flandres then line 1 to République–Beaux Arts.*

Gare Saint Sauveur Bd J-B Lebas, 59000 See page 188.

Le Majestic GP 54–56 rue de Béthune, 59000 ☎ 03 20 54 08 96
⌂ www.lemajesticlille.com [234 E5 & 236 E8] 🚊 *Rihour* *e** *Métro 2 to Gare Lille Flandres then line 1 to Rihour. Rue de la Vieille Comédie leads to rue de Béthune.*

Le Métropole S 26 rue des Ponts de Comines, 59000 ✆ 08 92 68 00 73 ⤴ www.lemetropole.com [235 G4 & 236 D6] 🚊 *Gare Lille Flandres* *e** *Av le Corbusier & right into rue Faidherbe, left on to rue des Ponts de Comines.*

MUSIC

The Orchestre Nationale de Lille is housed in the big, round Nouveau Siècle building to the side of Grand' Place. Surrounded by restaurants, the building might easily be dismissed by diners as just another office block and underground car park. But nothing is ever quite what it seems in Lille, as I realised on my first visit to the car park when I noticed that signs for motorists were disconcertingly, albeit politically correctly, translated into Braille. Full orchestral programmes alternate with chamber concerts. The all-too-rare, occasional Sunday morning recitals have always been firm favourites with locals. Nonetheless, other treats abound on other dates. Open rehearsals are fascinating and free to watch – check the ONL website for details – and there is a superb season of pre-concert talks. The orchestra's director, Jean Claude Casadesus, woos international soloists to his concerts with lunch at local fish restaurants. Concerts are not limited to the Nouveau Siècle hall. The musicians play at many other venues around the region, as well as many prestigious international events. Programme details are posted on the orchestra's website.

The other nationally acclaimed company is the Ballet du Nord. Performing all over Europe, its local base is the Colisée at Roubaix, a large theatre equally as popular with the world of rock as of dance. Opera has returned to the city centre thanks to the reopening of the Opéra de Lille on the place du Théâtre. Inspired by the Paris opera house, the elegant bars and salons can match the stage for opulence and theatricality. With soloists and choirs mixed and matched from the leading companies of Europe, the season here is amongst the continent's best bargains. Just before the place closed for renovation, a production of *Eugène Onegin* boasted a chorus imported from St Petersburg and tickets from under €30. The new regime, with an opening season featuring *Madame Butterfly* and *Don Giovanni*, promised to better that with a limited number of €5 seats available for every performance. A triumphant co-production (with the Brussels opera) of *Rigoletto*, with a witty beach hut design, showcased some of the most exciting new musical talent around and sold out almost instantly. The opera house opened itself up as a home to dance, with premières of new works and visits by ballet legends. The first season alone brought Bill T Jones and William Forsythe with the Frankfurt Ballet company. The stunning foyer, glittering with opulence and sheer dazzling style, hosts weekly recitals and performances every Wednesday evening at 18.00. Balconies and vast windows offer breathtaking views of the city, and the extraordinary rehearsal studio spaces in the attics have access to amazing terraces looking out over the new and the old towns.

As if that were not enough, the district has a second opera venue: the Atelier Lyrique in Tourcoing produces studio versions of contemporary and classic works. A cycle of all the Mozart-da Ponte comic operas shared the honours between the main house in Lille and this intimate space at Tourcoing.

Regular concerts and recitals are held at the various churches in central Lille and all venues are open during the year's many music festivals. The main event is the Mozart Festival running from November to April. November itself sees Lille Piano Festival. May brings accordion players from many lands to an annual ten-day festival in Wazemmes. Programmes for all these events are available at the tourist office.

Tourcoing hosts its own autumn jazz festival, with fringe events spilling over the Belgian border. Good jazz may be enjoyed in Lille every week of the year. Visit Moonlight Café, close to the bars of Solférino or the Bel Ouvrage in the Latin quarter, for a fix of something mellow by night.

For a harder edge, rock is obviously at home in a district of 100,000 youngsters. Six thousand people a night can raise the roof at the Zenith Arena; smaller crowds pack the Biplan, the essential rendezvous of Wazemmes, Le Splendid (a former cinema) and the Blue Note. Tickets for major events may be obtained through FNAC (see page 162). The Aeronef venue high above Euralille is a typical Lille curiosity. Originally an underground organisation for disaffected youth, the club moved to its new high-rise home amongst the banks and financial institutions of the business district when it was offered the venue by the city. Multinational corporations pitched in with generous grants, and the kids were left to organise their own fun. So much so that when a band offended public morals with their sexually explicit antics on stage, organisers, expecting a mass withdrawal of funding or legal action, were merely sent a memo from the authorities.

Whatever your musical taste, whatever the year, cancel sleep on 21 June. National Music Day, created by former culture minister Jack Lang (since then a *député* for Boulogne), is an amazing occasion. Free concerts are held everywhere – in villages, towns and cities – and Lille manages to upstage most of the country with performances in public spaces, matched by live entertainment inside and outside almost every restaurant, café and bar in town. If you can get a table anywhere, keep ordering food and drink as the performances continue through the evening and into the night. If not, just keep on moving from street to street as swing blends into rap and baroque into rock.

Lille 3000 seasons always bring exciting music events to unexpected venues, from Bollywood sounds in the inaugural programme to music from central Europe in the XXL fest of 2009. And don't forget that the new Gare Saint Sauveur, not far from the club district, has a music venue all of its own. The Maisons Folies are always worth checking out as well.

Aeronef S Av Willy Brandt, Centre Commercial, Euralille, 59777 ✆03 28 38 50 50 ⌂ www.aeronef-spectacles.com [235 H5] 🚉 *Gare Lille Europe or Gare Lille Flandres e* Av le Corbusier to av Willy Brandt, look for the signs, then scale the outside of the tower block.*

Atelier Lyrique 82 bd Gambetta, 59200 Tourcoing ✆03 20 70 66 66 🚉 *Carliers e* Métro 2 to Carliers.*

Ballet du Nord ✆03 20 24 66 66 ⌂ www.ccn-roubaix.com

Bel Ouvrage MK 4 parvis Saint Michel, 59800 ✆03 20 57 73 56 ⊙ Mon–Sat 17.30–02.00, closed Aug [234 D8] 🚉 *République–Beaux Arts e* Bus Citadine 1 to Douai-Arras, walk up rue Solférino to the parvis St Michel.* Arrive after 23.00 to get the feel of the place. Very friendly bar, interesting exhibitions & live music. Other sounds piped through at other times at a level to be enjoyed but which will not inhibit lively conversation.

Le Biplan 19 rue Colbert, 59000 ✆03 20 12 91 11 ⌂ www.chez.com /biplan [234 A4] 🚉 *Gambetta e* Bus 12 from Gare Lille Flandres to Colbert.*

Blue Note See page 134.

Colisée Roubaix Culture Rue de l'Epeule, 59100 Roubaix ✆03 20 24 07 07 🚉 *Gare Jean Lebas e* Métro 2 to Carliers. Walk down rue de L'Alouette.*

Gare Saint Sauveur See page 188.

Moonlight Café MK 56 rue des Stations, 59800 ✆03 20 57 79 72 ⌂ www.moonlight-cafe.fr [234 B5] ⊙ Mon–Thu 19.00–00.00, Fri–Sat 19.00–02.00 🚉 *Gambetta e* Bus Citadines 2 to Colbert, then walk south on rue Colbert & first right to rue des Stations.* The Pizza Jazz shopfront restaurant is open to 23.00 most nights (& lunchtimes Tue–Thu), the music venue later still. Jazz & blues are regularly on the programme (check website for current listings), but

Nightlife & entertainment Music

music shares the honours with comedy & spoken word. As well as the established professional acts, catch up with up-&-coming talent on open mike nights: comedians first Wednesday of the month, musicians on the last Thursday. Showtime around 21.30.

Opéra de Lille GP Pl du Théâtre, 59000 ☏ 03 28 38 40 40 ⌨ www.opera-lille.fr [235 F3 & 236 C5] 🚊 *Rihour* **e*** *Bus 12 from Gare Lille Flandres to Théâtre.*
See page 133.

Orchestre Nationale GP Nouveau Siècle, 30 pl Mendès France, 59000 ☏ 03 20 12 82 40 ⌨ www.onlille.com [234 E3 & 236 A5] 🚊 *Rihour* **e*** *Bus 12 from Gare Lille Flandres to de Gaulle.*

Le Splendid 1 pl du Mont de Terre, 59000 ☏ 03 20 56 46 16 [235 K8] 🚊 *Hellemmes* **e*** *Métro 2 to Porte de Douai, then bus 7 to pl du Mont de Terre in the Hellemmes quarter.*

Zenith S Lille Grand Palais, 1 bd des Cités Unies, 59777 ☏ 03 20 14 15 16 [235 J6] 🚊 *Lille Grand Palais* **e*** *Métro 2 to Lille Grand Palais then follow signs.*

BARS & CLUBS

Traditionally there have been only two rules to remember when setting out for a night's clubbing in Lille. Firstly, stay in the bars until late, since no one, but nobody, is seen in a club before well past midnight, however early the doors officially swing open. Secondly, if you really want to party on down, you go to Belgium. Move directly to Belgium, do not pass Go (see page 142).

Although the hardened merry-maker continues to make the cross-border trip to Brussels and other Belgian towns, and London's Ministry of Sound is on the main weekend agenda for the continental Eurostar set, the second tenet is perhaps a little unfair these days. Lille's smaller clubs are pretty cool and great for letting the evening spill into the night and flow towards the dawn. The night scene in Lille is pretty much an attitude-free zone of tolerance with fewer of the rigid barriers between crowds that one finds in Paris and London, yet manages to avoid the sorry air of piteous compromise found in many French provincial cities.

Nonetheless, it pays to choose a nightspot best suited to your age, musical tastes or sexuality. So do check out the *Ch'ti* guide at your hotel reception or online at ⌨ www.lechti.com for the views of the student community on which are the current clubs and bars to bless with your company. Listen to the word on the streets around Les Halles (see page 124) or find a stylish bar in Vieux Lille or student dive anywhere and pick up flyers for clubs. At the tourist office, the *Autour de Minuit* listings guide has the low-down on where to spend the midnight hour – thanks to the journalists at *La Voix du Nord*.

Admission is often free midweek. Where door charges are made, this often includes the cost of a first drink. Drinks usually cost around double or treble the price charged in bars.

Le Duke's Club MK 6 rue Gosselet, 59000 ☎ 03 20 52 97 98
☾ Thu–Sat 21.00–04.00 [234 E8] 🚇 *République–Beaux Arts* ✦* *Métro 2 to Gare Lille Flandres, changing to line 1 to République–Beaux Arts, then take rue Gaulthier de Châtillon to rue Jeanne d'Arc to rue Gosselet.*
Where men with unforgiveable eyes break their promises & girls whose lips are wishes pretend to believe, a riper crowd orders shorts from the bar & sips, talks & dances 'til late with the younger punters. Proudly advertises itself as the venue for the over-28s.

La Fabrik Rue Nicolas Appert, Lezzennes ⌂ www.fabrik-club.com
☾ Thu–Sun from 22.00 🚇 *Villeneuve d'Ascq* ✦* *Métro line 2 to Gare Lille Flandres, then métro 1 to the end of the line. Walk along av Poincaré to rue Nicolas Appert.*
On the site of the former 4 Cantons disco at the Villeneuve d'Ascq city limits, this is the latest club from Franck Duquesne. A spacious club with 4 bars & 2 dance floors, each with its own musical ambiance. Reversing the traditional trend for Lillois party animals to cross the border, the new nightspot attracts a lively international crowd from Belgium & Holland.

Le Flib MK 53 rue Gambetta, 59800 ☎ 03 20 30 16 16
⌂ www.flibclub.com ☾ 20.00–08.00 🚇 *République–Beaux Arts* ✦* *Métro 2 to Gare Lille Flandres changing to line 1 to République–Beaux Arts, then walk along rue Gambetta, & the club is on your left.*
Get into the mezzanine VIP area & you've either made it socially or you're so drop-dead gorgeous that you'll put the go-go girls to shame, & the club is keeping you out of sight. Contemporary mainstream club sounds. Arrive after midnight, leave at 8am, crash at a friend's place then go for brunch at the Gospel Café opposite.

Network Café MK 15 rue Faisan, 59800 ☎ 03 20 40 04 91
⌂ www.networkcafe.fr ☾ Tue–Sun 22.30–dawn [234 C4]
🚇 *République–Beaux Arts* ✦* *Métro 2 to Gare Lille Flandres changing to line 1 to République–Beaux Arts, then walk along bd de la Liberté & turn left onto rue Puebla leading to rue Faisan.*

Come early on a Sunday for salsa class (from 19.00) or from 21.30 on Thursday for a taste of rock-&-roll. Otherwise, 20- & 30-somethings hit the floor for house sounds at the weekend or ease back into real life with R&B from midnight on Sunday.

Palace Café MK 3 rue Deconynck, 59000 ✆ 03 20 57 04 16
🖰 www.snooker-palace-cafe.com ⊙ 14.00–dawn [234 C5]
🚇 *République–Beaux Arts* *e* Métro 2 to Gare Lille Flandres changing to line 1 to République–Beaux Arts, then take rue Gambetta to Solférino & bear right to the rue Deconynck.*
In Lille, this is the students' hangout of choice. Yvette is den mother to the youngsters who hang out here from mid-afternoon 'til breakfast time. The disco has its fun theme nights, some salsa, much rock, lots of retro & kitsch & plenty of party dates. But the karaoke sessions in front of 3 huge screens or the endless standing around in the pool room (around two dozen snooker & billiard tables) make this HQ for scores of new arrivals each freshers' season.

La Suite VL 32 pl Louise de Bettignies, 59800 ✆ 03 20 42 10 60
⊙ Mon–Sat 23.00–dawn [235 F2 & 236 D3] *e* Any Claire de Lune bus from Gare Lille Flandres to Lion d'Or.*
Laid-back yet lively, when this venue was known as the Scala, its varied music policy appealed to the discerning younger crowd without alienating veterans of the scene. Now proving popular with the over 35s, new name, newish look, same key location at the heart of the city.

La Tchouka MK 80 rue de Barthélémy Delespau, 59800 ✆ 03 20 14 37 50
⊙ Fri–Sat 23.00–06.00 [234 C8] 🚇 *Wazemmes* *e* Métro 2 to Gare Lille Flandres, changing to line 1 to Wazemmes. Rue des Postes leads to rue de Barthélémy Delespau.*
You may have known this venue in a past life as Le Tunnel. The name has changed, the décor has got camper (Barbie dolls, condoms & confetti) but the party atmosphere remains the same. House sounds, vodka cocktails & a mixed gay & straight crowd in their twenties & thirties.

Vice Versa See page 140.

GAY LISTINGS

Lille's gay and lesbian community is far less ghettoised than in other cities. Most gay bars stock a free map-guide listing other gay and gay-friendly establishments in town and across the region.

Coming Out VL 11 rue de Gand, 59000 ☎03 62 52 04 61 *e* comingout.
lille@gmail.com ⊙Mon–Thu 17.00–00.00, Fri & Sun 17.00–01.00, Sat 17.00–
02.00 [235 G1 & 236 E2] *e* Bus 3, 6 or 9 from Gare Lille Flandres to Lion d'Or.*
Newish gay bar has attracted a loyal crowd, since the demise of the
quarter's longer established venues. Thursday night brings a DJ to the
bar, every night promises new & imaginative cocktails scrawled on the
blackboard.

Le Pop Paradize VL 60 av du Peuple Belge, 59000 ☎03 28 38 14 27
e pop-paradize@hotmail.com ⊙23.00–08.00 [235 F1 & 236 D2] *e* Bus 3, 6 or
9 from Gare Lille Flandres to Lion d'Or. Cross pl Louise de Bettignies & turn left.*
Previously home to the Odali club, now pink champagne style but
manageable bar prices (glass of beer at under €5, coupe of fizz at under
€10) reign at this popular discotheque. Free admission weeknights, but
pay €8 after 02.00 at weekends, drinks included.

Le Privilège VL 2 rue Royale, 59000 ☎03 20 21 12 19 ⊙15.00–03.00
[234 E2 & 236 A4] *e* Bus 12 to de Gaulle, cross Grand' Place to rue
Esquermoise & onto rue Royale.*
A handful of small rooms for chilling out with friends. Welcoming bar
staff, & manageable prices for a late night last drink within an easy walk
of the Grand' Place. A small dance floor gets the boys on their feet when
the varying music policy veers towards the anthemic. Predominantly gay.

Le Miss Marple VL 18 rue du Gand, 59000 ☎03 20 39 85 92
⊙Mon–Thu 16.00–24.00, Fri 17.00–01.00, Sat 17.00–02.00, Sun 18.00–22.00
[235 G1 & 236 E2] *e* Bus 3, 6 or 9 from Gare Lille Flandres to Lion d'Or.*
No body in the library or any of the other original diversions of St Mary
Mead. Neither, despite the implication in the name, is this an exclusive
haunt of tweedy ladies of a certain vintage. Instead a friendly (mostly)
lesbian & (quite) gay crowd & their friends enjoy the evening in a
comfortable not-too-hip bar. The bar's website as listed in local
publications appeared at the time of writing to have been hijacked by the
official copyright holder to the Agatha Christie character, so no bar news
online, just updates on new editions of popular whodunnits!

Le Shower Bar MK 12 rue Inkerman, 59000 ☎09 51 36 54 47
⌐www.showerbar.fr ⊙Sun–Thu 17.00–00.00, Fri 17.00–01.00, Sat 17.00–
02.00 [234 D6] 🚇République–Beaux Arts *e* Métro 2 to Gare Lille Flandres,
changing to line 1 to République–Beaux Arts then cross square to rue Inkerman.*
Go-go boys are nothing new in Lille – Chippendale nights abound in
mainstream clubs, & the Bonheur des Dames offers little else, besides

smoked salmon starters & meat & two veg on a plate. Still, this bar-club has a unique slant on the now traditional flaunt & taunt moving wallpaper: a shower cubicle at the bar for showcasing the wet-look dancers. Advertised as gay & 'gay friendly'. Show times listed on the website

La Tchouka See page 138.

Vice Versa VL 3 rue de la Barre, 59800 ✆ 03 20 54 93 46 ⊘ Mon–Fri 11.00–03.00, Sat 14.00–03.00, Sun 16.00–03.00 [234 E2 & 236 A4] *e* Bus 3 or 6 from Gare Lille Flandres to Conservatoire. From rue Angleterre turn left into rue Royale & right into rue de la Barre.*
Popular with the gay crowd as much as with straight punters, this is cool without being cold. Friendly staff, happening sounds & a good mix of stylish punters make this a good halfway house for meeting up & debating 'where next?'

THE MORNING AFTER

If you are really lucky or truly blessed then, fortified with a sturdy breakfast at Paul (see page 115), you might cross Grand' Place in time for a second cup of coffee at the Nouveau Siècle concert hall. The occasional Sunday morning chamber concerts offer an ideal programme of music to face the world by. The only tough challenge for those who have made the most of their Saturday night is finding the correct doorway in a 360° building when they are pie-eyed! Otherwise, hope for a gospel brunch at the Gospel Café or check in advance with the tourist office for other concerts around town and budget your hangover accordingly.

Orchèstre Nationale GP Nouveau Siècle, 30 pl Mendès France, 59000 ✆ 03 20 12 82 40 ⊕ www.onlille.com [234 E3 & 236 A5] ₪ *Rihour e* Bus 12 from Gare Lille Flandres to de Gaulle.*

Gospel Café 78 rue Gambetta, 59000 ✆ 03 20 07 39 64 See page 75.

If you need more than a spiritual detox, then the Turkish bath spa at the Maison Folie Wazemmes (see page 190) could well prove your salvation.

TO XXXX OR NOT TO XXXX

Lille's appointment as European Capital of Culture for 2004 surely reflected the city's total commitment to the arts. A commitment that is found in the most surprising quarters. Some years ago, when a local theatre staged its acclaimed production of *Hamlet*, support came from radio stations, bookshops and even the porno sector. To tie in with the conventional production and a screening of Kenneth Branagh's movie version, a sex shop in the back streets near the station promoted its hardcore video adaptation that gave the lie to the perceived wisdom that there are few female parts in Shakespeare and featured a quantity of natural shocks that flesh is heir to and several consummations devoutly to be wish'd.

For current offerings, check out the sex shops on rue des Jardins **S**, rue de Roubaix **S** and rue Ponts de Comines **S** [235 G3–H3].

▼ *The Opera de Lille: grandeur at a price to suit every pocket.*

GOOD WALKS INTERRUPTED: THE GOLF COURSES OF LILLE

Justify those late nights on the lash, the pull, the dance-floor or the beer with a nice healthy walk in the name of sport on the morning after. As a distraction from the hedonistic lure of the city centre, the outskirts of Lille boast a fair selection of fairways, for 18 holes of wellbeing and fitness. And even if the weather is not at its best, you can still enjoy the virtual virtue of a round at an indoor golf course.

Golf de Lille Métropole Rond Point des Acacias, 59790 Ronchin ✆03 20 47 42 42 👆www.golfdelille.fr.
Public golf course with 9 & 18 holes.

Golf de Brigode 36 av du Golf, 59650, Villeneuve D'Ascq ✆03 20 91 17 86 👆www.golfbrigode.com.
18-hole course.

Lille Golf'IT - Simulateur Indoor 456 av de Lattre de Tassigny, 59350 Saint-André-lez-Lille ✆03 20 40 19 49 👆www.lille-golfit.com ⊘Mon & Wed–Fri 09.30–22.00, Tue 12.00–14.00 & 17.00–22.00, Sat 09.00–22.00, Sun (reservations only) 08.30–13.00 (last entry 30 mins before closing) €15 for 30 mins, €26 1 hour for up to 6 players.

The fickle weather of northern Europe need never interfere with playing a round: in 2009 Lille opened its virtual golf course, safely indoors. The Centre de Golf Indoor features 4 virtual golf course simulators, a 9-hole putting green & 5 practice areas.

LEAVE THE COUNTRY

When the bars in old Lille wind down, the punters break for the border. The designated driver earns the gratitude of as many who can squeeze into the car as possible, as the fun continues across national frontiers. The Belgian city of Tournai (within the Lille Métropole district) is home to the 747 club, Star Rock Café and Stephen's Café. Nearby Pecq is a party animal's natural habitat with the Axiome, Bush, H20 and Zoo clubs wooing the Lille bar crowd in the small hours.

The fun is not just for motorists. Just as Lille provides entertainment for the millions of people who live within an hour of the city, plenty of others exit aboard the high-speed trains which run in both directions. Once upon a time the weekend was an excuse for local teenagers to hop aboard the party trains to Amsterdam. These days, members of the speedily mobile social set use the fast trains to party in their capital city of choice. Brussels is the most popular cross-border break and most clubbing travellers aim for Fuse, which is within walking distance of the Eurostar terminal as well as countless other bars and clubs. Allow around 35 minutes by TGV, Thalys or Eurostar from Lille Europe. Tickets cost around €14. A shuttle bus on club nights at the Bush leaves Gare Lille Flandres for Pecq at midnight and returns at 05.30.

The last Eurostar to London is a favourite for clubbers heading for the Ministry of Sound or, these days, the Scala (a former cinema, just up the road from the Eurostar at St Pancras) and other cool clubs. Saturday sees *Lillois* day trippers heading to the West End for matinées of musicals and – since the British store closed its French outlets – shopping at Marks & Spencer.

France provides other lures. Paris is packed with clubbing, theatrical and gastronomic excuses for spending the evening away from home. In summer, the direct rail link from Lille to Disneyland is popular with the young, free and childless in search of the American dream during the late-night opening season. Since Marne La Vallée after midnight has little to offer, these superannuated *mousquetaires* tend to hit the nightclubs of Pigalle and the Bastille, then chill out at the after-parties in the capital before taking the return train home after lunch on Sunday (of course,

▼ *The afternoon before the evening to come – the essential daily and weekly listings magazines with updated information on events for every age, taste and budget.*

good-time people armed with the *Bradt Guide to Eurostar Cities* should have no problem in finding plenty to do, wherever they find themselves).

To be truly daring, take a TGV to Marseille, Montpellier, Lyon, Nice, Nantes or Bordeaux. But you might not get home in time for breakfast!

Brussels Le Fuse, 208 rue Blaes

Pecq L'Axiome, route de Tournai; La Bush, 180 chaussée de Tournai, Roquelmes; H20, 52 rue Albert 1er; The Zoo, 169 route de Tournai

Tournai 747, 7 pl de Lille; Star Rock Café, 5 pl Combez; Le Stephen's Café, 12 rue Duquesnoy

▼ *Trade meets a lullaby – the chiming* clocher *of the Chamber of Commerce.*

Shopping

There are four main shopping areas in Lille, and each one needs to be explored and exploited to the max. For sheer chic, absolute style and total magic, **Vieux Lille** has to be visited. Even if you have no money, it is worth pressing your nose against a window and inhaling the wealth. The second you step away from the squares of the town centre and take to the cobbles of the old town, the shops shriek class. And they drop names the way a starlet drips diamonds. Cartier, Chanel, Kenzo and co come into sharp focus within the first 50 metres. If you are an old hand at Lille shopping, you'll know that the antique dealers cluster around the roads just north of Grand' Place, but you might not have spotted the latest trends. Tableware is huge right now and Baccarat and Villeroy & Boch have their own *vitrines* in town (try rues de la Bourse and Esquermoise for that sort of thing). Rue Basse, long-time poor relation to the other streets looping around Notre Dame de la Treille, is being colonised by stylish new shopkeepers. Décor and furnishings are well worth the browsing, and the fun is in finding ever more antique dealers with tiny shops groaning under the weight of chandeliers and hiding Drouot bronze *animaliers*, intricate marquetry and lovely Lalique glassware. The place aux Oignons and its tributaries rue aux Vieux Murs and the variously spelled rue Peterinck (sometimes Peterynck) are a hive of good taste and creativity. Find wedding dresses made with antique fabrics, artists' studios, delicious specialist food shops and some amazing tableware in the galleries and *ateliers* tucked away behind the cathedral.

If proof were needed that Lille has the heart and passion of the Mediterranean, it may be found in a simple calendar. In recent years, and to raise money for charity, the male shopkeepers of Vieux Lille have presented themselves to their patrons (albeit via the camera lens) in all their rugged nakedness. No coy hiding behind flower arrangements à la WI: here the proud masculinity of rippling commerce is draped around historic buildings, noble statuary and the grandeur of the opera house. Making the headlines when they first posed shirtless for the millennium,

145

▲ *Vieux Lille is a treasure trove of little shops.*

by the 2003 edition the boys' flaunting had become more flagrant and they were dubbed by the press the *Ch'tippendales*!

From **Grand' Place**, the shopping possibilities fan out in all directions. Where Vieux Lille meets the squares are rows of extravagant footwear boutiques, whilst budget shoes, wedding gowns and books may be found along the rue Faidherbe stretching to the stations. The rue Nationale, with its banks and Printemps department store, has respected boutiques, whilst the pedestrian zone sprawling out towards the place République is shoppers' city. The rues Béthune, Neuve, Paris and Tanneurs, with all their spurs and back-doubles, boast all the major high-street names, and plenty more besides. Galeries Lafayette has been the big star arrival of recent seasons. Meanwhile H&M brings shoppers out into the sunlight whilst C&A provides the initial attraction to the new **Tanneurs** mall within the charmed quarter. This precinct [235 F4–5] and other galleries link an impressive area from rue Molinel to Grand' Place itself. As shopping centres go, the Tanneurs is a manageable and undaunting size, its big attraction for me the clusters of very comfy armchairs for much needed mid-spree recuperation. There is something remarkably decadent and exhibitionist about relaxing in soft furnishings in a public thoroughfare: a little like clothed nudism for the clinically coy. For those who can ignore the garish neon artwork/mission statement suspended above the chairs, it is practically a haven. Another rainy-day option featuring some of the same shops and more is the fabulous **Euralille** complex (see page 166), dominating the landscape between the two railway stations and a draw in its own right.

In a district best known for the Sunday market at Wazemmes, **rue Gambetta** is worth knowing about, if only for its Sunday opening hours, a boon for weekenders wanting to spend before travelling home. It is also the very cheapest side of town. Find mini-supermarkets for last-minute bottles of mineral water and hotel-room snacking. Kitschest of cheapo clothing from the Kilo Shop at number 25 and loads of bazaars selling everything under the sun. Les Aubanes is a Sunday morning favourite at number 298. Here you will find clothes, saucepans, household goods, toys and games from last year's mail-order catalogues: La Redoute uses this store to offload surplus stock, great for a budget Christmas list. There are literally hundreds of shops, boutiques, stores and stalls to discover in Lille. I have suggested a mere 60 or so that my friends and I like to visit. Follow your nose, your eyes, and trust in your budget and willpower!

True bargain hunters should take the tram or métro out to Roubaix, home of serious savings. The twin giants of factory-outlet shopping have long wooed visitors away from Lille, charmed by the prospects of designer labels at 30–70% off high-street prices. If you are planning to go to Roubaix, don't just visit the shops. As it's a cultural centre in its own right, make a day of it (see pages 197–203).

OPENING HOURS

Unless otherwise stated, shops usually open during the following hours:
Vieux Lille & the city centre ⊘ Mon 14.00–19.00, Tue–Sat 10.00–19.00, closed all day Sun. Smaller shops often close for lunch between 12.00 & 14.00.

Euralille ⊘ Mon–Sat 10.00–21.00, closed Sun. Carrefour opens 09.00–22.00; restaurants 10.00–24.00.

Les Tanneurs ⊘ Mon–Sat 08.30–19.45, closed Sun. Monoprix opens 08.30–20.30.

Rue Gambetta ⊘ Mon 14.00–19.00, Tue–Sat 10.00–19.00, Sun 09.00–13.00.

ACCESSORIES

Benjamin GP 45 rue de Béthune, 59000 ✆ 03 20 54 69 67 [235 E5]
🚇 Rihour *e** Métro 2 to Gare Lille Flandres then line 1 to Rihour. Rue de la Vieille
Comédie leads to rue de Béthune.

Hats, gloves, brollies & finishing touches for any outfit; Benjamin has
been accessorising Lille's best-dressed set since 1926.

La Droguerie See *Crafts*, page 155.

Sheriley 94 rue St André 59000 ✆ 03 20 14 00 37 *e** Bus 6 from Gare
Lille Flandres to Conservatoire.

Big name handbags & luggage at real discount prices. Worth the extra
couple of hundred metres of cobbles in Jimmy Choos to accessorise.

BOOKS

Le Bateau Livre GP 39 rue de la Clef, 59000 ✆ 03 20 78 16 30
☺ Tue–Sat 10.00–13.00 & 14.00–19.00, closed Sun & Mon [235 F3] *e** Av le
Corbusier & right into rue Faidherbe; walk behind the opera house to rue de la
Clef.

Even if your own French is rusty, your kids could become proficient if
you take them home a children's book in French. Most bookshops in
town have a juvenile section, but this *librairie* is strictly for the under
16s & is a temple to the joy of reading. Ask the staff what they would
recommend. Perhaps an original *Babar* story, or even a translation of
Harry Potter. Think how cool your kids would be considered if they
could drop the French for muggles & Hogwarts into the playground
conversation (*moldus* & *Poudlard*, by the way).

Books et Alia VL 10 rue de la Barre, 59000 ✆ 03 20 74 32 67
☺ Tue–Sat 10.00–13.00 & 14.00–19.00, closed Sun & Mon [234 D2] *e** Bus
3 or 6 from Gare Lille Flandres to Conservatoire. From rue Angleterre turn left
into rue Royale & right into rue de la Barre.

If, like me, you are prone to sudden lit-cravings in foreign lands, this is
an address to remember. I recall waking in Belgium at midnight with an
insatiable urge to read *Black Beauty*, & tramping through Paris at the
crack of dawn in search of *A Midsummer Night's Dream*. Find your
English language classics here, as well as the latest Helen Fielding or Ian
Rankin.

FNAC 20 rue St Nicolas, 59000
See *Home Entertainment/Music*, page 162.

Le Furet du Nord <u>GP</u> Pl Charles de Gaulle, 59000 ☎ 03 20 78 43 43 ⊘ Mon–Sat 09.30–19.30 [235 F4] 🚇 *Rihour* ***e***** Bus 12 from Gare Lille Flandres to de Gaulle. Or walk av le Corbusier & right into rue Faidherbe then left to Grand' Place.*

France's largest bookshop, an institution on Grand' Place (see page 184), has a respectable international section & good ground-floor travel department. A must for bibliophiles.

Godon <u>VL</u> 16 rue Masurel, 59000 ☎ 03 20 31 56 19 [235 F3] ***e***** Bus 12 from Gare Lille Flandres to de Gaulle. Walk along the débris St Etienne & bear left into rue Lepelletier until you reach rue Masurel.*

Antiquarian bookseller, for that first edition you always dreamt of owning.

Maxi-Livres <u>S</u> 54 rue Faidherbe ☎ 03 20 78 10 87 ⊘ Mon 14.00–19.00, Tue–Sat 10.00–19.00, Sun 10.00–13.00 [235 G4] 🚇 *Gare Lille Flandres* ***e***** Av le Corbusier & right into rue Faidherbe then left into rue des Ponts de Comines & right into rue de Paris.*

Discount book chain selling literary classics for under €2 & recipe books at silly prices. Other branches at 57 rue de Bethune & 246 rue Gambetta.

Relay The nationwide station news & book chain. Bestsellers & local maps.

Vieille Bourse <u>GP</u> ⊘ Tue–Sun aft [235 F4]

Antiquarian & secondhand book market (see page 183).

VO <u>S</u> 36 rue de Tournai, 59800 ☎ 03 20 14 33 96 ⊘ Tue–Sat 12.00–19.00, closed Sun & Mon [235 H5] 🚇 *Gare Lille Flandres* ***e***** Métro or walk to Gare Lille Flandres then turn left along rue de Tournai.*

The international bookshop of Lille for English, German & Italian books, untranslated, just as the author imagined 'em. Browsers welcome; you can even enjoy coffee or juice in store.

THE FAUBOURG OF FAB

Take the métro down to the end of Line One and step off **CHR B Calmette**, then follow your innate sense of style to the rue du Faubourg des Postes, aka the Faubourg of Fab. This new **Faubourg des Modes** is the new fashion district, as launched in 2007 by designer Agnès b. A dozen workshops along the street, set to grow to at least 18 by the end of 2009, are home to a new generation of designers selling direct from their studios to the public, cutting out middle-men, catwalks and fashion shows.

Shopping Books

CLOTHES

Fashion

Constance de Gonidec VL 1 pl Oignons 59800 ✆ 03 20 06 44 45
☺ by appointment only [235 F2] *e* Bus 3, 6 or 9 from Gare Lille Flandres to Lion d'Or. From rue de la Monnaie turn left into rue Peterinck & bear left again into the place.*

The rues Faidherbe & Molinel may have plenty of wedding dresses for the freshly affianced, but if you intend to swoon on the threshold of a whole new life, & be caught by anything of Darcy grade or above, then you really need to blush prettily in one of Constance de Gonidec's simply exquisite made-to-measure gowns. Each one a work of art & a joy to behold. Not a shop, but a workshop where the breathtaking creations are conjured to order & inspiration. Simply stunning outfits.

Cool Cat GP 56 rue de Béthune, 59800 ✆ 03 20 38 33 83
⌐ www.coolcat.nl [234 E5] 🚊 *Rihour e* Métro 2 to Gare Lille Flandres then Line 1 to Rihour & walk down rue de la Vieille Comédie to rue de Béthune.*
The Dutch line in don't-care-casual for students & clubbers comes to Lille with enough loud music pumped out through a good sound system, & plasma screens to keep the right crowd browsing & the wrong crowd at bay. Whatever-wear for a generation.

La Griffe VL 27 rue de la Barre, 59000 ✆ 03 20 57 47 20 ☺ Mon 14.30–19.00, Tue & Thu–Sat 13.00–19.00, closed Wed [234 D2] *e* Bus 3 or 6 from Gare Lille Flandres to Conservatoire. From rue Angleterre turn left into rue Royale & right into rue de la Barre.*
Secondhand clothes & shoes from the continent's leading fashion houses. Everything is in good condition & costs about a third of the original retail price.

Loding VL 13 rue Lepelletier, 59000 ✆ 03 20 40 08 47 [235 F3]
🚊 *Rihour e* Bus 12 from Gare Lille Flandres to Théâtre. Walk through the Alcide arch from Grand' Place towards rue Lepelletier.*
Happy Fathers' Day, or just welcome to your new moneyed lifestyle. Classy menswear – shoes, shirts, cufflinks & cashmere sweaters, plus classic gentlemen's club colours & décor. Reeks of tradition, but dates back to the late 1990s.

Michel Ruc VL 23–25 rue des Chats Bossus, 59000 ✆ 03 20 15 96 16
☺ Mon 14.00–19.00, Tue–Sat 10.30–19.00 [235 F2] *e* Bus 3, 6 or 9 from Gare Lille Flandres to Lion d'Or.*

The shopfront may be centuries old but the window features the latest looks from Milan & Paris. Gaultier for the girls, Boss for the boys & Armani for everyone.

Miss Sixty GP 12 rue de la Clef, 59000 ✆ 03 20 21 04 66 [235 F3]
🚋 *Gare Lille Flandres* ***e*** Bus 12 from Gare Lille Flandres to Théâtre & walk along bd Carnot.*
Even dungarees are cute here (the choice was between baby doll nightie style & a floppy-belted hot pant version in the 2009 collection). The popular name in mail order style has its Lille shopfront at the edge of the old town by the reality of bd Carnot.

Nathalie Chaize VL 43 rue Basse ✆ 03 20 51 27 17
🖰 www.nathaliechaize.com [234 E3] ***e*** Bus 12 from Gare Lille Flandres to de Gaulle. Walk up rue Esquermoise & turn right into rue Basse.*
One-time architect, all-time fashion designer, darling of the Paris art set, hands-on creator of posh frocks & luscious lingerie, Chaize is one of the characters of the French fashion scene. Her annual collections, presented on Paris catwalks by film stars, are on sale in her new boutique in the old town.

Rouge GP 15 rue de la Clef, 59000 ✆ 03 20 74 19 20 ⊙ Mon 14.00–19.00, Tue–Sat 10.30–12.30 & 14.00–19.00 [235 F3] ***e*** Av le Corbusier & right into rue Faidherbe; walk behind the opera house to rue de la Clef.*
Cool looks just outside Vieux Lille. This is where the younger designers showcase their outfits to a sympathetic, youthful market. Well-known names such as Comme des Garçons keep the place ticking over, whilst unknown labels get an early airing. Kit yourself out in Aem'Kei, Full Circle & Dirk Bikkembergs.

La 7ème Compagnie GP 11 rue Jean Sans Peur, 59000 ✆ 03 20 54 39 63 ⊙ Tue–Sat 10.00–12.00 & 14.00–19.00 [234 D5] 🚋 *République–Beaux Arts* ***e*** Métro 2 to Gare Lille Flandres, changing to line 1 to République–Beaux Arts. Walk north on bd de la Liberté to junction with rue Jean Sans Peur.*
Epaulettes, camouflage & good strong fabric. Outfits with a military look from practical combats & standard army-surplus clubwear to costume items such as British Guardsman's uniforms.

Tati S 12–14 rue Faidherbe, 59000 ✆ 03 20 74 00 00 🖰 www.tati.fr [235 G4]
See *Bargains*, page 152.

Bargains

See also *Factory outlets*, page 153.

Adéquat S 2 rue des Ponts de Comines, 59000 ☎ 03 20 78 14 60
☺ Mon 13.00–19.00, Tue–Wed 10.00–19.00, Thu–Sat 10.00–19.30 [235 G4]
🚉 *Gare Lille Flandres e* Av le Corbusier & right into rue Faidherbe.*
The street corners of the rue Faidherbe are lined with racks of shiny new shoes at discount prices. This store has a good range from trainers, winter boots & walkwear to classy dress shoes.

La Griffe VL 27 rue de la Barre, 59000 ☎ 03 20 57 47 20 [234 D2]
See *Fashion*, page 150.

Inside Out VL 9 rue Royale, 59000 ☎ 06 37 56 50 49 [234 E2] *e* Bus 3 or 6 from Gare Lille Flandres to Conservatoire. From rue Angleterre turn left into rue Royale*
Pedigree retreads: the stylish come here for retro, others for a bargain. Call it what you will (& the French use the word *friperie*) this has been a popular place for secondhand clothes for around a decade. Some outfits have been round the block enough times to be treated as old friends by the regular bargain hunters.

Tati S 12–14 rue Faidherbe, 59000 ☎ 03 20 74 00 00 ⌂ www.tati.fr
☺ Mon–Sat 09.30–19.00 [235 G4] 🚉 *Gare Lille Flandres e* Av le Corbusier & right into rue Faidherbe.*
Mikhail Gorbachev was once late for a meeting of world leaders because his wife, the radiant Raisa, she of the cover-girl style, had fallen for the charms of the main Parisian branch of Tati. This institution is France's bargain basement &, even in well-mannered Lille, the niceties have been known to be abandoned in the scrum for a pair of trousers for the price of a coffee, a skirt for the cost of a sandwich or an entire wedding trousseau for less than €75. Lille has a row of branches of the store at the top of the rue Faidherbe, selling everything from jewellery to beachwear, dinner jackets to posing pouches, terracotta candlesticks to pillowcases. Since Kylie Minogue sported an outfit inspired by Tati's trademark pink gingham, & Hockney iconised the pattern, the well-to-do have been known to venture through the doors even without their Hermès headscarves & dark glasses. So what if 90% of the stuff is ghastly, & the cheapest wedding dress so polyester rich it could raise enough static electricity to discipline the naughtiest pageboy at a single touch? Who cares? Cotton T-shirts are cotton T-shirts & the kids will

grow out of the €5 jeans long before the seams surrender. Anyone who has found angora & cashmere hidden behind the naffest velour cardies is hooked for life. I've found €3 corduroy slippers a godsend when staying in a cheap hotel, & on the one occasion that I discovered dubious signs of life in the bedsheets at a student hall of residence in Lille, I invested in a full set of linen, pillows & duvet in order to bed down on the floor – & paid Tati just €20 for the privilege. If you have over-shopped elsewhere, find extra luggage at knockdown prices; if you've left the camera at home, buy a disposable one here for next to nothing; & if you've decided to consummate the love of your life, pick up a pack of Tati's gingham-wrapped condoms (just ignore the disconcerting name, 'Soft Life').

Factory outlets

MacArthur Glen Mail de Lannoy, 59100 Roubaix ☏ 03 28 33 36 00
🖱 www.mcarthurglen.fr ☺ Mon–Sat 10.00–19.00 🚇 Eurotéléport *e** Métro 2 to Eurotéléport, or tram to Roubaix.
Confirming Roubaix's status as the home of bargain designer shopping, this open-air mall above the main métro station is an avenue of 52 outlet stores. Mostly French high-street names, the international firms offering permanent discounts of 30–70% on regular prices include Adidas, Reebok, Blanc Bleu, Cacherel & Carven. Even Disney's upmarket label Donaldson may be found here, featuring hacking jackets & tweeds with the most discreet Mickey Mouse buttons.

L'Usine 228 av Alfred Motte, 59100 Roubaix ☏ 03 20 83 16 20
🖱 www.lusine.fr ☺ Mon–Sat 10.00–19.00 *e** Métro 2 to Epeule Montesquieu then bus 25 to Les Hauts Champs.
Not as neatly laid out as MacArthur Glen, but this is where it all began 20 years ago, & where 4 million French & Belgian shoppers each year choose to eke out their euros. 3 storeys of a former factory, stuffed with linens, clothes & shoes at ludicrously low prices. Since Roubaix is the capital of France's mail-order industry, with Les Trois Suisses & La Redoute both based here, when new catalogues are published, old stock has to be sold off as swiftly as possible. End-of-range goods, factory seconds, everything from footwear to table linen at prices to raise the most plucked eyebrow. A children's playground, choice of restaurants & even a hairdressing salon on the premises for those planning to make a day of it, walking from room to room to pick up Etam, Lacoste, Nike, Dior, YSL, Wrangler & Levi products at well under half the shop price.

Shopping Clothes

XXL

Capel GP 88 rue Nationale, 59000 ℃ 03 20 57 48 17 [234 E4] 🚊 *Rihour*
e* Bus 12 from Gare Lille Flandres to rue Nationale.
Bienvenue chez Monsieur XXL. Suits & casual menswear for the taller
or wider punter.

Etre Ronde en Couleurs GP Passage des Tanneurs, 80 rue de Paris,
59800 ℃ 03 20 54 39 44 [235 F4] 🚊 *Rihour e* Métro 2 to Gare Lille Flandres
then line 1 to Rihour. Rue de la Vieille Comédie to rue du Sec Arembault, & the
new entrance to the Tanneurs arcade.*
Big girls don't cry, they dress up in pretty things, from frilly undies to
wafty, summery picnicky outfits.

Je m'Aime en Ronde MK 318–320 rue Gambetta, 59000 ℃ 03 20
54 50 82 ⤴ www.jemaimeenronde.com [234 B6] 🚊 *Gambetta e* Métro 2 to
Gare Lille Flandres, then line 1 to Gambetta, walk along rue de Flandre, turn left
into rue de la Paix d'Utrecht & into rue Gambetta.*
French couture for all. Stylish eye-catching outfits from size 16 to 30 &
beyond. Just ask Hélène Coquerelle & her team of *vendeuses* & you will
positively strut out of the store looking a million euros & turning heads
all the way to the Eurostar home. Flaunt it, flirt in it & carry it off. Don't
forget that the Gambetta shop is open Sunday morning too.

COSMETICS & PERFUME

Molinard VL 2 pl du Lion d'Or, 59000 ℃ 03 20 39 57 69 [235 F2]
🚊 *Rihour e* Bus 3, 6 or 9 from Gare Lille Flandres to Lion d'Or.*
Celebrated for classic bottles designed by Baccarat & Lalique, the oldest
family-run perfumiers in France has opened their first boutique in the
north of France. The family business is still based in the town of Grasse
in Provence.

Saga GP 3 rue Neuve, 59000 ℃ 03 20 39 25 60 ⤴ www.sagacosmetic.com
[235 F4] 🚊 *Rihour e* Métro 2 to Gare Lille Flandres then line 1 to Rihour, walk
to the corner of Grand' Place then right to rue Neuve.*
Pharmacies & department stores have a traditional grip on the cosmetics
market in France. Even baby soap bought at the chemist may belie the
no-more-tears promise when it comes to the price tag. Supermarkets
have nudged prices down at the popular end of the scale, but for the big
names in make-up, the province of the hyper-plucked eyebrowed
cosmetic technician in a white lab coat has remained pretty impregnable
– at least until 1999 when the first cut-price retailer elbowed its way into

the high street. It has been a slow revolution: Saga has but 13 stores nationwide, & the latest has now opened its doors in Lille. Not all the great *marques* may be found here but Revlon, Schwartzkopf & Balmain are on the shelves, with low price tags.

Sephora GP 7 pl du Général de Gaulle, 59000 ☎03 28 36 11 90
🖰 www.sephora.fr [235 F6] 🚇 *Rihour e* Métro 2 to Gare Lille Flandres then line 1 to Rihour, the shop is on the corner of Grand' Place.*
National cosmetic chain retailer, now with a branch on Grand' Place. The shop is open until 19.00. A second shop, in the Euralille complex (see page 166) remains open an hour later.

CRAFTS

Atelier de la Sorcière Verte See page 160.

La Droguerie VL 50 rue Basse, 59000 ☎03 20 55 36 80 [234 E3]
e* Bus 12 from Gare Lille Flandres to de Gaulle. Walk up rue Esquermoise & turn right into rue Basse.
If you're looking to accessorise or to tart up an old frock found in a flea market then come here, where fabrics, silks, wools & jars of buttons & beads are stacked along the walls in a Bohemian dressmaker's delight.

Loisirs et Créations S Euralille, 59777 ☎03 20 51 39 01 ⊘Mon–Sat 10.00–20.00 [235 H4] 🚇 *Lille Europe e* Opposite the station.*
Cross-stitch, watercolours or tie-dyeing: whatever your art or your craft, this spacious store has everything for the creative hobbyist. Visit the studio for workshops in new & different techniques.

FLORISTS

D'Autres Fleurs S 92 rue de Paris, 59000 ☎03 20 57 45 40
⊘10.00–13.00 & 14.30–19.00, closed Mon [235 F4] 🚇 *Gare Lille Flandres e* Av le Corbusier to Gare Lille Flandres, then left into rue de Priez; at the foot of rue Faidherbe walk around the church to rue de Paris.*
Martine Desmettre's lovely little florist shop has more than a hint of the Edwardian about it, with fin du siècle tea services & cherubim amongst the flowers.

Eté Country VL 27 rue des Vieux Murs, 59800 ☎03 20 78 06 53 [235 F2] *e* Bus 3, 6 or 9 from Gare Lille Flandres to Lion d'Or. From rue de la Monnaie turn left into rue Peterinck & pl aux Oignons.*

2 quaint little shops on either side of the cobbled street are the most unlikely garden centre you will ever discover. There is even a postage-stamp back-garden oasis of greenery. Discover enchantment from stone statuary to cast-iron sundials.

Jardins de Julie & Lea GP 4 rue des Molfonds, 59000 ℡ 03 20 06 59 60 [235 F4] 🚇 Rihour *e** Line 2 to Gare Lille Flandres then line 1 to Rihour. From rue de la Vieille Comedie turn right into rue des Fosses & left into rue des Malfonds.
See page 117 for more on this sweet florist/bar-café. Sit, sip & people-watch amongst the flowers.

Pomme Cannelle GP 5 rue du Curé St Etienne, 59000 ℡ 03 20 06 83 06 ⊙ Mon 14.00–19.00, Tue–Sat 10.00–19.00, closed Sun [235 F3] 🚇 Rihour *e** Bus 12 from Gare Lille Flandres to de Gaulle. Walk under the Alcide arch then turn left.
I love this tiny little florist shop. Dinky & dainty terracotta pots of perfect miniature rose bushes from €4.50, or unusual & exotic plants manicured to perfection.

Ultra Violet GP 19 rue Lepelletier, 59000 ℡ 03 20 06 00 15 [235 F3] 🚇 Rihour *e** Bus 12 from Gare Lille Flandres to Théâtre. Walk through the Alcide arch from Grand' Place towards rue Lepelletier.
This place looks rather like a cave thanks to the tangle of roots & branches along the ceiling. Pick up imaginative table arrangements mixing fruits, plants, mosses & twigs.

FOOD & WINE

The daily bread

Chez L'Ami des Arts Maison Brésard VL 44 rue Négrier, 59000 ℡ 03 28 36 90 58 ⊙ Mon–Sat 07.00–13.30 & 15.00–19.45, Sun 07.00–13.30 & 17.00–19.45 [234 E1] *e** Bus 6 from Gare Lille Flandres to Conservatoire, walk along rue Negrier.
A modest little chain of bread shops, for nice buttery croissants & good crusty loaves. Other branches at 28 rue des Postes & 38 pl Cormantaigne.

Paul See page 115.
Lille's original bakers & sandwich bar. Branches across the city & as far afield as St Pancras Station & the Mediterranean. Now but 3 baguettes & a crunchy wholegrain loaf away from world domination.

Silence Ca Cuit MK 26 Rue Manuel, 59000 ☎ 03 20 51 53 87
⌂ www.silencecacuit.com ☉ Mon–Sat 07.30–19.30 [234 C7] 🚊 *Gambetta*
e* Métro 2 to Gare Lille Flandres, then line 1 to Gambetta. Walk the length of rue Manuel.

At last a worthy alternative to the ubiquitous Paul. Just when it seemed that all the last quirky corner shop bakeries were inevitably branded with the logo that lights your route before you even step on the Eurostar in London, a new kid on the block begins his own tradition. Well, new to this block perhaps, but no stranger to Lille. Marc Lelieur runs half a dozen well-known eateries in the heart of town, from the Chicorée & La Paix to Le Square & La Baignoire & is also the driving force behind the Hotel Kanai. This block is way across town: just around the corner & then another turn or two from Sébastopol is the imposing bakery with the air of a venue. Flags around the building declare *maman's* eternal answer to her hungry children, with the signature statement *Pain by Marc* scrawled across the doorway. Samples of bread laid out for the tasting, viennoiseries & delicious pastries displayed as at an art gallery to whet the appetite. Find service with a brisk, efficient smile at the counter in front of the grand working kitchen. Hygiene rules, & cash transactions (coins at any rate) are handled by a dinky little change machine, whilst the vendeuse slips your purchase into a neat paper bag. Delicious chocky *crème pâtissière*, & to wash down your *pain au raisins*, stick with the produce of the vine. Some cracking Bordeaux & Champagnes are sold at the bread counter – from a St Estèphe for €7.50 to some fizz at under €25.

The food

See also *Supermarkets*, page 165.

L'Abbaye des Saveurs VL 13 rue des Vieux Murs, 59000 ☎ 03 28 07 70 06 ⌂ www.abbayedessaveurs.com ☉ Tue–Sat 10.00–19.30, Sun 10.00–14.30 [235 F2] *e* Bus 3, 6 or 9 from Gare Lille Flandres to Lion d'Or. From rue de la Monnaie turn left into rue Peterinck.*

For true beer lovers this is the place to find artisanal beers from across Flanders, *bières sans frontières*, with superb ranges of the best of Belgium to complement around two dozen local breweries represented on the shelves, available by the bottle or the barrel. Franck & Anthony, the faces of L'Abbaye des Saveurs, are both passionate about local produce & this is reflected in the range of meats, sweets & local delicacies from jars of *potjevlesch* to rounds of cheeses. Most items are supplied directly from the farmers, & shop staff will advise on which producers open their farms to visitors, should you fancy a day in the country. If you are planning a party in Lille, then rent a beer pump from the shop.

L'Arrière Pays VL 47 rue Basse, 59000 ☎03 20 13 80 07 [234 E3]
e* Bus 12 from Gare Lille Flandres to de Gaulle. Walk up rue Esquermoise & turn right into rue Basse.
A grocery shop selling incredible & wonderful preserves, oils & pâtés in little bottles & jars. The place doubles as a restaurant salon de thé (see page 81).

Benoit VL 77 rue de la Monnaie, 59000 ☎03 20 31 69 03 ⊙Tue–Sat 09.30–19.30, Sun 09.00–13.30 [235 F2] *e* Bus 3, 6 or 9 from Gare Lille Flandres to Lion d'Or.*
Belgium's Neuhaus & Leonidas have high-profile counters in Lille, but forsake them in favour of a taste of the domestic product. The famous chocolate shop of Lille has over 50 varieties of chocolates & truffles to tempt the sweet tooth.

Bottega VL 8b rue Peterinck, 59800 ☎03 20 21 16 85 �🖰 www.la-bottega.com [235 F2] *e* Bus 3, 6 or 9 from Gare Lille Flandres to Lion d'Or. From rue de la Monnaie turn left into rue Peterinck.*
Everything Italian, from espresso machines to beautifully turned Venetian carnival masks, pasta & pesto, coffee & Tuscan olive oil – a celebration of *la dolce vita* at the table in the heart of Vieux Lille. And if the Latin smile behind the counter looks familiar, but you cannot quite place it, perhaps you do not recognise its wearer with his clothes on. Gilberto Annunzio regularly displays his Latin credentials on the celebrated Vieux Lille calendar (see page 145).

Chocolat Passion GP 67 rue Nationale, 59800 ☎03 20 54 74 42 �🖰 www.chocolatpassion.com [234 E4] 🚊 Rihour *e* Métro 2 to Gare Lille Flandres then line 1 to Rihour, then walk up rue Roisin & turn left on to rue Nationale.*
Good for last-minute pressies, if a little souvenirish & not quite kitsch. Here amongst the serious chocolate boxes are 'novelty' items such as edible mobile phones & supersized euro coins. You can buy a gift for €5 though.

La Comtesse du Barry GP 21 rue Esquermoise, 59000 ☎03 20 54 00 43 ⊙Mon 14.00–19.30, Tue–Sat 09.30–19.30 [234 E3] 🚊 Rihour *e* Bus 12 from Gare Lille Flandres to de Gaulle.*
Pâtés in jars & tins of preserved delicacies from across France, but mostly from the farmyards of the southwest. *Foie gras*, smoked salmon,

prepared terrines & cold platters for lunch, or gift-wrapped as savoury presents.

Ferme en Ville GP 15 pl Mendès France, 59000 ☎ 03 20 55 42 53 **e** ferme.brabant@wanadoo.fr [234 E3] 🚇 *Rihour* **e*** *Métro 2 to Gare Lille Flandres then line 1 to Rihour. Rue Roisin into rue de Pas & pl Mendès France.*
Farm animals in the centre of the city do not stop the traffic. The *Lillois* are used to Grand' Place being transformed into agricultural plots, just as frequently as it becomes a ballroom or a Christmas grotto. But the static cow that stands outside 15 pl Mendès France is something of a permanent fixture, the little local landmark that tells passers-by that the city has a genuine farm shop in its midst. If you miss market day, then rely on Aurélie & Gladys to sell you the freshest leeks & endives, fine strings of ripe garlic, jars of farmyard pâtés & all other creamery, charcuterie, market garden or farmhouse table produce to perk up your picnic.

A l'Huîtrière VL [236 C4 (80)] See page 87.

Pâtisserie Meert GP [236 B5 (65)] See page 118.
When closed on a Monday, find the famous waffles at **Printemps** department store (see 165).

Philippe Olivier GP 3 rue du Curé St Etienne, 59000 ☎ 03 20 74 96 99 ⊘ Mon 14.30–19.30, Tue 10.00–12.30 & 14.30–19.30, Wed–Sat 10.00–19.30 [235 F3] 🚇 *Rihour* **e*** *Bus 12 from Gare Lille Flandres to de Gaulle. Walk under the Alcide arch then turn left.*
Maître Olivier is one of the country's grand masters of cheese. His main store in Boulogne supplies the Elysée Palace, the Vatican & the White House. Buy a Camembert marinated in Calvados or try a local Flanders speciality such as a Mont des Cats.

The wines & beers
L'Abbaye des Saveurs See page 157.

La Cave du Parvis St Maurice S 98 rue de Paris, 59800 ☎ 03 20 13 76 68 **e** caveduparvis@aol.com [235 F4] 🚇 *Gare Lille Flandres* **e*** *Av le Corbusier to Gare Lille Flandres, then left into rue de Priez; at the foot of rue Faidherbe, walk around the church to rue de Paris.*
My new favourite wine address stands in the shade of the St Maurice church on rue de Paris. Come here for wines, wine accessories & lots of wine wisdom. This knowledge & insight is dispensed to even the most casual of browsers, but by the figurative magnum to those who book for the special *soirée découverte et dégustation* tutored tasting sessions. You

may buy a place at one of these evenings as a gift. Don't be misled by the modest shopfront. As the sign in the window explains 'our window may be small, but our cellar is huge' & there are around 17,000 labels to be discovered here.

Au Gré du Vin See page 112.

Les Vins Gourmands <u>VL</u> 33 rue Esquermoise, 59000 ☎ 03 20 30 12 20 [234 E3] 🚇 *Rihour* ***e*** Bus 12 from Gare Lille Flandres to de Gaulle.*
Since Annie-Paule gave up her fabulous boutique shop around the corner & across the way, I've been seeking another shop where one's every purchase is a lesson. This will do nicely. Well-read & open-minded staff know not only their French *cépages* & vintages, but have a good knowledge of the wider world. So when talking of the picnic or dinner party you have in mind, do not be surprised to be offered a New Zealand white or South African red as well as a Burgundy & a Côtes du Rhône.

Silence Ca Cuit See page 156.
Bordeaux & bubbly at trendy new bread shop.

GIFTS

Artisanat Monastique <u>VL</u> Parvis Notre Dame de la Treille, pl Gilleson, 59000 ☎ 03 20 55 22 19 ⊙ Mon 14.00–18.30, Tue–Sat 09.30–18.30 [235 F2] ***e*** Bus 3, 6 or 9 from Gare Lille Flandres to Lion d'Or then walk from rue de la Monnaie to the cathedral.*
Religious & liturgical gifts, from monastic-themed accessories to devotional items.

Artisans du Monde <u>VL</u> 6 rue de Palais Rihour, 59000 ☎ 03 20 06 03 12 ⊙ Tue–Sat 11.00–19.00 [234 E4] 🚇 *Rihour* ***e*** Métro 2 to Gare Lille Flandres, then line 1 to Rihour. Walk beyond the tourist office towards rue de l'Hôpital Militaire.*
Assuage the guilt of a weekend's heavy consumerism by spending something at this shop built on the fair-trade principle. Whatever ethnic trinket or artefact catches your eye here, rest assured that your money goes directly to developing world community projects. Note the new address.

Atelier de la Sorcière Verte <u>GP</u> 19 rue de la Clef, 59800 ☎ 03 20 12 07 06 🖰 www.latelierdelasorciereverte.fr [235 F3] ***e*** Av le Corbusier & right into rue Faidherbe; walk behind the opera house to rue de la Clef.*
The good green witch sells lovely stationery, elegant nibs & inks for calligraphers, smart & elegant diaries & calligraphy papers.

Atelier Un Vrai Semblance VL 3 rue Peterinck, 59800 ℡03 20 15 08 99 **e** contact@abcome.net ⊙Tue–Sat 09.30–12.00 & 14.00–18.30 [235 F2] **e*** Bus 3, 6 or 9 from Gare Lille Flandres to Lion d'Or. From rue de la Monnaie turn left into rue Peterinck.

The price of Rembrandts these days is really quite shocking. You will hardly see any change out of £20million should you pop out for a Van Gogh landscape. No wonder people in the know pop into Guillaume Moisson's studio to see if he can run them up a quick Rubens or come up with a nice Cézanne for the spare bedroom. Moisson is a talented artist in his own right – well worth asking if you can see his private gallery – but he earns his living making copies of great artworks from the world's leading galleries. After a successful career recreating greatness as a scenic artist for the theatre, he set up this little studio, between the rue de la Monnaie & the cathedral, where he produces copies of Caravaggios on demand for something getting close to four figures & reproduction Monets from perhaps a little less. Commissions usually take 3 months.

Jadis Presse GP 25 rue de Paris, 59000 ℡03 20 13 04 06 [235 F4] 🚇 Rihour **e*** Bus 12 from Gare Lille Flandres to Théâtre & walk down rue de Paris. The sign above the doorway of this narrowest of shops says it all really: *Le Journal de Votre Anniversaire*. Pick up original vintage newspapers & magazines recalling momentous events or commemorating your own special day. A *Paris Match* or *Le Figaro* published on your wedding day, perhaps.

Nature et Découvertes S Euralille, 59777 ℡03 20 78 01 00 ⌃🖰 www.natureetdecouvertes.com [235 H4] 🚇 Lille Europe **e*** Cross parvis Mitterand to Centre Euralille.

A fabulous calming oasis in any shopping centre (there is another branch in the Galerie Grand' Place), here ecologically responsible shoppers can browse in a state of relaxation occasioned by the headphones playing sounds of nature & rainwater & cups of freshly infused herbal tea. Wooden toys, ramblers' accessories, books, gifts & a range of eclectic wonders. I love the store's suggestion of the perfect present to mark the birth of a child: an acorn & planter so that a tree grows with the new life.

HOME

Camille Stopin VL 14 pl Louise de Bettignies, 59800 ℡03 20 55 39 02 [235 G2] ⌃🖰 www.stopin.fr ⊙Mon–Fri 09.00–12.00 & 14.30–19.00, however, appointments are preferred **e*** Bus 3, 6 or 9 from Gare Lille Flandres to Lion d'Or.

Shopping Home

For something rather special, this family of cabinet makers has served Lille's stylish householders since 1860. Father & son craftsmen work on restoring & creating some choice pieces of furniture. The family have been called upon by France's museums to restore some of the nation's premier pieces of furniture. Should you find a battered *escritoire* or armoire at the Braderie or the fleamarket, this is the place to take your antiques. If you've bought the car, push the boat out.

Christofle VL 48 rue Grande Chaussée, 59000 ☎03 20 51 46 20 [235 F3] 🚊 *Rihour e* Bus 12 from Gare Lille Flandres to Théâtre, cross the pl du Théâtre & turn right up the rue de la Grande Chaussée.*
Buying a cake slice, or the full canteen of cutlery? Christofle's main Paris outlet has been selling flatware & table appointments to the well-to-do for nearly 200 years. If it was good enough for King Louis Philippe ...

La Puce à l'Oreille VL 10 pl Louise de Bettignies, 59000 ☎03 28 36 28 28 🖰 www.la-puce.com [235 G2] *e* Bus 3, 6 or 9 from Gare Lille Flandres to Lion d'Or.*
A mix of the genuine antique, reconditioned, worn-out & repro at this quaint interiors specialist. Sturdy & stylish wooden furniture, imaginative décor ideas & some luxurious linens within this highly browsable old building.

HOME ENTERTAINMENT/MUSIC

Carrefour See page 165.
The Carrefour hypermarket at Euralille has a good-sized department selling electrical goods, CDs & computer accessories. Their own-brand products often come with a 2-year warranty.

FNAC GP 20 rue St Nicolas, 59000 ☎0825 020 020 (premium rate) ⊙Mon–Sat 10.00–19.30 [235 F4] 🚊 *Rihour e* Bus 12 from Gare Lille Flandres to de Gaulle & walk through La Voix du Nord building, or av le Corbusier, right into rue Faidherbe, left on rue des Ponts de Comines, right to rue de Paris, & left to rue St Nicolas.*
Hi-fi & photographic equipment & accessories, books, discs & videos at the nation's favourite chain store & box office. A self-service gift-wrapping desk is located near the cashiers. Another entrance to the store is on Grand' Place itself.

O'CD GP 21 rue des Tanneurs, 59800 ☎03 20 40 04 62 🖰 www.ocd.net ⊙Mon 14.00–19.30, Tue–Sat 10.00–19.30, Sun 15.00–19.30 [235 F5]

🚇 Rihour *e** Métro 2 to Gare Lille Flandres then line 1 to Rihour. Rue de la Vieille Comédie leads to rue des Tanneurs.

Second-hand CDs & DVDs bought & sold daily. Priced at €2–13, & guaranteed to be good quality, all discs may be heard before you buy, thanks to rows of headphones around the shop.

JEWELLERY

Le Page GP 6–10 rue de la Bourse, 59000 ☎ 03 20 12 04 04 ⊘ Mon 14.00–19.00, Tue–Fri 10.00–12.30 & 14.00–19.00, Sat 10.00–19.00, closed Mon in Jul & Aug [235 F3] 🚇 *Rihour e** Bus 12 from Gare Lille Flandres to Théâtre. Walk past the opera house to rue de la Bourse.

A jewel-box of a shop, the ornate façade is always one of the treats of the town when the Christmas lights are switched on. Upstaging even the building are the watches & trinkets from Gucci, Cartier, Chanel & Rolex.

MARKETS

Braderie See page 12.

Marché de l'Art VL Rue Péterinck & pl aux Oignons ⊘ all day Sun [235 F2] *e** Bus 3, 6 or 9 from Gare Lille Flandres to Lion d'Or then follow rue de la Monnaie to the marketplace.

A civilised alternative to the rummage & scrummage of earthier quarters. You may find a little gem amongst the artworks on display, or you might not, but the fun is in the atmosphere as local artists both professional & amateur display their wares on the pavement. A nice weekend sideshow to the classy food at the place du Concert.

Place du Concert VL Pl du Concert, 59800 ⊘ Wed, Fri & Sun 07.00–14.00 [235 F1] *e** Bus 3, 6 or 9 from Gare Lille Flandres to Lion d'Or then follow rue de la Monnaie to the marketplace.

Chic, low-key & a treat in the centre of the old town. None of the bustle of Wazemmes, but quality goods, & walking distance from some fine restaurants, most of which are not averse to sourcing the dish of the day from these very stalls.

Sébastopol MK Pl Sébastopol, 59000 ⊘ Wed & Sat 07.00–14.00 [234 D6] 🚇 *République–Beaux Arts e** Métro 2 to Gare Lille Flandres, then line 1 to République–Beaux Arts; walk along rue Inkerman to the market square.

In the shadow of the extravagantly over-designed theatre come cheery

Shopping Markets

local traders with mainly a food market. Don't forget that chicory (known in France as *endive*) is the pepperiest & crunchiest accompaniment to any picnic. Dubbed *les perles du Nord*, they are the stars of the fruit & veg stalls. I have found some stylish jewellery here on occasions & friends swear by the bag stalls as excellent value.

Vieille Bourse GP [235 F4] See page 183.
Books.

Wazemmes Market MK Pl de la Nouvelle Aventure, 59000 ☉Sun morn; covered produce market ☉Tue–Sun from 06.00 until late aft [234 A6–7] 🚊 *Gambetta* **e*** *Métro 2 to Gare Lille Flandres, then line 1 to Gambetta. Cross the rue du Marché & walk around the church to pl de la Nouvelle Aventure.* Emerge from Gambetta métro station & prepare for all your senses to be ravaged. Surrender to the pulse of the city & simply follow the crowds past puppies & chickens, rabbits & budgerigars. Around the church of St Pierre & St Paul swims the tide of humanity, past antiques, bric-a-brac & junk, past piles of clothing. Into the pl de la Nouvelle Aventure the adventure continues, past mounds of gloriously plump fresh chicory, rose-red radishes & tear-blushed artichokes from the market gardens of Artois & Flanders, past puppets & playthings, smart coats & swimwear; shop doorways flung open on a Sunday; past promises of 'Special prices just for you Monsieur, Madame, only today from my cousin in Africa'. Into the red-brick market hall itself: past fresh North Sea fish on the slab & crates of seafood; past cheeses from the region & beyond; past exotic sausages & pristine plucked poultry. Through the hall to the flower market: past carnations & lilies; past spring blooms or Christmas wreaths.

From café doorways hear the sound of the accordion playing. An old man on a bicycle offers bunches of herbs from his panniers to passers-by & a younger biker steps off his Harley to try on a new leather jacket for €70. Backs are slapped, hands are shaken, noses are tapped & deals are struck. As the church bells toll for mass, traders' cries mingle with the sound of a barrel organ. At the back of a lorry blocking the rue des Sarrazins, gleaming saucepans are offered at never-to-be repeated prices, & in the midst of the whirlpool of the market square a salesman demonstrates his miracle wonder-broom or incredible, magical vegetable-slicing machine.

On street corners, enormous rotisseries drip the juices from turning chickens on to trays of roast potatoes & vegetables, the scent of a traditional Sunday lunch competing with the more exotic aromas from the enormous drums of couscous & paella as a French market merges into the multi-ethnic North African souk. Follow your nose & keep your hand on your wallet. All in all, Wazemmes on a Sunday morning is an unforgettable experience for bargain hunters & browsers alike.

SUPERMARKETS/DEPARTMENT STORES

Carrefour S Euralille shopping centre, 59777 ☎03 20 15 56 00
☺Mon–Sat 09.00–22.00 [235 H4] 🚆 *Lille Europe* *e** *Opposite the station.*
This massive hypermarket is the ideal place for stocking up before catching the train home (except on Sunday). The branch is so vast, staff use roller skates to whizz between checkouts & aisles. Look out for the logo featuring a belfry & a heart. This denotes local products, & the store sells a good selection of ales & prepared foods from the region & a large range of fresh halal meats. For free parking in the Euralille car park, get your ticket stamped at the checkout.

Monoprix S Les Tanneurs shopping centre, 80 rue Paris, 59000 ☎03 28 82 92 20 ☺Mon–Sat 08.30–20.30 [235 F4] 🚆 *Gare Lille Flandres*
e* *From Gare Lille Flandres take bus 13 to Molinel-Paris.*
Since moving from its larger home on rue Molinel, this modest supermarket has proved some solace to the town-centre workers who still mourn the passing of the Marks & Spencer food hall up the road. Good grocery section on the lower level, even a kosher counter. Upstairs, find a limited range of clothes & household wares.

Galeries Lafayette GP 31 rue de Béthune, 59000 ☎03 20 14 76 50
☺Mon–Thu 10.00–22.00, Fri–Sat 10.00–21.00 [235 F4] 🚆 *Rihour*
e* *Métro 2 to Gare Lille Flandres then line 1 to Rihour. Walk down rue de la Vieille Comédie, turn left on to rue des Fossés to rue de Béthune.*
The long-awaited validation of Lille as a key destination for the fashion conscious, France's premier department store opened its largest branch outside Paris here in the heart of the pedestrian zone with a glitzy launch party in 2007. A cinematic sweep of frontage amongst the movie houses of the rue de Bethune. All you'd expect from the A-listers' emporium, plus a branch of the Zein spa (see page 190).

Printemps GP 41–45 rue Nationale, 59000 ☎03 20 63 62 00
☺Tue–Thu & Sat 09.30–19.30, Fri 09.30–20.00 [234 E4] 🚆 *Rihour* *e** *Métro 2 to Gare Lille Flandres then line 1 to Rihour. Behind the tourist office is the rear entrance to the store.*
A branch of the famous Parisian department store. Fashion, classy luggage & decent tableware. Car park beneath the store.

▲ *Euralille, the shopping city within a city – all the boutiques and none of the cobbles!*

UNDER ONE ROOF

Euralille S Av le Corbusier, 59000 ☎ 03 20 14 52 20 (Euralille), 03 28 38 50 50 (Aeronef) [235 H4] 🚇 *Gare Lille Europe or Gare Lille Flandres* *e* Cross the parvis François Mitterand.*

Between the two railway stations, Euralille is one of France's biggest shopping centres. Hardcore consumers may squeak with excitement at the massive Carrefour hypermarket and specialist shops such as the temple to new-age consumerism, Nature et Découvertes, and the arts and crafts wonderland of Loisirs et Créations. Personally, I mourn the passing of the pet superstore that once advertised the special offer '15 caged birds for the price of 12', either the zenith or nadir of promotional hype. Exhibitions and displays in the centre have ranged from tableaux of zebra and rhino on loan from the Natural History Museum to a free circus with high wires and trapeze acts above the heads of bemused shoppers. The mall is more than merely 140 shops spread over two storeys of consumerism. Office units, hotel rooms and serviced short-stay apartments hide behind the smoked glass. Even the once-underground nightclub L'Aeronef is now to be found several levels above ground in the Euralille complex, with its programme of cutting-edge rock music and bad-taste film festivals. Together with Christian de Portzampac's 'ski-boot' Tour Crédit Lyonnais balanced over Lille Europe station and Rem Koolhaas' own Grand Palais exhibition centre and concert venue, Euralille is testament to Koolhaas' concept of 21st-century living, Lille's remarkable civic optimism and Mayor Mauroy's belief in the Eurostar dream. The interim 'temporary' casino was housed here: fine dining, floor shows and roulette within a barcode bleep of the family supermarket shop. Between Gare Europe and Euralille, the parvis François Mitterand has been colonised by the micro-scooter and rollerblade fraternity. A statue of President Mitterand waves passengers on their high-speed way, a gigantic bunch of tulips is a cheery legacy of Lille 2004 and the recently ripened Parc Matisse offers a comfortable walk towards Vieux Lille.

Walking tour

This favourite walk takes in the 'best of...' and provides the perfect appetiser to a weekend of self-indulgence. Straight from the Eurostar station*, it meanders through the three central squares, along the cobbles of the historic old town, and finishes amidst the wide-open spaces of the largest park and woodlands in the city centre.

It also brings you within a lip's smack of the most delicious little food stores in town, so bring a basket and shop for a picnic (following our suggestions on pages 156–60) to round off the hike and build up your energies for the return walk to your hotel. Another gastronomic subtext of my preferred stroll is that it takes you past many of the best restaurants in town, so you can always press your nose to a window and check out the menus for later!

Although the circuit is perfectly manageable within an hour for those who prefer a brisk constitutional, I would recommend that you allow two to three hours and take your time. Every other shop window is a digression-in-waiting and so many of the old buildings deserve a more leisurely appreciation.

If you would rather not start at the station, you could always pick up the trail at the place du Théâtre.

THE WALK

From the Gare Lille Europe, step down to the parvis François Mitterand, with its giant tulips. To your right is the Parc Matisse (see page 196) and the Porte de Roubaix (see page 183); to your left is Euralille (see page 166). Head towards the Gare Lille Flandres and perhaps check out an exhibition at the Tripostale. At the place de la Gare bear right along the rue Faidherbe towards the place du Théâtre, the belfry and the opera house (see page 182).

Step inside the Vieille Bourse (see page 183) and savour the timeless atmosphere of this unique enclave, then come out on to the place du

Général de Gaulle, or Grand' Place. This is the central square of Lille and its many façades reflect the varied and dazzling history of the city. Spot the gilded suns atop public buildings, symbol of Louis XIV, and admire the central fountain and La Déesse (see page 184).

Pass the archway inscribed with the name of the Brasserie Alcide, and instead follow rue de la Bourse, with its 17th-century houses adorned with images of innocence and corruption, to the rue de la Grande Chaussée. Follow the pointing arm above the first shopfront to direct you along the cobbled street lined with designer names, where D'Artagnan once lived (see page 10) in the house that is now La Botte Chantilly shoe shop, and pause at the spectacular art deco mosaic shopfront of L'Huîtrière (see page 87). Step inside just to admire the décor and peek in the restaurant (you could double back along rue Basse to visit the original site of the restaurant before it moved to its present location in 1928 if you have time). Follow the rue des Chats Bossus to the place Lion d'Or and walk down to 29 place Louise de Bettignies to admire the baroque façade of the Demeure Gilles de la Boë. You could always trot down towards the rue de Gand for some menu fantasising, but there is still plenty to see back in the oldest street in town.

You may have got hopelessly lost thanks to the sirens of so many boutiques and antique shops nudging into your peripheral vision.

So, turn back to place Lion d'Or and walk along Lille's first commercial centre, the rue de la Monnaie, with original shop signs above the doors denoting early merchants' trades. Stop off at the Musée de l'Hospice Comtesse (see page 173) and turn left into rue Peterinck, where 18th-century weavers' houses have now become very fashionable artists' studios, boutiques and eateries. This road leads to the place aux Oignons (see page 145), which may seem an appropriate name in light of the many small delicatessens in the area but is actually a corrupt spelling of the word *donjon* (dungeon). For here was the keep of the original fortress on the marshland that was the city's birthplace.

Having explored all the treats on offer in place aux Oignons and its tributaries, take the little alleyway that leads to place Gilleson, and climb the steps to the side entrance to Notre Dame de la Treille (see page 187). Walk through the magnificent church and leave by the brand-new doors. Turn left into rue du Cirque, stopping at any of the little art and antique shops that take your fancy. Turn right into rue Basse and take a sharp left into rue Lepelletier, at the tiny little bakery with the leaded-glass windows reading 'Au Notre Dame de la Treille'. This is now a branch of the ubiquitous Paul (see page 115), and if you have not already succumbed to the gastronomic temptations on the walk thus far, grab a pastry or some bread to sustain you for the rest of the trek!

By now you may have got hopelessly lost thanks to the sirens of so many boutiques and antique shops nudging into your peripheral vision and the fact that none of these streets follows any geometric rules. But if you are sticking closely to the map, you should be able to take the first turning on the right, the rue du Curé St Etienne, to lead you to rue Esquermoise (and the further enticement of Meert's tea rooms!).

Just across the rue Esquermoise is the rue St Etienne, a narrow street that takes you past the town's major Renaissance façade, the restaurant Le Compostelle (see page 99).

At the place Mendès France with the undistinguished circular Nouveau Siècle building (see page 133), turn sharp left into rue de Pas, crossing the bustling rue Nationale into rue Roisin. This leads you to the place Rihour (see page 180) and the tourist office and remains of the ducal Palais Rihour (see page 179). Worth a dawdle if brasserie-menu browsing or enjoying the stalls at the Christmas market; otherwise continue past the palace along the rue du Palais Rihour and turn right on the rue de l'Hôpital Militaire.

Cross over the rue Nationale once more and turn left along the thoroughfare until you come to the square Foch with its statue of the P'tit Quinquin (see page 183). Walk through the recently smartened-up gardens, where you may appreciate other statues including a bust of Maréchal Foch or the saucier Suzanne at her bath! Keep on walking through the leafy squares (the next garden is called square du Tilleul) until the road opens up to the canal basin, and stroll along the quai de Wault admiring swans until you come out by the square Daubanton. Look across at the charming and elegant Jardin Vauban, with its puppet theatre and manicured pathways (see page 194). But opposite you, across the pont de la Citadelle, is the Bois de Boulogne (see page 194), a perfect place to relax with a picnic.

▲ *Flaunting it: the never bashful windows of Lille.*

Museums
& sightseeing

THE UNMISSABLES

Palais des Beaux Arts (Fine Arts Museum) **GP** Pl de la République, 59000 ☎ 03 20 06 78 00 ⌂ www.pba-lille.fr 🖾 €5 (discounts for under 25s), but free admission on the 1st Sun of the month; free access to atrium ☺ Mon 14.00–18.00, Wed–Thu & Sat–Sun 10.00–18.00, Fri 10.00–19.00; closed Tue & public holidays [235 E6] 🚊 *République–Beaux Arts **e*** Métro 2 to Gare Lille Flandres, changing to line 1 to République–Beaux Arts.*

For years, in a modest office tucked away behind the magnificent splendour of the museum, the then curator Arnaud Brejon de Lavergnée pondered over the Palais des Beaux Arts' many treasures. France's second museum after the Louvre has Goyas & Rubens, Picassos, Lautrecs & Monets, but the greatest treasure of them all is Arnaud Brejon de Lavergnée himself. The passions of this modest & unassuming art lover are as much a part of this fabulous palace as the rich red walls, the floppy chairs, & the catalogue of some of the world's greatest artworks. During the renovations, Monsieur Brejon de Lavergnée could be seen at the station platform, clutching bubble-wrapped masterpieces to his chest as he personally escorted the Palais's jewels to be restored at the National Gallery in London. Until the day in 1997 that President Chirac inaugurated the new museum, every picture, every frame & every detail came under his exacting scrutiny. Monsieur Brejon has since handed over the reins to Alain Tapié, but may still be seen leading privileged visitors around the museum. On the eve of the legendary Rubens exhibition, I left my allotted tour group to tag along behind the master as Monsieur Brejon laid bare the genius of the artist to a privileged party including Prince Jean of France aka Duke of Orleans, banker, philosopher, MBA, erstwhile footballer & current Dauphin & pretender to the throne.

The breathtaking art collection was brought to Lille on the orders of Napoleon, who stripped the walls of palaces & private galleries throughout his European empire, from Italy to the Low Countries. The

▲ *Palais des Beaux Arts: grand gateway to the spoils of cultural looting on a massive scale.*

imposing palace was built from 1889 to 1892 by the Parisian architects Bérard et Delmas, & reinvented a century later by Jean-Marc Ibos & Myrto Vitart who, together with Monsieur Brejon de Lavergnée, were instructed by Mayor Mauroy to open up the museum to the town.

They redefined the ground floor as a light, airy atrium & terrace, open to the public as a meeting place or coffee stop – admission free. The plan paid off: what had been a pleasure for the cultured few is now a cherished symbol of civic pride, & was the triumph that awoke the world to the news that Lille had achieved greatness.

Today's visitors take one of the twin grand staircases adorned with leaded windows heralding the *arts et métiers* of Lille to the first floor, where room after room offers French, Flemish & European masterpieces from the 17th to the 19th centuries. Highlights include Rubens's *Descente de la Croix*, an entire room devoted to Jordaens, & a succession of high-ceilinged galleries housing the works of Van Dyck, Corot & Delacroix with Watteau, père et fils, the collection's first curators. Best of all is the celebrated pair of Goyas, *Les Jeunes & Les Vieilles*, the former a timeless portrayal of a teenage crush, as relevant to the SMS text generation as to its own time, & the latter a cruelly satirical dissection of old age: crones at one with their malevolence. With so many riches, it is easy to overlook the corridor devoted to the Impressionists. Make time for Monet, Van Gogh, Renoir & Sisley, not to mention a Lautrec & Rodin's *Burghers of Calais*.

Back on the ground floor, the sculpture gallery includes the best of 19th-century classical statuary, some imperial, some disturbing. A good halfway refreshment point for your visit, the collection leads to the rear courtyard & the modern architects' remarkable prism comprising the glass-fronted administration block & a sheet of water that turns the grey skies of the north into pure natural light to illuminate the basement galleries.

The underground rooms should not be missed. The Renaissance room includes Donatello's bas-relief *Festin d'Herod*, & many sketches by Raphaël. It also houses 19 of Vauban's detailed models of his fortified towns – among them Lille & Calais – frozen in time & space between sheets of glass in an otherwise blacked-out exhibition of the landscape of 18th-century France & Flanders.

The catalogue of treasures on every floor could never leave anybody feeling short-changed. And, in his day, anyone lucky enough to come across Monsieur Brejon de Lavergnée himself escorting his guests around his gallery, his infectious enthusiasm drawing total strangers to his enlightening discourse on a favourite painting, well, that was ever a bonus beyond price.

Musée de l'Hospice Comtesse VL 32 rue de la Monnaie, 59800
℡ 03 28 36 84 00 ✎ €3; joint tickets also available with Palais des Beaux Arts
☉ Mon 14.00–18.00, Wed–Sun 10.00–12.30 & 14.00–18.00; closed holidays
[235 F2 & 236 C3] *e* Bus 3, 6 or 9 from Gare Lille Flandres to Lion d'Or.*
I love the stillness of the old hospital ward, with its boatbuilder-vaulted ceiling. This most tranquil of sanctuaries is a season apart, even from the rest of the historic quarter. Tucked away behind the shops & archways of the oldest street in town, the former 13th-century hospital captures the life & talents of another Lille in another time. The city's benefactress Jeanne de Constantinople, Countess of Flanders, built the hospice for the needy in 1237, a charitable gesture that has echoed down the centuries in a city that nurtures the ideals of civic responsibilities. After all, the celebrated annual Braderie (see page 12) was born of a sense of *noblesse oblige*, when servants were granted the right to sell their masters' clothes in these very streets. Once both a hospital & a convent, the site has been restored as a museum of local arts & crafts. Outside is a medicinal herb garden. Inside, find an eclectic collection of carved furniture & rare musical instruments, domestic tableaux & wooden panels adorned with paintings of local children. The art collection includes paintings by Flemish & northern French masters, among them Louis & François Watteau, as well as tapestries by Lille's famous weaver Guillaume Werniers. The kitchen is typically tiled with the traditional blue-&-white tiles of the Low Countries, & vestiges of the original murals can be seen in the 17th-century convent chapel. The chapel, the 15th-century ward &

▲ *All aboard for a thousand years of history in one hour – the Lille City Tour.*

other buildings around the central courtyard are favourite locations for informal concerts & intimate musical recitals. Guided tours are available at no extra charge most afternoons.

La Piscine Roubaix See page 199.
A truly remarkable building that very nearly upstages the town's remarkable art collection.

Musée de l'Art Moderne Villeneuve d'Ascq See page 206.
Picasso, Braque, Modigliani & much, much more – well worth the métro ride out of town. Check for temporary exhibitions from the collection at other sites around the region whilst the museum closes for renovation.

MUSEUMS

The Lille City Pass (see page 46) includes free admission to the museums in Lille and the surrounding area, with unlimited use of the public transport system. See pages 197–209 for details of the excellent collections located just a bus, métro or tram ride out of town.

Musée de l'Art Religieux
See Notre Dame de la Treille, page 187.

Musée des Canonniers Sédentaires de Lille VL 44 rue des
Canonniers, 59800 ℃ 03 20 55 58 90 ✇ €6 ☺ Mon–Sat 14.00–17.00; closed holidays, 1st 3 weeks of Aug & 15 Dec–2 Feb [235 H2] 🚊 *Gare Lille Flandres*
e* Walk through the Parc Matisse & pass through the Porte de Roubaix to rue de Roubaix. Turn right into rue des Canonniers & 2nd right into rue des Urbanistes.

It is fitting that a garrison town should have a museum of military hardware, & over 3,000 weapons, documents & maps from 1777 to 1945 are on display in the former Urbanistes convent. The stars of the show are the magnificent cannons, most notably the Gribeauval – the Big Bertha of its day. Despite the postal address, the public entrance is in rue des Urbanistes.

Musée d'Histoire Naturelle et de Géologie (Natural History Museum) **MK** 19 rue de Bruxelles, 59000 ℃ 03 28 55 30 80 ⌂ free midweek & 1st Sun of the month; €3 Sun ☉ Mon & Wed–Fri 9.00–12.00 & 14.00–17.00, Sun 10.00–13.00 & 14.00–18.00; closed Tue & Sat [234 E8] 🚊 *République–Beaux Arts e* Bus 13 from Gare Lille Flandres to Jeanne d'Arc.* This is among my favourite time warps, more for the rooms themselves than the collections. I always feel as though I have entered a Victorian draper's shop that does a nice line in sabre-toothed tigers. A typical 19th-century museum, with its glass cases, iron walkways & spiral staircases, this very old-fashioned throwback to the days of hands-off musty scholarship is an oddity in a city that prides itself on cutting-edge exhibitions. There is something comfortingly nostalgic about the place, with its whale skeletons suspended from the ceiling, irresistibly camp tableaux of stuffed birds & animals & studiously catalogued trays of geological specimens & fossils.

Musée de l'Hospice Comtesse VL 32 rue de la Monnaie, 59000 ℃ 03 28 36 84 00 [235 F2 & 236 C3]
See page 173.

Maison de l'Architecture et de la Ville S Pl François Mitterrand, 59777 ℃ 03 20 14 61 15 🖰 www.mav-npdc.com ⌂ free ☉ Tue–Thu 10.00–12.30 & 14.00–17.00, Sat 11.00–18.00; exhibition & festival dates vary [235 H4] 🚊 *Gare Lille Europe e* Leave the Eurostar, cross the piazza below the station & the museum is under the viaduct.* Legacy of the 2004 festivities, this gallery devoted to urban architecture is sited slap bang in the heart of the Euralille district, underneath – & almost propping up – the concrete viaduct that is the av Corbusier. Not merely a showcase for town planning, the venue plays a key role in city festivals & hosts workshops & talks on architecture past & present across the region. Slightly more offbeat are the special dinners when chefs & architects work together to illustrate design concepts on a plate.

Maison Natale du Général de Gaulle (Général de Gaulle's birthplace) **VL** 9 rue Princesse, 59000 ℃ 03 28 38 12 05 🖰 www.maison-natale-de-gaulle.org 🎧 €5 ⊘ Wed–Sat 10.00–13.00 & 14.00–18.00, Sun 13.30–17.30; closed holidays *e** *Bus 3 or 6 from Gare Lille Flandres to Magasin. Take rue St André to rue Princesse.*

War hero, statesman & Europe's most celebrated Anglosceptic, Charles de Gaulle was born here, in his grandmother's house, on 22 November 1890, opposite the Eglise St André where the once & future president was baptised. See his christening robes when the refurbished museum devoted to the life of Lille's most famous son eventually reopens. The exhibition tells the story of the first president of the Fifth Republic with lesser-known tales from his early life, & documents his refusal to accept Marshal Pétain's 1940 truce with Nazi Germany, then rallying the Free French army with his historic broadcast from London that same year. Dramatic episodes are well illustrated, with the very Citroën DS in which the president was travelling outside Paris when he survived an assassin's bullet. The long-awaited reopening promises multimedia displays & a conference centre. Last admission is one hour before the museum closes.

Palais des Beaux Arts (Fine Arts Museum) **GP** Pl de la République, 59000 ✆ 03 20 06 78 00 [234 E6]
See page 171.

SITES & MONUMENTS

Citadelle VL Av du 43ème Régiment d'Infanterie, 59000 ✆ 08 91 56 20 04 (€0.225/min, tourist office) 🎧 €7 ⊘ advance reservation essential: guided tours only on selected dates in summer [234 B1] *e** *Métro 2 to Gare Lille Flandres, then line 1 to République–Beaux Arts. Bus 14 to Jardin Vauban.*

A town in its own right, France's Queen of Citadels was the greatest fortress of the reign of Louis XIV. When the Sun King commissioned the great military architect Sébastien Le Prestre de Vauban to protect his kingdom with a ring of 100 fortified towns, this imposing & impenetrable, pentagonal, star-shaped Citadelle was hailed as the masterpiece of the world's finest military engineer. Built by 400 men in just 3 years using 16 million newly baked bricks, the garrison opened in 1670 as home to 1,200 soldiers. 300 years on, it remains the nucleus of the modern army with 1,000 French soldiers & foreign legionnaires stationed here.

In April, 14 of the 28 northern fortresses hold an open day; otherwise the public are permitted to tour the site only on summer Sunday guided tours. Visitors are expected to behave themselves. When a couple of schoolchildren sat on the parade-ground rostrum, the young soldier of the *43ème régiment* accompanying our group was confined to barracks, a sharp reminder that this is no museum, but a working garrison. Its 5-sided design is as effective a security measure today as it was in the 17th century – & is said to have inspired the US Pentagon. Soil banks the ramparts to absorb artillery shells, & the main walls are 4m thick. The principal entrance, the Porte Royale, was built at an angle to the drawbridge to avoid direct hits. This gateway, facing the old quarter of Lille, was a major strategic & symbolic feature with regal motifs & Latin mottos representing the king himself. In the centre of the pentagonal parade ground is a ship's mast, a reminder that the fortress was built along the banks of a river & was originally protected by the navy. The soldiers stationed here today still wear naval badges. Around the parade ground are the renovated barracks, arsenal, chapel & officers' quarters.

The king, a regular visitor, appointed Vauban as the first governor of the Citadelle. His successor, Charles, Comte d'Artagnan (best known as hero of Dumas's *Three Musketeers*), died in 1673. The original governor's residence is no more, but traces may still be found in the chapel of the gubernatorial doorway. Vauban's original models for the fortified towns of the north are displayed at the Palais des Beaux Arts (see page 171). The rest of the collection is housed at Les Invalides in Paris.

▼ *The royal entrance to the Citadelle.*

▲ *A dramatic gesture at the opera house.*

La Déesse (the Goddess of the Grand' Place) **GP** [235 F4]
See page 184.

L'Hermitage Gantois **S** 224 rue de Paris, 59800 ℂ 03 20 85 30 30
🖰 www.hotels-slih.com [235 F6] 🚋 *Mairie de Lille* **e*** *Métro 2 to Mairie de Lille.*
Walk westwards along av du Président Kennedy then turn left on to rue de Paris.
See page 54 for more on this restored historic building.

Hôtel de Ville (Town Hall) **S** Pl Roger Salengro, 59000 ℂ 03 20 49 50 00
[235 G7] 🚋 *Mairie de Lille* **e*** *Métro 2 to Mairie de Lille.*
Although the Christmas Ferris wheel on Grand' Place offers the best
view in town, there is a summer alternative. From April to September
(check with the tourist office first), take a detour from the main historic
& shopping quarters & climb to the top of the 104m belfry of the town
hall (a lift takes you most of the way). Completed in 1932, the tower
crowned Emile Dubuisson's striking Hôtel de Ville, which replaced the
original Gothic Palais Rihour building with a ferro-concrete tribute to the
gabled houses of Flanders. More than merely a nice place to enjoy a
pleasant view, in 1950 the top of the tower became the first regional
television studio, *Télé-Lille*. Holding up the tower are the figures of
giants Lydéric & Phinaert, the Romulus, Remus, Bambi, Sirius Black &
Voldemort of Lille. Lydéric was raised by wild deer & a hermit after his
family was killed by the tyrant Phinaert. On 15 June, 605, the two
fought: Lydéric was the victor & he founded the town. The history of
Lille is told in a huge cartoon-strip fresco inside the building, painted by
the Icelandic artist Erro. The building was constructed over the ruins of
the original working-class quarter of St Sauveur where, in the long-
demolished bar, La Liberté, local wood turner Pierre Degeyter composed
& played the music for Eugène Pottier's socialist anthem
L'Internationale for the very first time in 1888.

Maison Coillot MK 14 rue Fleurus, 59000 [234 D7]

🚇 République–Beaux Arts e* Métro 2 to Gare Lille Flandres changing to line 1 to République–Beaux Arts. Take rue Nicolas Leblanc to place Lebon, into rue Fleurus.

An unexpected flourish of art nouveau in a quiet residential street off the place Lebon. All the houses around the church of St Michel are identical. All but one, that is. If 14 rue Fleurus looks more like a Paris métro station than a private home, then thanks are due to its original owner, Monsieur Coillot, a ceramics maker who commissioned Hector Guimard to redesign his house. Guimard's celebrated flourishes, dark-green swirls & horticultural sweeps are the hallmark of the capital's subway system. His reinvention of the domestic townhouse is no less flamboyant, using Coillot's own ceramics alongside cast iron & volcanic rock. These remarkable windows, balconies, gables & even a suggestion of a pagoda on the roof are worth a modest detour when trekking between local museums, for although still a private address, the house was so designed that the interiors appear open to the street.

Palais Rihour GP Pl Rihour, 59002 ☎ 03 59 57 94 00 *💶 free ☉ tourist office hours Mon–Sat 09.30–18.30, Sun & holidays 10.00–12.00 & 14.00–17.00; 1st floor by appointment* [234 E4] *🚇 Rihour e* Métro 2 to Gare Lille Flandres, then line 1 to Rihour.*

To most people this old building behind the monumental war memorial is merely a rather quaint tourist office. I've even heard some visitors dismiss the Gothic arches & mullioned windows as a Victorian folly. Heresy. Cross the threshold & you are standing in the remains of a ducal palace, seat of power in Lille for over 450 years & boasting an A-list guest list that has included England's Henry VIII & France's Louis XV. The original Palais Rihour was built by Philippe le Bon, Duke of Burgundy, when he moved the court to the city in 1453. His son Charles le Téméraire completed the palace 20 years later. It was through the Burgundian line that Lille passed to the Hapsburgs when Marie de Bourgogne married Maximilien of Austria in 1474. When Philip IV of Spain sold the palace to the city in the 17th century it began a new life as the town hall & continued to serve the community until ravaged by fire in 1916. The stairwell & chapels, among the finest surviving examples of flamboyant Gothic architecture in town, could hardly house a city's local government, so a new Hôtel de Ville was built in the St Sauveur district (see page 178). The ground-floor guards' chapel is now the main tourist office. Climb the winding stairs to the upper chapel to admire the trefoil windows & vaulted ceiling. Burgundian coats of arms adorn the walls, & a real sense of the original palace remains.

▲ *In memoriam: the imposing war memorial on the place Rihour.*

Exhibitions & concerts are sometimes held here. Do take time to admire the beautifully restored glass of the sacristy.

Place du Général de Gaulle (Grand' Place) **GP** [235 F4]
See page 184.

Place Philippe Lebon **MK** [234 D7] 🚊 *République–Beaux Arts*
e* Métro 2 to Gare Lille Flandres changing to line 1 to République–Beaux Arts. Take rue Nicolas Leblanc to place Lebon.
This intersection of the rue Solférino boasts the kitschest statue in town. On the edge of the original university district, this is a lavish homage to Louis Pasteur, first dean of the science faculty. As the microbiologist who first discovered that germs cause disease & the pioneer of pasteurisation, the great man is shown surrounded by grateful mothers offering their babies aloft. And you thought science could not be camp. This is a cult classic. Totally fab. Across the square is the Romanesque-Byzantine church of St Michel surrounded by identikit townhouses. The Maison Coillot (see page 179) is on the rue Fleurus. Walking south, Solférino leads to an equestrian statue of Joan of Arc. To the north are the Théâtre Sébastopol & Les Halles (see page 124).

Place Rihour **GP** [234 E4] 🚊 *Rihour e* Métro 2 to Gare Lille Flandres then line 1 to Rihour.*
Place de Gaulle trickles into place Rihour, home of the Palais Rihour (see page 179) & tourist office, by way of a row of restaurants, cafés & bars where late-night revellers adjourn for an onion-soup breakfast in the small hours. A massive war memorial dominates the square, & is the

scene of civic remembrance services on Armistice Day. Some rather disturbing coloured lighting illuminates the fountain that rinses the glass pyramid above the métro station. The result varies from fairground garish to an effect not unlike spilt hospital custard. In winter, a Christmas market of wooden chalets sells hot mulled wine & handmade gifts. The rue de la Vieille Comédie is named after Voltaire's visit to Lille in 1741 for the première of his play *Mohamet*.

Place du Théâtre GP [235 F3] 🚊 *Gare Lille Flandres* ***e*** *Bus 12 from Gare Lille Flandres to Théâtre. Or walk av le Corbusier & right into rue Faidherbe.* Behind the Vieille Bourse (see page 183), & looking down towards the old station, is the place du Théâtre. Only recently pedestrianised as part of the city's millennium renovations, this is the junction of Lille ancient & modern. Spot the iron arm hanging above the junction of rue de la Bourse & rue de la Grande Chaussée pointing visitors to Vieux Lille. The two most striking buildings on the square are surprisingly new, dating from the 20th century: the neo-classical opera house, with its monumental sculptures of Apollo & the Muses, & the splendid 76m neo-Flemish belfry of the imposing Chambre de Commerce et d'Industrie – both built by Louis Cordonnier. The Opéra's lavish restored interiors are even more dazzling than ever. Inspired by the Palais Garnier in Paris, the Opéra de Lille has always been a place to be seen, & its programme usually features popular classics in productions from other European companies with an international cast of principals (see page 133). It now truly belongs to the square, with its lights from the chandeliers spilling

▼ *A helping hand – no language barriers en route to the old town.*

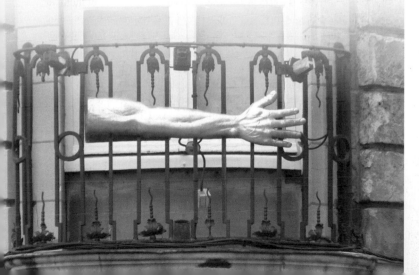

into the streets. Opposite is the Rang de Beauregard, an extraordinarily ornate terrace of 14 three-storey houses & shops constructed in 1687 to complement the Vieille Bourse, & undergoing painstaking restoration. Look closely at the elegant shopfronts: still embedded in the walls are cannonballs from the siege of 1792. A favourite shopfront is that of Morel et Fils, legendary lingerie from days of yore until the millennium. Today, the vintage mannequins welcome guests to the emporium's reincarnation as a charming café, Maison du Moulin d'Or (see page 118).

Porte de Gand **VL** Rue de Gand [235 H1] *e** *Bus 3, 6 or 9 from Gare Lille Flandres to Lion d'Or. Cross pl Louise de Bettignies to rue de Gand.*
The last remaining fortified entrance to Vieux Lille stands astride the rue de Gand, looking down over the cobbles & menus of this fashionable dining area. From the old town, admire the coloured patterns in the brickwork above the archways. The windows at the top belong to a restaurant (see *La Terrasse des Ramparts*, page 103). From the other side, the Porte de Gand can be seen as part of some serious defensive walls. The original perimeter was strengthened twice in the 17th century, the *porte* & ramparts built in 1621 by the Spanish authorities against the French, & an extra line of defence added by Vauban against everybody else. Between the two walls are gardens that can be seen from the restaurant terrace in summer when diners may sit at tables on the ramparts. Since the winding road leading from the gate still serves a working barracks, the rue de Gand has serviced the many appetites of young soldiers since long before the restaurants arrived on the scene. Pools of lamplight under the trees beneath the city walls continue to offer late-night comforts à la Lili Marlène.

Porte de Paris **S** Pl Simon Volant [235 F7] 🚈 *Lille Grand Palais* *e** *Métro 2 to Lille Grand Palais. Take rue des Déportés past the Hôtel de Ville.*
On the traffic roundabout named after the porte's architect stands the greatest of the three remaining city gates. Unlike the portes des Roubaix & Gand, this is an unashamed piece of monumental triumphalism, a lavish declaration of the might and majesty of Louis XIV & celebration of Lille's embrace into the Kingdom of France. Unveiled in 1692, this *arc de triomphe* has an image of the king himself surrounded by angels & cherubim. Columns frame niches holding classical images of war & power, Hercules & Mars paying tribute to France's own Sun King. Originally the gateway rose above the town's fortifications. The walls were torn down in 1858 to make way for boulevards, & the rest of the

district of St Sauveur was demolished in the slum-clearance programmes of the 1920s. A small landscaped garden replaces the moat, once spanned by a drawbridge, & the baroque arch itself is as imposing as ever. Impress your new friends with the trivial nugget that the gateway was not dubbed the Porte de Paris until the Revolution. Despite its regal statuary, it was originally called the Porte des Malades ('Sick People's Gate') because it led to the hospital!

Porte de Roubaix S Parc Matisse or rue de Roubaix [235 H3] 🚇 *Gare Lille Europe e* From the station enter the park & follow the footpath to the city walls.*

From the rue de Roubaix, this nearly neglected old gateway long presented a rather sorry & run-down appearance, & most passers-by simply pass it by. Yet this is the door that saved a city. The Parc Matisse offers a far more appropriate perspective from which to view this remnant of the old fortifications. Here the crenellations & drawbridge channels may be seen to best advantage, & you can imagine the moment in 1792 when the door was slammed in the face of the Austrian duke of Saxe-Teschen & his army of 35,000 men. If the two smaller archways seem to give the gate an air of a triumphal arch, blame it on the commuters. The side walls were opened up in the 19th century for a long-forgotten tramway to the suburbs. The gateway took a belated bow with architectural Botox & celebratory illumination as part of Lille 2004.

P'tit Quinquin GP Sq Foch, rue Nationale, 59000 [234 D4] 🚇 *Rihour e* Bus 12 from Gare Lille Flandres to Foch.*

This is the statue to a lullaby that won the heart of a town (see page XV): the sentimental patois melodrama of a poor lacemaker whose child would not stop crying. *Le P'tit Quinquin* was composed in 1852 by town-hall clerk Alexandre Desrousseaux, & was soon adopted as a bedtime ballad by every mother in town. When the composer died in 1892 it was adapted as his funeral march, & the town commissioned Eugène Deplechin to build a memorial to the songwriter. The statue of Desrousseaux's working-class *Madonna & Child* is an as unashamed manipulator of the heartstrings as the song itself. If you would like to hear the tune, make your way to the place du Théâtre, where the bells of the clock tower chime the lullaby every day at noon.

Vieille Bourse GP Pl du Général de Gaulle, 59000 🎟 free ☉ Tue–Sun aft [235 F4] 🚇 *Rihour e* Bus 12 from Gare Lille Flandres to Théâtre. Or walk av le Corbusier & right into rue Faidherbe.*

Museums & sightseeing Sites & monuments

Exquisite & unmissable, the most beautiful building in town has been restored to its original Flemish Renaissance brilliance. The greatest legacy of the Spanish occupation of the city was this jewel-box of a Bourse de Commerce merchants' exchange between the two main squares. In fact the Bourse comprises 24 individual 17th-century houses ranged around a cloistered courtyard. Although at first glance the houses, with their ground-floor shops, may seem identical, the intricate carvings & mouldings on each façade are unique, thanks to the skills of builder Julien Destrez who worked on the project from 1652 to 1653. Destrez had already won a distinguished reputation as a carpenter & sculptor, & he dressed his masterpiece with ornate flourishes of masks & garlands on the outer walls. Lions of Flanders adorn the four doorways into the courtyard, which is itself decked with floral & fruit motifs. Today, above the symbols of the original guilds that once traded here, is a discreet row of contemporary logos representing the private enterprises sponsoring the restoration. As the sun rises over Lille, it catches the gilded bell tower on the roof & radiates golden beams across the Grand' Place. Step inside the contemplative cloister to find a charming weekday market selling antiquarian books under the gaze of busts of local pioneers of science & literature. A sanctuary from summer sun & winter winds alike, people come here to sit & read or play chess from mid-morning until early evening. Sunday brings impromptu tea dances, with the old walls echoing to the sound of the waltzes & salsa.

PLACE DU GENERAL DE GAULLE

GP [235 F4] 🚊 *Rihour e* Bus 12 from Gare Lille Flandres to de Gaulle. Or walk av le Corbusier & right into rue Faidherbe then left to Grand' Place.*
Named after Lille's most famous son, but known to everyone simply as the Grand' Place, the main square is the very heartbeat of the city. Almost pedestrianised, although a serpentine trail of traffic slithers safely along two sides, this is a veritable forum where shoppers break their day, friends plot an evening and revellers celebrate the night.

The essential rendezvous is the central fountain around the column of the Déesse, the goddess and symbol of the spirit of the city. The statue commemorates the bravery of the townsfolk, withstanding the siege of Lille by 35,000 Austrian soldiers in 1792. The original idea, mooted the day after the victory, was to build a monument by melting down all royal statues (the Revolution was at its height and Marie Antoinette had not yet been executed). Enthusiasm waned, but eventually the Déesse was cast by

Théophile Bra, with the intention of placing her atop his Arc de Triomphe in Paris. That plan too was abandoned, and the goddess returned to Lille, standing for three years in place Rihour before moving to Charles Benvignat's column on Grand' Place in 1845. Her crown represents Lille's ramparts, her right hand ever ready to fire another cannon, her left pointing to a plaque inscribed with the brave words of Mayor André's rebuttal of Austria's demands. Tongues soon began to wag, since from upper windows locals noted the goddess's uncanny resemblance to Mme Bigodanel, the 54-year-old wife of the then mayor. It seems her fuller figure had not gone unnoticed by the artist.

Under her watchful gaze, students hold their protest rallies, bands play on Gay Pride Weekend and the city's tame giants parade during the Fêtes de Lille. Grand' Place has a habit of dressing for every occasion: most famously as a Christmas grotto in December and January when, surrounded by Cinderella candelabra, a huge Ferris wheel swings sensation seekers into the skies to take in the panorama of gables and belfries from a swaying cradle high above the cobblestones. The wheel turns from mid-morning until well past midnight. Sometimes the cobbles are covered with plants, lawns and box hedges as the city gardeners decide to transform the square into a park. Perhaps the whole area will become a farmyard, with rows of market-garden cabbages in front of the theatre, and a herd of cows grazing contentedly outside McDonald's. On one memorable visit, thousands of screaming fans turned out for a free pop concert on a sultry summer's night, and obliging students on rooftops sprayed the crowd from mineral water bottles.

▼ *Grand' Place is the rendezvous for all seasons.*

Around the square, look out for carved and gilded images of the sun, symbol of King Louis XIV, whose royal bodyguard lived in the Grande Garde, a splendid galleried building that today houses the Théâtre du Nord. Alongside the theatre is the striking frontage of the home of *La Voix du Nord*, once a wartime Resistance news-sheet and now the regional daily newspaper. Dominating the square, its tiered roof is topped out by three golden Graces, symbolising the regional provinces of Artois, Flanders and Hainaut. Continental Europe's biggest bookshop, the Furet du Nord, boasts half a million volumes in stock, and is spread over eight storeys on different levels served by a complicated arrangement of lifts, staircases and walkways. Across the square, linking Grand' Place with place du Théâtre, is the stunning Vieille Bourse. The gateway to Vieux Lille is the archway bearing the name of the Brasserie Alcide. Brasseries, bars and cafés abound, the square and its arteries liberally sprinkled with tables for al fresco dining and people-watching.

CHURCHES

Eglise Ste Cathérine <u>VL</u> Pl Jean-Jacques Louchard, 59000 ☏ 03 20 55 45 92 ⬚ free ☺ Sat 14.30–17.00 (16.30 in winter), 1st & 3rd Sun, & 2nd & 4th Thu 14.30–16.00 [234 D2] *e** *Bus 3 from Gare Lille Flandres to Conservatoire, walk west along rue d'Angleterre, left to rue Royale & right to rue de la Barre then sharp right to rue St Jean.*

Out-of-towners rarely discover this 13th-century church. Yet until work started on Notre Dame de la Treille, this was home to the town's precious statue of the Virgin Mary (see page 188). Rubens's *Martyrdom of Sainte Cathérine*, now in the Palais des Beaux Arts (see page 171), hung here for years, & many striking works by lesser-known artists may still be seen in the spacious & bright interior. The altar is graced by some excellent artworks including adoration of the shepherds & images inspired by Leonardo's *Last Supper*. Over the centuries the parish church of the rural suburb of Faubourg de Weppes expanded to become a traditional Flemish *hallekerque* (see *St Maurice*, opposite). Its three spacious naves were probably saved from demolition during the Revolution when the building was called into service as a barn, returning to the Catholic Church in 1797. By then it had lost the ornate iron partition grilles & other elaborate furnishings. Other splendid items remain, from the carved choir stalls to the beautifully painted pillars, & Ste Cathérine has at last won historic monument listing status.

Eglise Ste Marie Madeleine VL Rue du Pont Neuf, 59000 ℂ 03 20 74 46 83 ⊘ Mon & Fri 14.00–18.00, Sun 15.00–18.00; closed mid-Jul–mid-Aug *e* Bus 9 from Flandres les Bataliers & walk back along the av du Peuple Belge to turn left on to rue du Pont Neuf.*

One of the most exciting concepts of Lille 2004 was the project that lured some of the world's leading cinematographers to illuminate & interpret the interior of this deconsecrated church. Peter Greenaway, Miwa Yanagi, Chiharu Shiota, Emir Kusturica & Erwin Redl each designed their own 2-month reinterpretation of the building, which reintroduced Lille to one of its forgotten treasures. The unassuming flat frontage belies the magnificence within, notably the dome, so painstakingly restored in the 18th century. Now reclaimed as an exhibition venue.

Eglise St Maurice S Parvis St Maurice, rue de Paris, 59000 ℂ 03 20 06 07 21 ⊘ Mon 13.15–18.00, Tue–Sat 10.15–12.15 & 13.15–18.00, Sun 15.30–20.00; guided visits (French) Sun 15.00–17.00; telephone for English & signed tours [235 G4 & 236 D7] 🚉 *Gare Lille Flandres e* Av le Corbusier to Gare Lille Flandres, left into rue de Priez at the foot of rue Faidherbe.*

The first of the sudden surprises that make Lille so special. Unless you decide to take a short cut from the station to the pedestrian shopping streets, you might never see this magnificent 15th-century church, its gleaming white stone façades restored to pristine condition – at the cost of many a summer night's sleep to neighbours within earshot of the sandblasting. Built on marshland, it has 5 high naves to distribute its weight equally across a wide area, in a style known as *Hallekerque Flamande* – literally 'Flemish Market Church' – after the airy market hall-style interior. Yet another unsung art collection may be viewed here, even if many original treasures have since found their way into the Palais des Beaux Arts. The dramatic stained-glass windows of *The Passion* were inspired by the heroic 19th-century style of Ingres. Summer Sunday organ recitals are worth catching, as are the occasional Saturday night concerts by local musicians.

Notre Dame de la Treille VL Pl Gilleson, 59000 ℂ 03 20 55 28 72 🎟 free ⊘ Mon–Wed & Fri–Sat 10.00–12.00 & 14.00–18.30, Thu 10.00–18.30, Sun: respect service times; remains open 1 hour later May–Sep [235 F2 & 236 C3] *e* Bus 3, 6 or 9 from Gare Lille Flandres to Lion d'Or. Take rue de la Monnaie then 1st left to pl Gilleson.*

For most of the last century, Lille was a city with three-quarters of a cathedral. Notre Dame de la Treille had not only a fine Gothic chapel and apse, but also the largest expanse of corrugated iron in northern Europe. For, although the foundation stone had been laid in 1854 & the bulk of

GARE SAINT SAUVEUR

Bd Jean-Baptiste Lebas, 59800 ☎ 03 28 52 30 00 ♿ free ☉ Wed–Sun
11.00–19.00 [235 G8] *e** *Bus 13 from Gare Lille Flandres to Lille-Lebas.*
The legacy of Lille 3000's Europe XXL season in 2009 is beyond
question the reinvention of an old railway station and goods yard
between the city centre and the residential Moulins quarter. Instead of
demolishing the site and imposing yet another office block or sports
stadium on the landscape, the city opted to inspire a new community
straddling the 19th and 21st centuries. More than merely another arts
centre, the Gare Saint Sauveur, opposite the new parc Lebas (itself the
legacy of the previous Lille 3000 event – see page XVI), at the foot of
the great thoroughfares of Liberté and Solférino, is a grand space
designed for living. With the original railway tracks still embedded in the
ground and the distinctive thick, red walls of the industrial revolution,
some 21 hectares of land cordoned off for generations from the people of
Lille, was handed over, parcelled and portioned by architects Franklin
Azzi. The two striking station buildings are linked by a south-facing

the edifice completed by the turn of the 19th century, work during the
20th century finally ground to a halt when the money ran out in 1947.
What should have been the great front entrance was hastily boarded up.
By 1999, in the golden age of accountancy, funding had finally been
found & Lille was able to unveil its cathedral. From the outside, architect
P L Carlier's designs are very much of the age of the out-of-town
shopping mall: B&Q perpendicular. But inside, it is quite a different
story: imposing yet welcoming, a delicate blend of light & shade. The
new rose window by Kijno produces a powerful effect within, & the
remarkable doors created by Holocaust survivor sculptor George
Jeanclos, representing a barbed-wire vine of human suffering & dignity,
are quite magnificent. The cathedral stands on the Îlot Comtesse, site of
the former château of the counts of Flanders, & the surrounding streets
follow the line of the old fortifications, with traces of a moat still visible.
A Museum of Religious Art in the crypt opens on Saturday afternoons
from 16.00 to 17.00, housing 200 works of art & historic objects,
including the original statue of Notre Dame de la Treille, dating from
1270.

terrace for lazy summer days and nights. One hall is now a cinema and brasserie, the exposed timbers and revitalised brickwork framing more modern concepts of interior design. The other space has been left empty, the blank canvas a grand exhibition centre, performance area, theatre or concert hall that is ripe and ready for constant reinvention.

The social anarchy of festival fever allowed the inaugural season a free-flow feel. A visitor might set up a table or pitch a tent on the site, or hang out at the book exchange café, where paperbacks were dropped and picked up by strangers. A huge wall was erected in summer 2009 for visitors to scrawl their thoughts and, across the site, the Bradérie tradition of anarchic free trade was celebrated as anyone who wished might set up stall to sell their attic trove and rummage through a neighbour's unwanted treasure. You could nip out for a coffee and a mooch and end up invited to an al fresco dinner party with strangers. At this long-forgotten railway station at the far end of the boulevard of respectability and best behaviour, Lille's twin passions of art and hospitality are consummated over coffee, a beer, a good book and a bargain.

MAISONS FOLIES

'Folly' is too frivolous a word since, in reviving abandoned or forgotten buildings, this audacious project has breathed new life into many a community: exciting spaces able to adapt to the imagination of each quarter. The longest-lasting legacy of the Capital of Culture is the fabulous scheme that created a dozen permanent arts centres in Lille and across the region into Belgium. Transforming abandoned buildings and creating entire new community spaces, the Maisons Folies are at once a celebration of the past, an indulgence for the present and a magnificent gift to future generations. Former industrial, military and religious buildings become galleries, theatres, nightclubs, party venues and recording studios, with artists in residence, gardens in the sky and libraries. Named for the architectural follies that were the brick-and-mortar whims of the wealthy aristocrats of the *ancien régime* and industrial *nouveaux riches*, these projects should revive and inspire local communities and entertain their visitors for years, even decades, to come. Unlike Marie Antoinette's model farm and other mini-châteaux and fairytale boathouses, the Maisons Folies belong to the people: kitchens and dining rooms, where local people can prepare and serve their own meals; gardens for those who want to get their

▲ *Reinventing the past: the Maison Folie at Wazemmes is a retreat, spa, and playground for a multicultural community.*

hands dirty; libraries with books in many languages; not to mention the opportunity for local children to meet and work with artists living on site. Folies came of age with Lille 2004, a focus for the diverse communities of the 21st century. The project has evolved comfortably over its first half-decade. The sites, once forbidden to their communities, have become so much a part of everyday life that their involvement in all activities and occasions is a given. Lille 3000 sets out its diary across these venues with ease, so that festival time is not contained within strict city limits, but is carried across into the wider community, generating a previously unimaginable sense of involvement.

Lille

Maison Folie Wazemmes <u>MK</u> Usine Leclercq, 70 rue des Sarrazins, 59000 ✆ 03 20 31 47 80 ⌂ http://zeinorientalspa.fr 🚊 *Gambetta e* Métro 2 to Gare Lille Flandres then line 1 to Wazemmes. Walk west along rue d'Ién, then take the 4th turning on your right, rue d'Austerlitz.*

A 19th-century textile factory which finally closed its doors in 1990 is reinvented with a stunning yet sympathetic building alongside the original structure, a brand new, undulating, red-brick road & public square in the vibrant Wazemmes district. Indoor & outdoor spaces, conceived by the architect Lars Spuybroek, are thrilling, eyecatching & versatile. Alongside studios, exhibition hall & urban orchard is a well-judged theatre space. The Folie is set to become a permanent home to many local arts & performance groups. However, to the locals its allure is far more practical. They wanted a Turkish bath, so the architect created a luxurious sauna & steam complex incorporating the warm red-brick vaulting with some beautiful tiling & interior design. The Zeïn Oriental Spa is open to women 11.00–21.00 (Mon, Wed, Thu & Sat) & 11.00–18.00 (Tue & Fri); to men 18.00–21.00 (Tue & Fri) & is mixed for families on market day, Sunday, 11.00–21.00.

Maison Folie des Trois Moulins 47–49 rue d'Arras, 59000 ℡ 03 28 52 20 04 🚇 *Porte d'Arras ℮* Line 1 to Porte d'Arras & walk along the rue d'Arras.*

This former brewery, an abandoned site of brick & copper, is set to become the very heart of the Moulins district, which already has a thriving arts scene (the Prato Theatre & Univers Cinema are both within a short walk). An imposing 140m² exhibition hall doubles as a theatrical rehearsal space, & the recording studios open out into a weekend nightclub dedicated to contemporary sounds. Two interior courtyards will host open-air performances & the building's original function is reflected in a new bar-brasserie on site.

Arras

Hôtel de Guines Rue des Jongleurs, 62000 ℡ 03 21 71 66 17

Next to the Musée des Beaux Arts in the St Vaast Abbey, a grand 18th-century private house has 2 wings embracing an enclosed courtyard. Its grand façade had already been listed as a national monument before the Maisons Folies project was launched. The stylish rooms are perfect artists' salons for many a cultural rendezvous, & experts from the nearby theatre have helped create performance areas for concerts & cabarets.

Lambersart

Maison de la Plaine Plaine de Lambersart, Berges de la Deûle, 59130 ℡ 03 20 08 44 44

This is the open-space folie by the waterside. Here, where Vauban once built a fortress, is where locals once came to dance by the banks of the Deûle. Thus the architects conceived the house of the future & set it in a meadow, where once again people may come to take the air.

Maubeuge

Les Cantuaines La Porte de Mons, pl Vauban, 59600 ℡ 03 27 62 11 93

This is an artists' retreat within a former convent on the site of a 16th-century hospice at La Porte de Mons, the last great town gate to be constructed for Louis XIV by Vauban. 7 cells near the chapel have been converted into studios for artists in residence. The gardens will host exhibitions & performances, & the grand gateway itself, long-time home to the local tourist office, has been converted into a brasserie & art gallery.

Mons-en-baroeul

Fort de Mons Rue de Normandie, 59700 ℡ 03 20 61 78 90

This place thrills me as a performance space: brick & sky crying out for open-air theatre & screaming with potential. An elegant 19th-century moated fortress with 3 paved courtyards, rather than the traditional central parade ground, now houses a cinema, restaurant & library, with exhibition halls & music & dance venues within the fortified walls.

Roubaix

La Condition Publique See page 201.

Tourcoing

L'Hospice d'Havré See page 205.

Villeneuve d'Ascq

La Ferme d'en Haut See page 207.

Belgium

Courtrai

Lille sur l'Isle L'Isle Buda, 9 Budastraat, 8500 ℡ 056 51 81 00
On an island on the River Lys, warehouses & cloisters become theatres & museums. The Limelight Centre for Contemporary Arts boasts a cinema, restaurant & galleries, & even the river itself becomes an exhibition space with floating billboards presenting art on the waters.

Mons

Les Arbalestriers 8 rue des Arbalestriers, 7000 ℡ 065 39 98 01
Outside, an open-air summer theatre; within, a café-concert, *médiatheque*, exhibition hall & auditorium. And so a former school in the heart of the town becomes the cultural crossroads of Mons, working with theatre companies across the French border in Maubeuge.

Tournai

Seminaire de Choiseul 11 rue des Soeurs de Charité, 7500 ℡ 069 44 38 82
The original 13th-century church of Ste Marguerite was mostly destroyed by fire & rebuilt in 1760 in the style of a neo-classical temple. An earlier 16th-century tower remains & is a landmark in the centre of the Belgian town. As a Maison Folie, the church will host visiting exhibitions, stage concerts & creative workshops & be at the heart of local fairs, markets & carnivals.

A VARIETY OF VENUES

As well as the Maisons Folies, Lille 2004 opened up many overlooked or forgotten buildings to the public. Three in particular were taken very much to the hearts of the *Lillois* and their visitors. The Eglise Ste Marie Madeleine (**VL** Rue du Pont Neuf, 59000 ☎ 03 20 74 46 83; see page 187) is to continue to stage exhibitions after its stunning debut. The remarkable horticultural hall, the Palais Rameau on boulevard Vauban (**MK** [234 B3]; see *Jardin Vauban*, page 194), has a habit of stepping out of retirement time and again, should occasion demand it. Check with the tourist office for exhibitions. It may be run-down, but it is an essential diversion for anyone with a soul.

The other surprise star of the City of Culture season was the old postal sorting office by the railway tracks that served as cultural HQ and itinerant exhibition centre and party venue. Le Tripostale (**GP** Av Willy Brandt, 59777 [235 H4]), stands between the Gare Lille Flandres and Euralille shopping centre. Martine Aubry, charismatic mayor and superwoman, wrested Le Tripostale from its landlords to allow it to remain open for five more years. It is still going strong. Shows in its first year included futuristic robots, Buckingham Palace reinvented as a council estate, and a sensual tickling machine. Now, the Gare Saint Sauveur (see page 188) is the latest slice of railway real estate to be appropriated by the city. Time, and the tourist office, will tell what new surprises may be discovered within these many refurbished walls.

▼ *Frankie goes to Lille: the statue of president François Mitterand welcomes visitors to the Parc Matisse, the new green space linking the old town with the new Europe District.*

PARKS & GARDENS

Lille boasts 350ha of green spaces within the city limits, and the wider region stretches out into open country (see page 212 for the lakes and hilly walks of the nature reserve at Villeneuve d'Ascq). Even if you do not have time to head to the sand dunes by Dunkerque or the farmland beyond the city, enjoy a breath of fresh air within a few minutes of your next urban adventure.

Bois de Boulogne **VL** Av Mathias Delobel, 59000 ✆ (zoo) 03 28 52 07 00 🖝 free ⊘ zoo: Mon–Fri 09.00–17.30 Apr–Oct & 10.00–17.00 Nov–Mar, Sat–Sun & holidays 09.00–18.30 Apr–Oct & 10.00–17.00 Nov–Mar; closed 2nd Sun in Dec, 2nd Sun in Feb [234 A–B2] *e** *Métro 2 to Gare Lille Flandres, then line 1 to République–Beaux Arts. Bus 14 to Jardin Vauban.*
The countryside comes to town where panthers prowl, joggers run & families take the air. Neatly tied up in a loop of the River Deûle's canals are 125 acres of greenery, picturesque towpaths & an island filled with monkeys. Home to the famous fortress (see *Citadelle*, page 206), the Bois de Boulogne is where the city loosens its tie on weekends & holidays. Children love the zoo, free to all, with its *Ile des Singes* (Monkey Island) & contented rhinos & zebras. There is also a playground for dodgems, side-shows & candyfloss moments. Outside the zoo is a cobbled pathway that forms part of the arduous Paris–Roubaix cycle race, known colloquially as 'The Hell of the North'. Fitness fanatics pace themselves running around the former moat, following the signposted route between the ramparts & the willow trees. You can always tell the soldiers & foreign legionnaires by their blue tracksuits. Lovers wander into the woods, whilst more decorous strollers prefer the esplanade, landscaped in 1675 by Vauban himself, or the Champ de Mars where funfairs pitch their tents during school holidays. If all seems carefree & inconsequential, take a moment to pause by the Monument aux Fusillées on square Daubenton at the edge of the Bois. Félix Desruelle's memorial pays tribute to those *Lillois* members of the French Resistance shot by the Nazis against the walls of the Citadelle.

Jardin Vauban **VL** Bd Vauban, 59000 [234 A3–B3] *e** *Métro 2 to Gare Lille Flandres, then line 1 to République–Beaux Arts. Bus 14 to Jardin Vauban.*
A delightful 19th-century park, often overshadowed by the large lush expanses of the Bois de Boulogne across the River Deûle, this is a pretty confection of dainty flowerbeds, waterfalls, lawns & grottos, landscaped in 1865 by Paris's chief gardener, the aptly named Barillet Deschamps.

Poets' Corner contains memorials to writers & musicians, & a monument to Charles de Gaulle stands at the square Daubenton entrance. Locals visit the immaculate miniature orchard to meet the present-day gardeners who are always willing to give advice & tips on growing fruit & vegetables at home. The most famous corner of the park is the puppet theatre in Monsieur Rameau's Goat House, where every Sunday & Wednesday Jacques le Lillois performs for local children. This *Chalet aux Chèvres* was one of Charles Rameau's many eccentric legacies to the town. He was a noted horticulturist who gave Lille the splendid Palais Rameau at the junction of rue Solférino & bd Vauban, a vast horticultural hall that doubles as a circus & performing-arts venue. In need of renovation, the hall is nonetheless a gem of its time & type. These munificent bequests were given freely on the condition that his grave at the Cimetière du Sud is always marked by a bed of potatoes, a tomato plant, strawberries, a vine, rosebush & dahlias.

Jardin des Plantes Rue du Jardin des Plantes, 59000 ✆ 03 28 36 13 50 ☺ daily 07.30–21.00 Apr–Sep & 08.30–18.30 Oct–Mar; greenhouses ☺ 09.00–12.00 & 13.30–17.00 🚇 *Porte de Douai or Porte d'Arras* *e** Métro 2 to Porte de Douai, follow the rue Carrel south & turn right on the rue Cap Michel towards the park.
Waterfalls & tropical greenhouses, rare plants & trees from many lands, all to be found just a little too far south for most visitors to bother with. Yet just below the ring-road is one of the most romantic escapes in the city, where many a troth has been plighted at the top level of the conservatory, or in the cooling summer shade of the *orangerie*. Botanists are not the only visitors to feel their pulses quickening when they wander through the lovingly maintained gardens. Sense the sultry south in the most unlikely corner of northern France.

Parc Jean-Baptiste Lebas S/MK Bd Jean-Baptiste Lebas [235 F8] *e** Bus 13 from Gare Lille Flandres to Lille-Lebas.
Proof that Lille does not need an international title to come up with fresh projects, this conversion of a car park into a haven of greenery was 2005's gift from the city to its residents & guests, opening midway through the year. Where the Porte de Paris & bd de la Liberté come to their natural conclusions, the tarmac is being laid to lawns & century-old chestnut trees augmented by more than 12 dozen new lindens in 3ha of unexpected city-centre garden. Naturally there are nice chairs, lamps, with of course a *bouledrome* for the grown-ups & a children's play area too, & all wrapped in high railings with monumental gateways to the

▲ *Another legacy: Monsieur Rameau's palace, like his goat house and market garden grave, was a gift to the people of Lille.*

various boulevards back into town, & to the Gare Saint Sauveur by the railway tracks.

Parc Henri Matisse S Euralille, 59000 [235 H3] 🚆 *Lille Europe*
e* Step out of the station & it is right there!

Part of another grand project within a grand project (the wish to create a green belt around the old city walls), the Parc Matisse was chosen to be one of the installation-art sites of Lille 2004. Happily, this newest of city parks has ripened & weathered itself to sit well in the urban landscape. Spindly saplings are now emerging as adolescent trees, lawns mellowing to meadow, wild flowers sitting comfortably against centuries-old walls as a foreground to the futuristic glass empire of Lille Europe that rises from the gardens. Popular with picnickers as much as with those looking for a short cut through the Porte de Roubaix (see page 183), the park has come of age & proven itself as a treasured haven. You can tell it works – even office workers hold hands as they stroll through its 8 green hectares.

Parc Barbieux Roubaix
See page 202.

Beyond the City

Pretty gardens of the Parc Barbieux and Disney-quaint houses line the roads on the half-hour tram route to the two major satellite towns of Tourcoing and Roubaix. These days, the extended métro cuts journey times in half, blurring the boundaries between the city of Lille and the other towns that make up Lille Métropole. The metropolitan population is almost a million, and the artistic honours of the conurbation are now shared fairly around Lille's immediate neighbours. So the Ballet du Nord performs at the huge Colisée theatre in Roubaix, and the Atelier Lyrique at Tourcoing stages intimate productions of favourites from Mozart to Bernstein. Tourcoing has its annual jazz festival, whilst Roubaix holds an open-air art market. Villeneuve d'Ascq may now be a university centre, but the area was once famous for its windmills and watermills. Lille's tourist office has information on events in all the surrounding towns and offers plenty of seasonal alternatives to conventional public transport – canal boats and vintage trams amongst them. Wherever you roam, remember to dial ℂ 3265 from any phone in France and you will be put through to the local tourist information centre (French and English spoken), be it a village, town or city.

ROUBAIX

The town of a thousand chimneys evolved from the 15th to the 19th centuries, as Roubaix developed its textile industry. Originally a useful sideline for farmers in winter, the manufacture of fabric and clothes created a boom town during the industrial revolution, its wealth matched only by its social conscience. A succession of enlightened civic and business leaders (see page 1) saw the town pioneering crèches, social housing, family allowance benefits, allotments and hospitals for the workers. Meanwhile, the town fathers accumulated an incredible collection of sample books, fabrics, fashion designs and ephemera: a comprehensive catalogue of styles from the ancient Egyptians to the 20th century. This archive is now displayed to best effect at the Art and Industry

© Bradt Travel Guides Ltd

Bradt

20km
16 miles

Straits of Dover

Calais

Boulogne

Dunkerque

Cassel

St Omer

BELGIUM

Courtrai

Tourcoing

Wattrelos

Roubaix

Villeneuve d'Ascq

Tournai

Wambrechies

Marcq-en-Baroeul

Lambersart

LILLE

Seclin

Lens

Arras

Cambrai

Le Cateau-Cambrésis

Museum (see below), alongside the private art collections of the entrepreneurs who owned the original mills. The only Ingres in town (even Lille's Palais des Beaux Arts cannot claim that), Picassos and works of local artists Cogghe and Weerts are to be seen there. The exhibits' original home was destroyed in World War II: however, architect Jean-Paul Philippon has reinvented one of the great buildings of Roubaix's heyday to provide a worthy successor, within the one place in town where citizens of all classes would mingle as equals. For years before the Maisons Folies project breathed new life into abandoned factories and sites, Roubaix was reinventing its architecture to serve future generations.

Tourist information

Roubaix Tourist Office 12 pl de la Liberté, 59100 Roubaix
℡ 03 20 65 31 90 🖰 www.roubaixtourisme.com ⊘ Mon–Sat 09.30–18.00; closed Sun

AlloVisit A guided tour via your mobile phone. Dial ℡ 08 92 68 25 11, then 010 007 & follow instructions for a full English commentary & interviews relating to each of 6 local sites, following the walking map available from the tourist office. Costs 34 cents a minute.

What to see & do

La Piscine – Musée d'Art et d'Industrie (Art & Industry Museum) 23 rue de l'Espérance, 59100 Roubaix ℡ 03 20 69 23 60
🖫 €4.50 ⊘ Tue–Thu 11.00–18.00, Fri 11.00–20.00, Sat–Sun 13.00–18.00
🚉 Gare Jean Lebas *e** Métro 2 to Gare Jean Lebas. Walk down av Jean Lebas & turn right to rue des Champs & left onto rue de l'Espérance.
The sun also rises at the former municipal swimming pool: a dramatic stained-glass window radiates stylised sunbeams over this most ambitious project. With the Palais des Beaux Arts in Lille, this is one of the musts of the area. An exciting, eclectic & always stimulating collection housed in a building that is itself the town's greatest art treasure of them all. Albert Baert's art deco swimming pool is listed as the finest example of the genre in the land. Even when I was picking my way through the site, 10 years after it had been abandoned & as work was beginning on its renaissance, the building still had the power to thrill. Restored & reinvented as a combination art gallery & sensual archive of textiles, it takes the breath away. The original floors & walls are impressive enough, but the form & shape of the place is a ravishing assault on the senses.

It is built in the fashion of a Cistercian abbey, around a central courtyard, once a rose garden, now a *jardin des plantes* reflecting the textile industry (flax, mulberry & the like having played their roles in Roubaix's past). To one side is the magnificent vaulted swimming pool, to the other the municipal bath house, where some of the tiled bathrooms remain. The rest of the wings house the art collection.

And what a collection, with Bonnard, Dufy & Gallé among the big-name draws. Most dating from the end of the 19th & the first half of the 20th century, the artworks provide a forensic examination of the lives & people of Roubaix. Originally housed in the textile college across the way, the museum grew from a collection of fabrics from the textile factories to include works of art accumulated & acquired by the industrialist families of the town. Some of these works show remarkable glimpses into the lives of the working men & women of the town. Others are camply hilarious: Shaw's middle-class morality, with allegorical images of high ideals. I love the whore rising above her surroundings, the rose symbol of her baser trade being replaced by the lily of purity as she rejects sin in favour of redemption. Others show a more perceptive grasp of reality: the initially enchanting idyll of children playing in a field takes on a grimmer aspect when you notice the eldest little girl burying her dolls, as factory chimneys beckon her beyond ambrosia to an adult life of toil. Social politics merge with artistic merit in a gallery devoted to the emancipation of women through art. A wry evocation of the *Mona Lisa* shows a modern woman of learning; Camille Claudel's evocative bust of a child was a challenge to Rodin, her mentor & former lover, to acknowledge the paternity of her own daughter.

As you wander through the galleries, the occasional sound of splashing & shrieking within the unmistakable acoustic of swimming baths leads you to the heart of the museum, the pool itself. The witty sound effect is even more effective in situ. A sheet of water still runs almost the length of the Olympic baths, fed by the fountain head of Neptune at the end of the dazzling mosaic basin. This continues to reflect brilliant-coloured glass sunrise & sunset windows at each end of the building. Catch your breath then walk along the boardwalks lined with 19th- & 20th-century sculpture. These, like Cogghe & Weerts' paintings in earlier galleries, reflect the social history of the town. Some are worthy religious icons, others starkly socialist interpretations of the dignity of the working man. A massive Moorish arch in Sèvres porcelain dominates the room, & along each side of the pool are ranged tiers of original shower & changing cubicles. Glazed to protect their exhibits, these are now treasure houses, including a remarkable range of ceramics by Picasso. On upper levels the textile collection brings gowns & underwear, accessories & shoes of bygone ages. The *tissuthèque* is an archive of thousands of years of material patterns, from ancient Egypt to the present day. Around the museum, filing-cabinet drawers of fabrics allow visitors to plunge their hands in a sensory wonderland of the soft & silky, matted & furred.

Take time to reflect on the day with a cool drink in the restaurant or on its terrace, run by Meert of Lille (see page 118), flicking through an art book from the excellent museum shop.

Manufacture des Flandres (Jacquard Museum) 25 rue de la Prudence, 59100 Roubaix ℂ 03 20 65 31 90 ⌂ http://madefla.50g.com ⌂ free ⊘ Tue–Sun 14.00–18.00, closed Mon, holidays & 3 weeks in Aug; guided visits 14.00, 15.00, 16.00 & 17.00 *e* Roubaix tram or Métro 2 to Roubaix-Eurotéléport, then bus 20, 24 or 42 to pl de la Fraternité.*
A loom with a view on the history of the weaving industry at this working museum that explains the story of mass production of textiles. See looms, from the original hand-operated contraptions, through the growth of the Jacquard machines, to contemporary computer-operated systems. The museum is a great place to shop for faux-medieval wall hangings, arts & crafts tableware & contemporary scatter cushions.

Maison Folie – La Condition Publique Pl Faidherbe, 59100 Roubaix ℂ 03 28 33 57 57 ⌂ www.laconditionpublique.com ⊘ Tue–Sat 12.30–18.30 *e* Métro 2 to Roubaix Eurotéléport then bus 29 to Roubaix Faidherbe.*
I have loved this Maison Folie (see page 189) ever since it was still just a construction site, when I visited the work in progress in summer 2003. A magnificent building, irresistibly reminiscent of a Victorian railway station without the trains, this was the place where wool would come to be treated & packed. In recent years it has hosted many a local festival & concert, its cobbled driveway between the 2 vast warehouses giving it a sense of a town within a town. One aspect of the original building that will remain unchanged is the eccentric sloping lawn on the glass roofs. In order to provide a constant year-round temperature, the glazed roof was turfed over & workers would often lie down & doze on this incidental meadow in the sky. The new plan features an undulating roof garden to continue the tradition, & promises an experimental suspended garden within the complex. Indoors, discover the exhibition halls, arts space & facilities of the Maisons Folies projects, a grand *estaminet* & local heritage centre.

▲ *Heritage beyond the city limits: Notre Dame Hospital, Seclin.*

Chez Rita 49 rue Daubenton, 59100 Roubaix ✆ 03 20 26 22 88
⌂ http://librairiedesartistes.free.fr ⊙ Thu 17.00–22.00 (shop); phone for other opening times 🚉 *Gare Jean Lebas* *e** *Métro 2 to Gare Jean Lebas then bus 25 to Flandre.*

Is it a biscuit or is it art? Once upon a time, the Rita waffle factory closed down. Since the family who ran the business wanted to leave something to the local community that had served the company so well for so many years, they handed over the factory building to a community of artists, who now work, rest & play in the nooks & crannies, workshops & loading bays. Every corner has been converted into an individual's creative space, with easels, divans, installation art & canvases personalising each artist's studio. With superb art deco etched glass, wide industrial doorways & a romantic roof where invited guests might sit to watch a sunset, the building has a personality to rival any of the artworks on display & on sale. Some lunchtimes, the artists open their *estaminet* bar & café, where modestly priced pâté, salads & locally brewed ale are always on the menu. The Thursday evening *librairie* is a co-operative affair shop selling books, CDs, artworks etc.

Le Parc Barbieux Av Jean Jaurès, 59100 Roubaix *e** *Tram (towards Roubaix) to Parc Barbieux.*

The Tourcoing & Roubaix trams run alongside this prettiest of gardens where, for generations, middle-class families have pushed prams & strolled away the hours of sunny Sunday afternoons. Delightful flowerbeds, some rare trees & hidden statuary punctuate the manicured lawns. You may be forgiven for imagining that these long narrow strips of colour might have been laid out to complement the tramway. In fact they were created in the 18th century by Georges Aumont, a Parisian landscape gardener, on a site earmarked for development as a canal.

Objets du Hasard La Resourcerie, 9 rue St Hubert, 59100 Roubaix; ☎ 03 20 02 50 88 ⊘ Mon–Fri 14.00–19.00, Sat 10.00–12.00 & 14.00–19.00 *e* Métro 2 to Roubaix Eurotéléport then bus 42 to Roubaix Fraternité; walk south along rue de Lannoy to rue St Hubert.*

This is a sensational recycling project, rapidly becoming the hippest place to buy cutting-edge design. For this is where unwanted household objects are rescued from the civic dump & reborn as art & furniture. Drums from washing machines become tables & lamps, & a stylish showroom presents other people's trash as the ultimate wish-list. Out back, carpenters restore doors & drawers, while a *zingeur* tacks zincs onto abandoned desks & cabinets to create the desirable & the fashionable. Behind the stylish store is a splendid collection of old TVs, fridges, teddy bears & bookcases, sewing machines & broken chairs, all waiting patiently for their own reincarnations. Come, look, admire, buy or just reconsider your next trip to the skip.

MacArthur Glen Mail de Lannoy, 59100 Roubaix See page 153.

L'Usine 228 av Alfred Motte, 59100 Roubaix See page 153.

SECLIN

If you have time, visit the Notre Dame Hospital founded by the great Marguerite de Flandres with its 13th-century architecture and fine garden. Like the town's monumental cemetery archway and 13th-century Collégiale Saint Piat, the hospital is listed in the register of historic monuments.

Tourist information
Seclin Tourist Office 70 Roger Bouvry, 59113 Seclin ☎ 03 20 90 12 12 ⌂ www.seclin-tourisme.com

What to see & do
Domaine Mandarine Napoléon 204 rue de Burgault, 59113 Seclin

℡ 03 20 32 54 93 **e** mandarine.napoleon@wanadoo.fr ⊙ Tue–Sat 10.00–17.00 **e*** *Métro 2 to Lille Porte des Postes, then bus 55 to Burgault.*

A hit with readers of my Bradt guides, thanks to the *chambre d'hôte* in the old manor house (see page 66), this is worth a visit even if you are not planning on spending the night in imperial splendour. 10 mins outside town at exit 19 of the A1 is the new home of the Mandarine Napoléon distillery. The liqueur, a firm favourite of the short man with big ideas, so we are told, is actually a Belgian tipple, but the distillery has now moved its operations across the border to this wonderfully restored farm with arboretum & butterfly gardens. Visitors may tour the distillery & a superb private collection of memorabilia of the great military man himself. George Fourcroy, head of the drinks company & descendant of the creator of the original recipe, personally created the Napoléon Bonaparte Museum with artefacts spanning 28 years from the legend's rise to political power to his death. From letters & uniforms to the bronze death mask, the collection is well displayed in a specially designed showroom. The complex also houses banqueting suites for weddings & conferences. An area is set aside for private games of *pétanque*, & a tasting lounge & gift shop cater to museum visitors.

TOURCOING

In a region famous for its bell towers, Tourcoing, renowned as a centre of the arts ancient and modern, makes space for a museum of bell-ringing (⊙ 1st & 3rd Sun aft May–Oct). Not only does the Musée du Carillon include some 62 bells weighing more than six tons, but the bell-ringer's cabin offers the best view of the town!

Tourist information

Tourcoing Tourist Office 9 rue de Tournai, 59200 Tourcoing ℡ 03 20 26 89 03 ◌ www.tourcoing-tourisme.com ⊙ Mon–Sat 09.30–12.30 & 13.30–18.30; closed Sun

What to see & do

Le Fresnoy Studio National des Arts Contemporains
22 rue du Fresnoy, 59202 Tourcoing ℡ 03 20 28 38 00 ◌ www.lefresnoy.net ◌ free admission to site, exhibition charges vary ⊙ Mon–Fri 09.00–12.30 & 14.00–17.30 ⊞ Alsace **e*** *Métro 2 to Alsace. Walk south on bd d'Armentières then right to rue du Capitaine Aubert into rue du Fresnoy.*

The arts centre & college on the site of an old bowling alley, dance hall & fleapit cinema has a lively programme of exhibitions, but any event is easily upstaged by the building itself & the vision of architect Tschumi. Le Fresnoy is perhaps the only building ever to have been designed to pander to human nature. Its charm lies in the 'in-between', a magical hinterland between two roofs. Tschumi decided to retain the original shells of the 1905 movie theatre & hall & create a footpath between the old tiles & the futuristic canopy of the modern centre. And so it is that students, locals & visitors alike can wander hand in hand around the chimney-stacks on a network of suspended metal gantries & steps. One path leads to a dead end behind a sloping roof. 'Why?' I asked. The answer was simple: 'The architect said that young people need somewhere to, you know, to kiss!' On summer nights they may hold hands as well, since the design also incorporates a mini-grandstand for watching old movies projected on to the tiles. Films are also screened in the art centre's 2 small cinemas. During Lille 2004 Le Fresnoy twinned itself with the home & studio of film-making legend Jean-Luc Godard & ran live feeds of the master's works in progress.

Musée des Beaux Arts 2 rue Paul Doumer, 59200 Tourcoing ✆ 03 20 28 91 60 **e** museebeauxarts@ville-tourcoing.fr 🖋 free ⊘ Wed–Mon 13.30–18.00 🚉 Tourcoing Centre **e*** Tram or métro to Tourcoing Centre. Rue Leclerc to rue Paul Doumer.

Eclectic, imaginative & never less than stimulating, Tourcoing's art collection spans the artistic spectrum from Brueghelesque Flemish works to the Cubists, & the archives are regularly ransacked by the curator to keep exhibitions fresh & nicely incongruous. So find a Rembrandt next to some local artist's portrait of a much-loved grandmother or discover a Picasso between a couple of mundane still lives. My favourite painting is the deliciously grand portrait of *Mlle Croisette en Costume d'Amazon*, a prim & proper bourgeois equestrian pose with more than a hint of passion beneath the unseen corsetry. The pictures are housed in elegant galleries dating from the 1930s. If the pick-&-mix nature of the museum appeals to you, cast your eye over the front of the nearby Maison du Collectionneur, an architectural buffet of a house whose original owner wanted to combine as many styles as possible in one building, at 3 sq Winston Churchill.

Maison Folie – L'Hospice d'Havré Rue d'Havré, 59200 Tourcoing ✆ 03 59 63 43 53 ⊘ 13.30–18.00; closed Tue & holidays **e*** Métro line 2 to Tourcoing Centre; follow rue de Tournai to turn right on to rue Havré.

Known locally as Notre Dame des Anges, this former monastery & poorhouse has retained all of its original buildings, & its various wings & cloister are a living record of styles from Lille baroque to Louis XIV's 18th-century influences. The chapel, gardens, hospice & baths now house an exhibition hall, artists' workshops, concert hall, restaurant & strip-cartoon centre in its new incarnation as Tourcoing's Maison Folie (see page 189). The blend of historical monument & free-for-all accessibility is rather exciting & like so many of the Maisons Folies lends a supercharge to the most modest occasion. The chapel gives chamber music a deserved home in a town better known for jazz. Guided tours on the first Sunday of each month (except Aug) at 11.00.

VILLENEUVE D'ASCQ

Renowned as home to Lille's university campus and boasting a vast shopping mall, it might be easy to forget that there is a strong rural heritage to be explored in this bustling satellite. Just outside the centre is the museum of windmills, a fascinating and unexpected little treat, as is the farming Musée du Terroir. Get outdoors at the Parc Urbain and use your field glasses at the Héron nature reserve with its lake and forested artificial hillside that welcomes 200, mostly migratory, types of bird. The tourist office has walking maps to some 30km of country footpaths over 155,000ha of open spaces and six lakes. Take métro line 1 to Pont de Bois, and then bus 41 to Contre Escarpe for the Parc Urbain Visitor Centre (☎ 03 20 91 77 33).

Tourist information

Villeneuve d'Ascq Tourist Office Château de Flers, Chemin du Chat Botté, 59650 Villeneuve d'Ascq ☎ 03 20 43 55 75

What to see & do

Musée d'Art Moderne 1 allée du Musée, 59650 Villeneuve d'Ascq ☎ 03 20 19 68 68 ☝ http://mam.cudl-lille.fr ☺ Wed–Mon 10.00–18.00; closed 1 Jan, 1 May & 25 Dec *e** *Métro 2 to Gare Lille Flandres then line 1 to Pont de Bois, then bus 41 to Parc Urbain-Musée, & follow the footpath into the park.* Discover the greatest artists of the 20th century in the galleries & gardens of this unexpected cultural park in Villeneuve d'Ascq, Lille's university campus suburb. To be renamed the 'LAM' for its grand reopening sometime in 2010, the light & unassuming brick building makes no attempt to upstage the top-notch collection that it houses. A comprehensive tour through the most influential painters of each of the key artistic movements of the past 100 years includes a half-dozen Picassos, Braque's *Maisons et Arbres*, works by Rouault, Miró & Masson, & some renowned canvases by Modigliani, including his *Nu Assis à la Chemise*. The bulk of the museum's wealth comes from generous bequests to the community from the private collections of Roger Dutilleul, & Jean & Geneviève Masurel. The Fauvist & Cubist rooms arc most popular, but post-war artists are equally well represented through more recent acquisitions. Temporary exhibitions vary in style & quality. If you are lucky you may spot an engaging new genius. Of course, you may have to wade through more than a few luminaries of the post-talent movement to find it. As you step between eras, huge plate-glass windows look out on the lawns where locals walk their dogs, ride their micro-scooters & kick footballs between installation sculptures, including Picasso's *Femme aux Bras Ecartés* & Alexander Calder's *Southern Cross*. Jewellery & other objects by local artists are sold in the museum shop, & the café & restaurant on site provide plenty of opportunity to continue the 'Yes, but is it Art?' debates. Until the grand reopening in mid or late 2010, many of the museum's treasures may be displayed in other galleries around the region, so check with Lille & Villeneuve d'Ascq's tourist offices for news of temporary exhibitions.

Forum des Sciences Centre François Mitterand

(Science Museum & Planetarium) 1 pl Hôtel de Ville, 59650 Villeneuve d'Ascq ☏ 03 20 19 36 36 ⌂ www.forum-des-sciences.tm.fr ₰ €3, €7.50 or €9.50 depending on how many attractions you visit; free admission 1st Sun of the month ⊙ Tue–Fri 10.00–17.30, Sat, Sun & holidays 14.30–18.30, hours may differ during French school holidays; closed Mon, 1 Jan, 1 May, 25 Dec ▣ Hôtel de Ville *e** Métro 2 to Gare Lille Flandres then line 1 to Hôtel de Ville. See Lille's night sky by day at the planetarium. You will probably not want to take the trip to Villeneuve d'Ascq simply to see the planetarium, but if you are travelling with children, this science centre makes an enjoyable diversion & bargaining counter for buying your own time at the modern art museum. The entertaining & informative shows (some in English) at the planetarium range from speculation as to life on Mars to the history of time itself. All presentations begin with a simulation of the Lille sky at dusk. A splashy, hands-on activity centre appeals to little ones, & adults will like the thought-provoking temporary exhibitions.

Maison Folie – La Ferme d'en Haut

268 rue Jules Guesde, Flers Bourg, 59650 Villeneuve d'Ascq ☏ 03 20 61 01 46 *e** Métro 2 to Mons en

Baroeul Fort de Mons then bus 43 to Villeneuve d'Ascq Faidherbe, follow signs to tourist office on rue Guesde.

The Upper Farm of the former Château de Flers (which is itself home of the tourist office & archaeological museum) is a typical red-brick & white-stone building of the region. In its Maison Folie incarnation (see page 189) farming heritage can be explored in an experimental kitchen, & many dance, drama or cabaret performances may well be accompanied by a meal in the performance space. I visited the place in its very early days & found an exhibition of circuses. The town has a long love affair with the big top & even involves acrobats & performers in its work with disabled & special needs children. As I was browsing the fascinating displays, & discovering a charming & unsung aspect of the local community, I could hear jazz musicians preparing for a performance later the same day.

Musée du Souvenir (Museum of Remembrance) 77 rue Mangain, 59650 Villeneuve d'Ascq ☎ 03 20 91 87 57 ⊘ Sun 14.30–17.30, Wed 09.00–12.00 & 14.30–17.30 year round; Tue & Thu 14.30–17.30 Jul–Aug *e* Métro 2 to Gare Lille Flandres then line 1 to Pont de Bois, then bus 43 to Massena.*

If you come to Villeneuve d'Ascq on a Sunday, find time to pay your respects to the memory of the victims of the Ascq Massacre, on Palm Sunday 1944. When local members of the Resistance blew up a train on the Tournai–Lille railway line, even though no one was injured, an SS convoy from the Russian front rounded up every man in the little community of Ascq. Some were shot in their homes, others taken to this site to be executed. In total, 86 died in the massacre, some as young as 15 years old. This simple museum has the usual wartime posters, but far more poignant are the clusters of personal effects of the victims that make the tragedy horribly personal. In the 1960s, when the area was swallowed up by the expanding city of Lille, it was decided to rename the district as Villeneuve d'Ascq in tribute to those who died.

WAMBRECHIES

What to see & do

Mairie 5 pl Général de Gaulle, 59118 Wambrechies ☎ 03 28 38 84 00; Information ☎ 03 28 42 44 58 ⌂ www.amitram.asso.fr

A vintage tram from 1906 runs every 15 mins along the canal bank between Wambrechies & Marquette on Sunday & public holidays between April & September, 14.30–19.00. Passengers may join the tram at Vent de Bise at Wambrechies or rue de la Deûle at Marquette. Pay €4 return fare & sit on authentic wooden benches, as refurbished in 1926.

Distillerie Claeyssens 1 rue de la Distillerie, 59118 Wambrechies ℓ 03 20 14 91 91 ⁀ www.wambrechies.com ⏍ €6, reservation essential ⊙ tours 09.30–12.30 & 13.30–17.30; closed holidays *e** *Bus 9 from Gare Lille Flandres to Wambrechies Château or bus 3 from Gare Lille Flandres to Wambrechies Mairie. From rue 11 Nov 1918 take rue Leclerc to rue de la Distillerie.* There is nothing high-tech about this distillery that has been making *genièvre* gin from junipers for the past 200 years. The original wooden equipment still sifts seeds, mills flour & heats, cools & distils the spirit, just as it did in Napoleonic times, when the waterways of the Deûle brought grain from Belgium after an edict banned the use of French crops. The hour-long tour is an anecdote-filled meander through a past that can hold its own in the present. An opportunity to taste the robust tipple follows the tour & a shop sells not only the *genièvre* itself, but 2 rather special by-products: beer made during the fermenting process, & a single malt of Highland quality. You may also combine the distillery tour with a canal trip from Lille on Claeyssens's private barge.

Musée de la Poupée et du Jouet Ancien (Doll & Antique Toy Museum) Château de Robersart, 59118 Wambrechies ℓ 03 20 39 69 28 ⁀ www.musee-du-jouet-ancien.com ⏍ €4 ⊙ Sun, Wed & school holidays 14.00–18.00; closed 25 Dec & 1 Jan *e** *Bus 9 from Gare Lille Flandres to Wambrechies Château.* At last, they tie the knot. The wedding of Barbie & Ken is a glittering occasion, the guest list itself reads like a who's who of Barbie. There's Beach Barbie, & Beautician Barbie & Trolley Dolly Barbie &, for all I know, Feng Shui Consultant Dietician Barbie, in the biggest gathering of big hair on plastic heads since *Dynasty* slipped off the TV listings pages. The nuptial tableau featuring scores of versions of the doll from each year of her long career is staged in a model of a Gothic cathedral, & is typical of the imaginative displays at this charming museum of childhood. The setting of the museum itself is something of a happy ever after, housed in the family château of Juliette, the last countess of Robersart. 2 galleries feature dolls & toys from every era. Victorian playthings & latter-day train sets provide plenty of 'ooh ahh' moments. Among the most interesting items in the permanent display are miniature fashion outfits made to patterns printed in the leading women's magazines of the last century.

ALSO WORTH A VISIT

The Maisons Folies network stretches far beyond Lille Métropole, even across the border into Belgium. So if you have a day to spare for exploring, check out the list on pages 189–92. This is a land rich in shared history, with Henry V's Agincourt less than 70 miles away (visit the battle museum built to resemble a row of English bowmen – I was the token Shakespeare-loving Brit on the French selection committee that chose the design), Henry VIII's Field of the Cloth of Gold on the road back to the ferry in Calais and the mustering station for Napoleon's putative invasion of Britain outside Boulogne. And, of course, Flanders fields lie all around you.

Arras

When you visit the Maison Folie (see page 191), do explore the rest of this stunning town. Incredibly, the 17th- and 18th-century squares are not the real thing, but recreated faithfully from the original architects' plans rescued from the rubble when the town was razed in two wars. Climb the belfry for views, and descend into the bowels of the town to see the remarkable network of underground passages that links the cellars of the old houses and was commandeered by the Allies in World War I as a command post. Railways ran under the city to the front line. Don't miss the unforgettable Canadian memorial and trenches at Vimy Ridge.

Tourist Office ☏ 03 21 51 26 95 ✉ arras-tourisme@wanadoo.fr

Boulogne-sur-mer

The delightful port with its old town perched on the hill is as charming as ever. Visit the Château Museum and walk the ramparts. By the port, Nausicaa, an interactive museum of the sea with sharks and sea lions, is a fascinating day out in its own right and an ardent exponent of green issues.

Tourist Office ☏ 03 21 10 88 10 🖑 www.ville-boulogne-sur-mer.fr

Calais

The Channel port best known for booze cruisers may not be as quaint as its neighbours, but take time to explore. The Musée des Beaux Arts et de la Dentelle, with its arts and fashion exhibits, was a major player in Lille 2004. Other worthy diversions include a war museum in a bunker, the lighthouse and many fine restaurants.

Tourist Office ☏ 03 21 96 62 40 🖑 www.calais-cotedopale.com

Cassel

The true spirit of Flanders, with windmills and *estaminets*.

Tourist Office ℓ 03 28 40 52 55 ℮ cassel@tourisme.norsys.fr

Dunkerque

The port of privateers and adventure has museums of fine arts, maritime heritage and piracy.

Tourist Office ℓ 03 28 66 79 21 ⌂ www.ot-dunkerque.fr

Le Cateau-cambresis

Birthplace of Henri Matisse: visit the fabulously restored museum devoted to the artist and his works.

Tourist Office ℓ 03 27 84 10 94 ⌂ www.tourisme-lecateau.fr

Lens

When the Louvre comes to the north in 2010 (see page 7), Lens will be on every cultural itinerary. Follow the progress of the new project online at ⌂ www.louvrelens.fr. Meanwhile, like Arras (see page 210), it is surrounded by wartime memories.

Tourist Office ℓ 03 21 67 66 66 ⌂ www.tourisme-lenslievin.fr

Marcq-en-baroeul

For generations this was Lille's Sunday in the country, the racecourse itself proving a magnet for the working man on his day off. Another attraction is the Septentrion gallery housed in a magnificent building in its 60-acre park, and the Château du Vert Bois and its museum of telecomunications.

Tourist Office ℓ 03 20 72 60 87 ⌂ www.ot-marcqenbaroeul.com

St Omer

For the Musée Sandelin to see how a table should be laid; for Arc International, better known as Crystal d'Arques, Europe's greatest glassmaking empire; for the fabulous Marais Audemarois's hidden world of floating market gardens, the chicory and wildlife, explored by canoe or tour boat from the café-restaurant Le Bon Accueil at Salperwick. Most importantly, for La Coupole, a Nazi V2 bunker just out of town, housing twin museums of life in occupied France and the space race. Do take time out to visit the aerodrome. The Royal Flying Corps was based here during the Great War and you will find a rarity – an RAF memorial away from British soil.

Tourist Office ☏ 03 21 98 08 51 ⌨ www.tourisme-saintomer.com

Wattrelos

Party on dudes. This is where the northern passion for good times beats its heart. March has the annual Salon des Artistes, April brings the great parade of giants and September boasts Les Berlouffes, France's second biggest fleamarket on the weekend after the Braderie of Lille itself. The art of fun is explored in a museum of popular arts and traditions.

Tourist Office ☏ 03 20 75 85 86 ⌨ www.ville-wattrelos.fr

HIKING & BIKING

If you've a yen for the great outdoors, rather than simply site-hopping on four wheels, then leave the city behind and explore the countryside of the Nord department. The Comité Départemental de Tourisme (CDT) (see page 38) publishes imaginative hiking and biking itineraries for exploring the trails of buccaneers, bandits and garlic smokers. Walk the Flanders Opal Coast in the path of legendary corsair and buccaneer Jean Bart; ride the frontiers where smugglers once toted their contraband between Belgium and France; enjoy the intimate and welcoming country *estaminet* bars in the front rooms of village houses; or simply head out into the natural and regional parks within reasonable reach of Lille.

Two English-language packs for walkers and cyclists have been created by the Nord Tourist Board and offer practical and easy-to-use trails, with plenty of information on sites and diversions en route, as well as recommended IGN maps. The packs may be downloaded free of charge from ⌨ www.cdt-nord.fr or obtained directly from the tourist office on ☏ 03 20 57 59 59.

Pack One suggests 30 excellent walks through the area, ranging from coastal hikes through the sand dunes to trails highlighting more gastronomic traditions, such as the *genièvre* gin distilleries (see page 209) and the Hainaut village of Arleux, famous for its smoked garlic soup. A waymarked 12km monastic trail is useful for building up an appetite, since it takes in the greatly appreciated Trappist sidelines of brewing and cheesemaking, as well as the windmills and ornate altarpieces! Trails through the Avesnois regional natural park combine the beauty of nature with the opportunity to learn traditional skills of earlier times, such as glassblowing.

The second pack has 22 trails for all-terrain bikers. Like the hikers' guide, it features a range of treats, from Paris-Roubaix cobbled circuits within Lille Métropole to the smugglers and *estaminets* trail through Flanders, along the cat-and-mouse footsteps of customs officers and their prey as well as excursions through the wetlands of the Scarpe-Escaut regional park and the hideaway habitats of wild deer.

IN FLANDERS FIELDS

The Flanders of recent memory, the fields where poppies grow beneath the crosses, is to be found in small hamlets and the grander memorials of Vimy Ridge and the Mennen Gate. An essential drive by car, since so many of these monuments and cemeteries are close to the city. For visitors without their own car, a coach tour leaves the Tourist Office every Saturday from April until mid-December at 13.30. An English-speaking guide explains the *lieux de memoires* en route to Ypres in Belgium, taking in the vast Tyne Cot Commonwealth cemetery and Essex Farm, inspiration of John McCrae's immortal poem, *In Flanders Fields*. The coach returns to Place de la République at 5.30.
Price €35; information & bookings 7 days a week on ☎ *0033 359 579 400 or* ✉ *info@lilletourism.com.*

Beyond the city Hiking & biking

Language

The principal language of Lille is, of course, French, but with its historical and geographical history, the Flemish side of the city is comfortable speaking Dutch. After all, until Eurostar awakened Britain to this gem on its doorstep, virtually every visitor came from Belgium. The Flemish for Lille is *Rijsel*, by the way.

The locals have their own patois, *Ch'ti*, a variation of the *Picard* argot spoken across northern France. You will rarely come across an entire conversation in the northern tongue; however, local cabarets aimed at domestic rather than visiting audiences will feature a smattering of phrases, and should you hang around a genuine *estaminet* you may well pick up some words that would baffle a Parisian! If you fancy trying your hand at a few words, do so in the comfort of your own home with an online dictionary (such as ⌐www.freelang.com/dictionnaire/chti.html). But don't worry if you don't get it. Local variants on language the world over, from rhyming slang to Yiddish, are designed for local communities. Outsiders are meant to be baffled! And you will probably have to let playground and street slang pass you by. *Verlan* (from *l'envers*) is popular 'backslang' (try *beur* for *arabe*), and is the most commonly spoken.

Around Wazemmes market you may well hear Arabic, so a few choice words and phrases from your wider travels may stand you in good stead.

FRENCH

The French are in general better mannered than their anglophone friends and neighbours, and simple courtesies are a way of life, with the lack of them making a negative impression.

The simple greetings *Bonjour* ('Good day') or *Bonsoir* ('Good evening') are essentials.

When a shopkeeper says '*Bonne journée*' or '*Bonne soirée*', that is the equivalent of the American salutation 'Have a nice day!'

Always use the courtesy titles *Monsieur* (Sir), *Madame* (Madam) or

Mademoiselle (Miss) when speaking to strangers – and remember that it is still more polite to refer to a mature woman as *Madame*, whether or not she sports a wedding ring. 'Ms' does not exist in France. Oh, and courtesy applies to waiters as well: it is considered ill-bred to snap the fingers and yell '*garçon*'. Restaurant staff in France are considered professionals: many will have studied for years from the age of 14 in order to perfect their art.

Shake hands whenever humanly possible. The French love doing it. The kissing on both cheeks business has its own rules that remain practically Masonic. Between men it is rarely done except 'twixt father and son or heads of state who hate each other, but if a woman is being introduced or encountered on a social basis (at a dinner party perhaps), the brushing of proffered cheeks is the thing to do. Usually twice, although between friends this may become three pecks, and within families four times is not unknown. (I have finally worked out the rules for cheek air-kissing: once = rude, twice = polite, thrice = friendly, four times = familial, five times = foreplay.) Shake hands on entering a room, meeting someone for the first time in the day and on ending a conversation. The only exception would be at a urinal or during an autopsy. However, I've found hands extended my way in an abattoir. To refuse would have gone down as well as a discussion on the many uses of tofu.

Then comes the heady question of pronouns, the second person in particular. In school we learn that *tu* and *toi* are the familiar version of 'you', with *vous* being the more formal usage. Of course there are no hard and fast rules, but I strongly recommend using *vous* to start any conversation and be guided by the local as to how you should continue. There are exceptions. These days young people – and Lille is a student town – tend towards *tutoyer* (ie: use *toi*) as a matter of course, and in trendy or gay bars the informal form is the norm, rather as the words 'love', 'darling' or 'mate' might be bandied in a British pub. Rule of thumb: always use *vous* when talking to someone of a different generation.

Remember your p's and q's. *S'il vous plaît* and *merci* cost nothing and should be used whenever possible.

In Lille, you will find that English is pretty widely spoken. A huge percentage of the population is involved with further education. The city's international business community and canny shopkeepers can handle most conversations in your native tongue. However, it is always appreciated when visitors make at least a modest attempt to speak the local language. So the following words should be used – even if you bashfully return to English after the initial contact:

Bonjour/bonsoir   Good day/good evening

Au revoir	Goodbye
Bonne nuit	Good night
Merci	Thank you
S'il vous plaît	Please
Oui	Yes
Non	No (see Charles de Gaulle)
Comment allez-vous?/Ça va?	How are you?
Très bien, merci	Very well, thank you
Au secours!	Help!
Aidez-moi!	Help me!

Only once you have memorised thus far may you learn the following phrase:

Parlez-vous anglais?	Do you speak English?

However, if you can remember that, then surely the following nuggets cannot be too difficult to deliver:

Je ne comprends pas	I don't understand
Parlez moins vite, s'il vous plaît	Speak a little slower, please
Je ne sais pas	I don't know
Je suis anglais/écossais/gallois/ *irlandais/américain/canadien/* *australien**	I am English/Scottish/Welsh/Irish/ American/Canadian/Australian
Avez vous une chambre à deux lits/ *grand lit?*	Have you a twin/double room?
Avec bain/douche	With bath/shower
Veuillez me réveiller à huit heures?	Could you wake me at 08.00?
Où est...?	Where is...?
Où?	Where?
Comment?	How?
Quand?	When?
Pourquoi?	Why?
Je voudrais...	I would like...
Combien?	How much?
Bon marché	Cheap
Cher/chère	Expensive
L'addition, s'il vous plaît	The bill, please
Je suis végétarien(ne)	I am vegetarian

Je suis malade   I am ill

* The examples given are in the masculine; women should add an 'e' (or 'ne') to each national adjective.

If you are still reading this chapter, the chances are your French grammar is pretty rusty and you want to know which words are masculine (using *le* or *un*) and which feminine (*la* or *une*). Well, I hate to break it to you, but you are hardly going to squeeze in a decent education between the top of this page and the index, so allow me, in my unorthodox way, to suggest an extremely useful compromise: learn essential nouns, use gestures, smile and remember to say *merci* (that sound that you just heard was Mrs Stockton, my third-form French mistress… fainting).

Useful nouns

beer	*une bière* (see page 70)	passport	*un passeport*
bread	*le pain*	park	*un parc*
breakfast	*le petit déjeuner*	petrol	*l'essence*
bus	*un car*	postcard	*une carte postale*
bus station	*la gare routière*	soup	*potage, consommé,*
car	*une voiture*		*soupe, bouillon*
chemist	*la pharmacie*	stamp	*un timbre*
condom	*le préservatif*	station	*la gare* (train),
credit card	*carte de crédit*		*la station* (subway)
dinner	*le dîner*	telephone	*le téléphone*
doctor	*le médecin*	ticket	*le billet/ticket*
fish	*le poisson*	toilet	*les toilettes/WC*
hospital	*l'hôpital*		(pronounced
letter	*une lettre*		doob-levay-say)
luggage	*les bagages*	town	*la ville*
lunch	*le déjeuner*	train	*le train*
meat	*la viande*	water	*l'eau*
menu	*la carte*	(mineral)	*(minérale)*
money	*l'argent*	wine	*le vin*
motorway	*l'autoroute*		

Days & months

Monday	*lundi*	Friday	*vendredi*
Tuesday	*mardi*	Saturday	*samedi*
Wednesday	*mercredi*	Sunday	*dimanche*
Thursday	*jeudi*		
January	*janvier*	February	*février*

March	*mars*	August	*août*
April	*avril*	September	*septembre*
May	*mai*	October	*octobre*
June	*juin*	November	*novembre*
July	*juillet*	December	*décembre*
day	*le jour*	noon	*midi*
today	*aujourd'hui*	afternoon	*l'après-midi*
yesterday	*hier*	evening	*le soir*
tomorrow	*demain*	night	*la nuit*
morning	*le matin*		

Numbers

1	*un/une*	16	*seize*
2	*deux*	17	*dix-sept*
3	*trois*	18	*dix-huit*
4	*quatre*	19	*dix-neuf*
5	*cinq*	20	*vingt*
6	*six*	30	*trente*
7	*sept*	40	*quarante*
8	*huit*	50	*cinquante*
9	*neuf*	60	*soixante*
10	*dix*	70	*soixante-dix* (except for
11	*onze*		Belgians who say *septante*)
12	*douze*	80	*quatre-vingt*
13	*treize*	90	*quatre-vingt-dix*
14	*quatorze*	100	*cent*
15	*quinze*	1,000	*mille*

Note: During sporting fixtures between the UK and France, I adopt Australian or Canadian nationality and accent if outnumbered on public transport.

Phrasebook

If you are considering buying a phrasebook, then the best in the business is *Hide This French Book* from Berlitz, priced £6.99. Very little use at the hairdresser or for buying stamps, it has genuinely invaluable stuff for real conversations, with sections on flirting, over-indulging, regretting and all aspects of a lively young social life from first meeting to the antibiotics after the night before. The slang is up to date and it even includes texting and email patois. Check it out (together with audio pronunciation files) online at ⊕www.berlitzpublishing.com.

Language French

Further information

ESSENTIALS

Lille Tourist Office ⌐🖰 www.lilletourism.com

ENTERTAINMENT

A range of daily freesheet newspapers, handed out at métro stations and especially around Gare Lille Flandres, are aimed at local commuters and have up-to-date listings and reviews. Also check out the day's *La Voix du Nord* at your hotel (see page 41).

Sortir magazine, a weekly entertainment listings magazine, is published on Wednesdays and is available from the tourist office (free), hotels and bars.

Autour de Minuit nightlife guide is free from the tourist office.

Nightpeople free from bars around town is packed with club news, photos and listings.

LOCAL TRANSPORT

⌐🖰 www.transpole.fr

⌐🖰 www.voyages-sncf.com

⌐🖰 www.eurostar.com

⌐🖰 www.raileurope.co.uk

⌐🖰 www.ter-sncf.com (for local trains)

DISABLED TRAVELLERS

Consider the *Smooth Ride Guide To France* by July Ramsay: ⌐🖰 www.smoothrideguides.com. Always worth keeping to hand in France is the Michelin Red Guide (£15.99 or €24) which now features a wheelchair symbol indicating hotels and restaurants with sensible facilities/access for disabled visitors. The free guide *Handi-Tourisme* with listings of hotels and attractions is available from the CDT Nord (see page 38).

VEGETARIAN TRAVELLERS

Visit ☝ www.focusguides.com for all guidebooks, but especially guidebooks for vegetarian travellers, including Andrew Sanger's hard-to-get-your-hands-on *Vegetarian Traveller* and Alex Bourke and Alan Todd's *Vegetarian France*.

GAY LILLE

A free guide and map listing all gay venues in the region is available from bars, clubs and other gay establishments in the city (see pages 138–40).

MODERN LILLE

A book of photographs by Jean-Pierre Duplan and Eric Le Brun, *Lille, Voyage en Métropole* (Ravet-Anceau), features six essays by leading French journalists on life in modern Lille. Available from bookshops in and around the city.

MAPS

Michelin Regional map 511 covers the Nord-Pas de Calais and the larger-scale Local 302 features greater Lille (including the Belgian towns). Online route finders can be found at ☝ www.viamichelin.com and ☝ www.mappy.fr.

TRAVEL GUIDES

Eurostar travel to Paris & Brussels

Paris, Lille, Brussels: The Bradt Guide to Eurostar Cities (£11.95) is the original award-winning guide for Eurostar travellers. Perfect if you have enjoyed this book, are planning a trip to Paris or Brussels, and want more personal reviews of the more eccentic and offbeat places to see.

Nord Pas de Calais

Due in August 2010, *Nord Pas de Calais: The Bradt Travel Guide* is the perfect companion to the region surrounding Lille. It delves not only into the port towns, but also into the forgotten France that's rarely reached.

It takes visitors to sample Vieux Bologne, the smelliest cheese in the world, and to climb the hill at Cassel, up (and down) which the Grand Old Duke of York marched his 10,000 men. It leads them to Agincourt, site of Henry V's famous battle (and where Bradt author Laurence Phillips was the token Shakespeare-loving Brit on the French selection committee that chose the design of the museum), and takes in more recent history from the trenches of World War I to the World War II beaches of Dunkirk. It also reveals where visitors can shop for cut-price goods; where they can cycle, walk and ride horses; how to enjoy the Festival of the Giants; and which are the top seaside resorts for children.

Index

Page numbers in **bold** indicate major entries

227

▲ The Bois de Boulogne is open country in the heart of town and prime cycling territory around the Citadelle (p.194).

(MD)

▲ Corners for reflection in the Jardin des Plantes (p.195).

(MD)

▲ A presidential welcome to new arrivals with the François Mitterand statue by the Parc Matisse, linking Euralille with the old town (p.196).

(LP)

(Z/A/SP)

▲ *The museum that upstages its own exhibits: the perpetual sunrise at La Piscine's sculpture gallery (p.199). (Below) Paris in miniature, the Opéra de Lille is an occasion in itself (p.181).*

(L/A/SP)

(MD)

(T/A/SP)

(DN/PCL)

▲ *The Fine Arts: (above) Ste Marie Madeleine, a truly spiritual home to the arts (p.187); (top right) a tuba player from Lille's National Orchestra; (right) still life at the Palais des Beaux Arts sculpture gallery (p.171).*

(MD)

▲ *The Fun Arts: over the top architecture at the people's playhouse; the Sebastapol theatre is home to knockabout comedies and concerts (p.128).*

(MD)

(DT)

(LP)

(YG/PCL)

▲ Le p'tit Quinquin - Lille's most cuddled
monument (p.183); monumental Lille:
(top left) the Goddess statue dominates
Flemish gables on the squares (p.178);
(middle left) Spanish Renaissance
confection at La Vielle Bourse (p.183);
(bottom left) 20th century pastiche
at the Chamber of Commerce (p.181);
(below) pure Art Nouveau at La Maison
Coillot (p.179).

(MD)

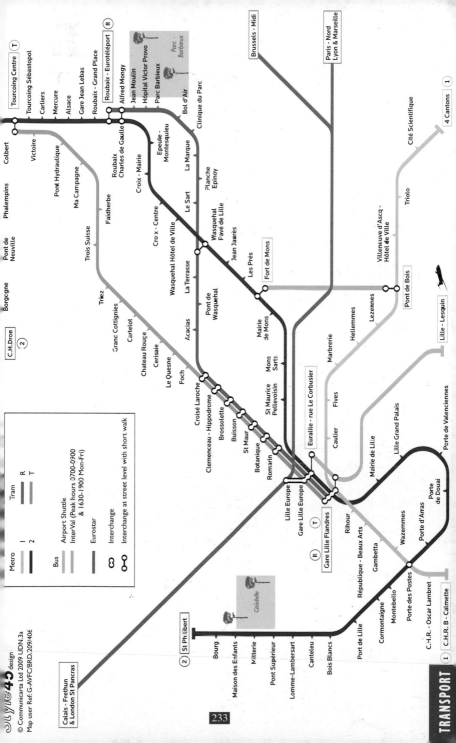

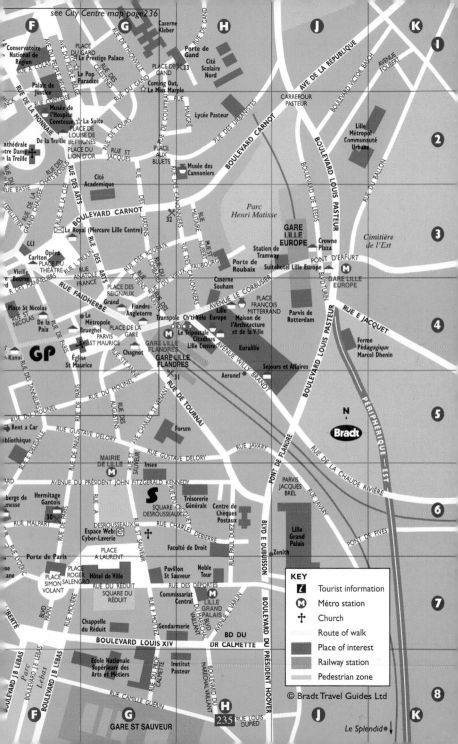

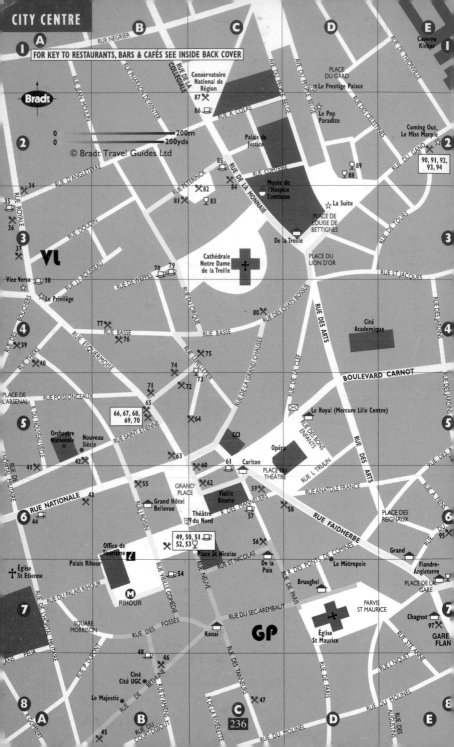